BUSINESSES WITH A DIFFERENCE:
BALANCING THE SOCIAL AND THE ECONOMIC

Edited by Laurie Mook, Jack Quarter, and Sherida Ryan

Market-based social economy firms such as social enterprises, social purpose businesses, co-operatives, credit unions, and community economic
development corporations aim to meet distinct social needs while making a profit. Do these types of businesses have the potential for growth
in today's economy? Are they destined to function only in areas where
conventional firms cannot achieve a sufficient rate of return? Or will the
role of social economy organizations change as businesses begin placing
more emphasis on corporate social responsibility?

Building on their popular 2010 collection *Researching the Social Economy*, editors Laurie Mook, Jack Quarter, and Sherida Ryan bring together contributors with diverse backgrounds to explore the challenges
and opportunities faced by firms that seek a genuine balance between
their social and economic objectives. Through international research,
case studies, and comparative analyses, this innovative collection highlights the unique issues that must be addressed when businesses are accountable not only to their investors and shareholders, but also to their
clients, workers, local communities, and the broader society.

LAURIE MOOK is an assistant professor in the School of Community
Resources and Development at Arizona State University.

JACK QUARTER is a professor and co-director of the Social Economy
Centre at the Ontario Institute for Studies in Education, University of
Toronto.

SHERIDA RYAN is the co-ordinator of the Community University Research Alliance on Social Business for Marginalized Business Groups at
the Ontario Institute for Studies in Education, University of Toronto.

Businesses with a Difference

Balancing the Social and the Economic

EDITED BY LAURIE MOOK, JACK QUARTER, AND SHERIDA RYAN

UNIVERSITY OF TORONTO PRESS
Toronto Buffalo London

© University of Toronto Press 2012
Toronto Buffalo London
www.utppublishing.com
Printed in Canada

ISBN 978-1-4426-4264-5 (cloth)
ISBN 978-1-4426-1147-4 (paper)

Printed on acid-free, 100% post-consumer recycled paper with vegetable-based inks.

Library and Archives Canada Cataloguing in Publication

Businesses with a difference: balancing the social and the economic/edited by Laurie Mook, Jack Quarter, and Sherida Ryan.

Includes bibliographical references.
ISBN 978-1-4264-5 (bound.) – ISBN 978-1-4426-1147-4 (pbk.)

1. Nonprofit organizations – Canada.   2. Cooperative societies – Canada.
3. Social entrepreneurship – Canada.   4. Economics – Canada – Sociological aspects.   5. Nonprofit organizations – Case studies.   6. Cooperative societies – Case studies.   7. Social enterpreneurship – Case studies.   8. Economics – Sociological aspects.   I. Quarter, Jack, 1941–   II. Mook, Laurie   III. Ryan, Sherida, 1949–

HD2769.2.C3B852012   306.30971   C2012-900209-7

University of Toronto Press acknowledges the financial assistance to its publishing program of the Canada Council for the Arts and the Ontario Arts Council.

University of Toronto Press acknowledges the financial support of the Government of Canada through the Canada Book Fund for its publishing activities.

Contents

Preface

Businesses with a Difference flows from a body of research funded through a series of research grants on the social economy from 2005 to 2010 from the Social Sciences and Humanities Research Council of Canada (SSHRC). The chapters in *Businesses with a Difference* are based primarily on Canadian research, but also include materials on the United States, the United Kingdom, and Latin America, particularly Venezuela and Argentina.

Outside of Western European countries and Quebec, the term 'social economy' is rarely heard, either in public discourse or among academics. A major objective of *Businesses with a Difference* is to address this lack of currency. The social economy involves a broad array of organizations that balance their social and economic functions. Not all of these organizations rely on the market to earn their revenues. This edited collection focuses on those that do – social economy businesses – including nonprofits, co-operatives, credit unions/caisses populaires that compete within the market for their revenues, as well as social enterprises and community economic development organizations.

This book recognizes that the term 'social economy' is highly contested, not only in its defining characteristics but also in how it is viewed in relation to the rest of society, and brings to the fore a fresh way of interpreting the social economy (see also Quarter, Mook, & Armstrong, 2009; Mook, Quarter, & Ryan, 2010). This point is addressed in detail within the introduction, which goes through the differing definitions of the social economy and argues that its characteristics are less important than the differing forms of interaction between organizations within the social economy, often functioning within social networks, and the rest of society.

Since SSHRC funded its network of research nodes across Canada, there is a growing interest in the social economy in universities as well as community organizations. Some indicators of this growing interest are recent books such as *Understanding the Social Economy* and *Researching the Social Economy* (University of Toronto Press, 2009 and 2010, respectively) and *Living Economics* (Emond Montgomery Publishing, 2010). In addition, there is now a learned society, the Association of Nonprofit and Social Economy Research (ANSER), which publishes the *Canadian Journal of Nonprofit and Social Economy Research*, with papers in both English and French. *Businesses with a Difference* is both a reflection of and an addition to the growing scholarship and interest in the social economy.

We are indebted to Jennifer DiDomenico, Acquisitions Editor, Business and Economics, of the University of Toronto Press, who has guided us from the beginning of this initiative and who been unfailing in her support of this work.

Laurie Mook
Jack Quarter
Sherida Ryan

BUSINESSES WITH A DIFFERENCE:
BALANCING THE SOCIAL AND THE ECONOMIC

Introduction

LAURIE MOOK, JACK QUARTER,
AND SHERIDA RYAN

This research collection focuses on businesses that balance an economic agenda with a social mission – that is, market-exchange social economy organizations. These social economy organizations generally take the form of nonprofit social enterprises and co-operatives. In this collection, some organizational variations are also discussed. We differentiate the market-exchange social economy from conventional businesses that engage in actions under the umbrella of corporate social responsibility, such as being good corporate citizens, fostering diversity in the workplace, putting in place environmental policies, donating to community programs, investing responsibly, and providing good wages and benefits. Although these actions may be considered socially responsible, conventional businesses are still ruled by the bottom line of financial profit and return to the owners or shareholders.

In contrast, the various manifestations of organizations in *Businesses with a Difference* are ruled by both financial and social bottom lines, and the needs of a wider group of stakeholders. The notion of the social economy flies in the face of *homo economicus*, the concept of humans as governed by a narrow economic self-interest that is divorced from broader social interactions. Social economy businesses are based on the idea that the social and economic are reciprocal and must be in balance. They take a stakeholder perspective and are set up not simply to meet the needs of owners, as is the case with conventional businesses, but to meet the needs of stakeholders, more broadly defined. This stakeholder perspective reflects the balance between the social and economic. This book explores the emergence, establishment, and adaptation of market-exchange social economy organizations as they operate in changing contexts in both prosperous and difficult times.

One critique of this approach is that social economy organizations are not real businesses. They are alternatives, suitable for the hinterlands, and not necessarily for where real businesses operate. This collection, we hope, will help lay this stereotype to rest. The chapters in this book include examples of businesses that operate in the market, yet have a relationship to stakeholders that differs from that of conventional businesses. Some dimensions of this difference are democratic work structures, employee owners, greater respect for ecology and society, and a transformative vision – that is, an image of a society in which the economy and its actors are governed by more than narrow economic self-interest.

The theoretical roots of thinking about a social entity with responsibilities to a range of stakeholders, not simply the owners or shareholders, comes from sociology and social theory and goes back at least to the 1950s with Karl Polanyi's (1957) concept of the economy as an 'instituted process.' Sociologist Mark Granovetter (1985) used the concept of 'embeddedness,' arguing that the economy was part of a society, not a distinct entity. Robert Putnam's more recent exploration of these ideas uses the concept of social capital (Putnam, 1993, 1995, 1996, 2000) to understand why some societies have a prosperous business culture and others do not. While all of these social theories differ, they share the idea that the economy is not an end unto itself but is part of, or embedded within, a broader society to whom it has responsibilities. Moreover, not only are the economy and the businesses within it part of a society, but the culture of that society influences how businesses behave and perform. Therefore, within these social constructs, the relationship between business and society could be viewed as reciprocal. If the two are in harmony, business contributes to the broader society and the broader society benefits from business.

Economists have also taken up this argument, widely known as alternative economics, and presented a fundamental critique of conventional economics, particularly its impact on human society. Among the alternative economists are critics of environmental exploitation (Ekins, Hillman, & Hutchinson, 1992; Henderson, 1991; Milani, 2000; Sachs, Loske, & Lindz, 1998), the exploitation of women (Mies, 1986; Shiva, 1989; Waring, 1996, 1999), the inadequacy of conventional methods of growth and the need for alternatives (Daly & Cobb, 1994; Ekins, 1986; Schumacher, 1973), including new methods of accounting for social value (Gray, Owen, & Adams, 1996; Hopwood, Burchell, & Clubb, 1994; Mathews, 1997; Mook, Quarter, & Richmond, 2007; Tinker, 1985). This latter field is also labelled as 'social and environmental accounting,' and it too attempts to broaden the domain that is normally considered in accounting frameworks.

We often look askance at new structures created within any society, in part because they are different, and difference can be disturbing, and in part because they face the additional challenges of operating within a less-than-conducive environment. The contributors to this collection do not ignore these challenges, but discuss them openly. They strike a balance between developing theoretical analyses and providing examples of cases that should be of use to instructors of courses in the social sciences and business as well as policy makers and practitioners. This book serves as a companion to *Researching the Social Economy* (2010). Whereas that volume addresses the social economy more broadly, this volume focuses on organizations that we classify as social economy businesses (see the categorization further down in this chapter). Although the bulk of the chapters concern Canada, the models presented within the book come also from the United Kingdom, the United States, Venezuela, and Argentina.

Not everyone is familiar with the concept of the social economy. Therefore, this chapter begins with an introduction to that concept, leading to the categorization of social economy organizations that are businesses, but businesses with a difference, because they create an appropriate balance between the social and economic.

A Brief Introduction to the Social Economy

This book recognizes that the term 'social economy' is highly contested, not simply in its defining characteristics but in how it is viewed in relation to the rest of society. It therefore interprets the social economy as an interactive approach and focuses on how the various components of the social economy interact with other sectors of society (see also Quarter, Mook, & Armstrong, 2009; Mook, Quarter, & Ryan, 2010).

This interactive approach contrasts with the sectoral approach, which focuses on the distinct characteristics of social economy organizations and tends to view the social economy as different from the rest of society (Bouchard, Ferraton, & Michaud, 2006). In Canada, the strongest expression of the sectoral approach is in Quebec, where the Chantier de l'économie sociale has taken the lead in defining the characteristics of the social economy (Mendell, 2010; Mendell & Neamtan, 2010). These are:

- The mission is services to members and community and not profit-oriented.
- Management is independent of government.
- Workers and/or users use a democratic process for decision making.
- People have priority over capital.
- Participation, empowerment, and individual and collective responsibility are key values. (Chantier de l'économie sociale, 2011)

The Quebec model also has utopian characteristics, in that its intent is to have the social economy be the dominant form in society (Shragge & Fontan, 2000). This utopian perspective is found in earlier variations of the social economy, for example, the 'co-operative commonwealth' (Webb & Webb, 1920, 1921).

Our concern with the sectoral approach is that it tends to view the social economy and its related organizations as isolated from the rest of society. Our approach, in contrast, emphasizes the relationship between the organizations in the social economy and the other parts of society, and how the social economy interacts with and relates to the private and public sectors. This idea has been underdeveloped in Canada, where sectoral approaches prevail, although there are some interesting international examples of it (Ben-Ner, 1986; Billis, 2010; Evers, 1995; Hansmann, 1980; Pestoff, 1998; Salamon, 1987, 1995; Weisbrod, 1974, 1977).

The model presented in this introductory chapter is interactive and emphasizes the myriad functions, sometimes conflicted, between organizations within the social economy, often functioning within social networks, and other parts of society. The differing forms of interaction between the social economy and other parts of society are portrayed below through a Venn diagram (see figure 1.1) and presented as forms of overlap. In brief, these various forms of interaction are:

- **Social Economy Businesses** – defined as nonprofits and co-operatives that operate in the market, alongside privately owned and publicly traded businesses, but which find a balance between their social and business objectives;
- **Community Economic Development (CED)** – organizations classified as a form of CED that also operate within the market, but typically serve regions and social groups experiencing inequalities and thereby rely upon government support of one sort or another;

- **Social Enterprises** – relatively new variations of CED that are a by-product of the neo-liberal agenda of smaller government and place a greater emphasis on the market than traditional CED;
- **Public Sector Nonprofits** – nonprofits operating within the social economy to deliver public services, but with one leg in the public sector in that they rely on government funds and can be influenced by government policies;
- **Civil Society Organizations** – either mutual associations serving a membership or publicly oriented nonprofits that are funded primarily by members, donations, and foundations.

This book focuses on the overlap of the private sector and the social economy, where we find social economy businesses, and on the overlap between the public and private sectors and the social economy, where we find community economic development and social enterprises, as these are the forms of organizations that engage in market-exchange activities. Understanding this overlap is important because it presents the challenge of building new social forms. Although their unique characteristics can be contemplated, implementing them requires interacting with a broader society and that interaction can shape the potential for change. For example, Favreau (2006) points out that even though Quebec's social economy envisages a distinct social order, activists have sought to influence government policies because government funding is essential to its development.

While market forces influence the operation of social economy organizations, the relationship is not unidirectional. Corporate social responsibility (CSR), the mantra of progressive businesses, attempts to seek a better equilibrium between commercial and social goals. However, businesses engaged in CSR use a conventional corporate structure, and their social focus is in large part determined by the actions of current leadership. When leadership changes, so can the focus on CSR.

Nonprofits and co-operatives, on the other hand, have a social mission built into their bylaws that they are expected to adhere to. Moreover, it is expected that this social mission will guide the corporation's practices, or as stated by Quarter et al. (2009), 'the prerogatives of capital (e.g., rate of return, capital valuation) do not dominate over the social objectives in the organization's decision-making' (p. 43). Some such organizations experience what is labelled as 'mission drift,' and depart from an appropriate equilibrium, but those are the exceptions, in our view. An

Figure I.1. The social economy in relation to the private and public sectors

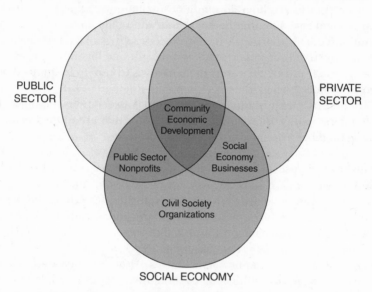

example of this is shown in chapter 3 by Jorge Sousa, who explores factors leading to the demutualization of co-operatives.

Differing Organizational Forms in the Commercial Social Economy

There are differing organizational forms in the overlap between the social economy and the private sector, as shown in figure I.1. Social economy businesses include commercial co-operatives and nonprofits. While they are different in form, they all have a mission that considers both business and social goals.

Co-operatives

The co-operative tradition is based on social economy businesses, in that co-operatives combine a social mission with commercial objectives that sustain them. This balance between the commercial and social is highlighted in the definition used by the International Co-operative Alliance, the umbrella federation for co-operatives internationally, and related associations such as the Canadian Co-operative Association. They state that 'a co-operative is an autonomous association of persons united voluntarily to meet their common economic, social, and cultural needs and aspirations through a jointly-owned and democratically-controlled enterprise' (ICA, 2009).

Co-operatives also use seven principles, adapted from those developed by the Rochdale Pioneers (Rochdale, England) in 1844. The most recent adaptation in Manchester, England, in 1995, is: voluntary and open membership; democratic member control; member economic participation; autonomy and independence; education, training, and information; co-operation among co-operatives; and concern for community. Although the definition and the accompanying principles emphasize the duality of co-operatives as both social and economic, some forms of co-operatives are very much businesses and others are derivative of government programs intended to provide public services, for example, housing, childcare, and health and homecare. Therefore, within our framework we categorize the latter forms of co-operatives within the overlap with the public sector and the social economy as public sector nonprofits, and differentiate them from co-operative businesses (see chapter 2 by Quarter, Mook, and Hann, and chapter 1 by Ian MacPherson). As noted in chapter 2, about half of the co-operatives in Canada are public sector nonprofits, predominantly housing co-operatives, but the economic muscle of the sector is among co-operative businesses, particularly producer co-operatives and consumer co-operatives.

As also noted in chapter 2 by Quarter, Mook, and Hann, about half of the revenues of co-operatives in Canada are generated by those engaged in farm marketing, farm supply, and related services labelled as producer co-operatives. Some large agricultural co-operatives have demutualized and become conventional businesses, an issue discussed in chapter 3 by Jorge Sousa. Agricultural co-operatives also are being bought out or merged into larger units. Nevertheless, non-financial co-operatives in Canada are dominated by the agricultural sector. The 2009 report of the Top 50 Non-financial Co-operatives in Canada (Co-operatives Secretariat, 2011) indicates that ten of the fifteen largest co-operatives in Canada are in the main agricultural co-operatives (farm marketing/farm supply). The most recent statistical summary of non-financial co-operatives published by the Co-operatives Secretariat indicates that there are 896 co-operatives in Canada engaged in agriculture with 346,000 members and with revenues of $13 billion, or 47 per cent of all revenues by non-financial co-operatives (Co-operatives Secretariat, 2007).

A variant of the typical co-operative framework based on users of a service is the worker co-operative in which the employees are members. In Canada, worker co-operatives tend to be relatively small enterprises in which members eke out a living, the exceptions being forestry co-operatives in Quebec. Chapter 6, by Marcelo Vieta, Manuel Larrabure, and Daniel Schugurensky, discusses the adaptation of the worker co-operative model that has emerged in Latin America, in part in response to plant closings.

Another form of co-operative is based on financial services, as discussed in chapter 1 by Ian MacPherson. Financial co-operatives in Canada have a storied history from their founding in Lévis, Québec, by Alphonse and Dormène Desjardins in 1900. The Desjardins Group is the sixth largest financial institution in Canada, with assets of $172.3 billion in 2010, a membership of 5.8 million in 451 caisses populaires, 42,641 employees, and returns to the community (sponsorships, donations, bursaries) of $80 million (Desjardins, 2010). Desjardins caisses populaires are predominantly seen in Quebec, but are found also in francophone communities across Canada and, to a lesser extent, in parts of English Canada.

The anglophone credit union system, which is not as powerful as Desjardins, is organized provincially through the Credit Union Central of Canada. There are 525 local credit unions affiliated with the system, a number that continues to decline because of mergers into larger units; nevertheless, the system reported assets of $119.2 billion for the third quarter of 2009. Membership in the system was at 5.1 million. Together, credit unions/caisses populaires in Canada have assets of about $270 billion, or approximately half the size of TD Bank, Canada's second largest financial institution, and about $60 billion less than CIBC, the fifth largest chartered bank, and almost double the size of the National Bank (Credit Union Central of Canada, 2010). In other words, the credit union/caisses populaires system is a major player in Canada's financial system.

Commercial Nonprofits

The words commercial and nonprofit may seem antithetical since the stereotype of a nonprofit is a service provider that most often depends on government and private donors for funding. However, a 2003 study by Statistics Canada estimates that the revenues of nonprofits in Canada was

$112 billion and about 35 per cent of this was classified as 'earned' (Hall et al., 2005). Subsequent research by Statistics Canada estimates that nonprofits contributed $80.3 billion to Canada's gross domestic product (GDP), or 7.1 per cent (Statistics Canada, 2006). In other words, there is a substantial amount of market activities by nonprofits. There are no annual reports that capture this, as in the case for co-operatives and credit unions; therefore, our presentation is anecdotal.

Some well-known examples of commercial nonprofits are the Canadian Automobile Association and its association of clubs across Canada embracing 4.9 million members (CAA, 2007); the Blue Cross (2009) insurance plans covering about seven million Canadians as a supplement to Medicare; Travel Cuts (2009), a business founded originally to assist university students making travel plans and owned by the Canadian Federation of Students and the Canadian Student Horizons Group; and the University of Toronto Press (2009), a nonprofit that owns a series of businesses whose revenues help it meet its primary objective of serving the scholarly books market. Other university presses across Canada have a similar structure. The network of YMCAs across Canada can be viewed as a nonprofit alternative that competes successfully with privately owned health clubs.

Variations of Form in Community Economic Development

The Canadian CED Network (CEDNet) defines community economic development as 'a community-based and community-directed process that explicitly combines social and economic development and fosters the economic, social, ecological and cultural well being of communities' (CCEDNet, 2007). In figure I.1, community economic development (CED) is situated in the overlap between the private sector, the government, and the social economy because these initiatives generally are undertaken through social economy organizations that attempt to sell their services through the marketplace but also rely on government funding. The reliance on government funding, both during start-up and for ongoing support, differentiates CED from social economy businesses, as discussed above. Part of the reason for this is that CED groups tend to be situated in so-called underdeveloped areas in which it is challenging to sustain a business strictly through the market (that is, from earned revenues). Historically, Canada has had an array of regional development programs designed to correct regional equalities associated with the market. These programs are administered through government agencies, such as the Atlantic Canada Opportunities Agency and Enterprise Cape Breton, as well as through an elaborate network of Community Futures Development Corporations, consisting of public sector nonprofits closely tied to government programs. Some provincial governments also have their own CED programs – for example, the Community and Regional Development Act of Nova Scotia, the Saskatchewan Program for Urban Community Development, and the Manitoba CED Framework.

Community development corporations are local hubs, incorporated as nonprofits, and are central to CED initiatives in Canada. The first was New Dawn, incorporated in 1976 in Cape Breton, which has been a leader in creating a community infrastructure in that region. CED and New Dawn are discussed in chapter 5 by Greg MacLeod, a founder of that organization. Chapter 7, by Laura Ryser and Greg Halseth, discusses CED in the context of small communities on the West Coast.

Some community-based enterprises also function without monetary exchange, that is, outside the formal market. Chapter 4, by Ana María Peredo, focuses on community-based enterprises which involve nonmarket exchange of services, a growing phenomenon.

Businesses owned by Aboriginal communities through nonprofit community development corporations are another example of social enterprises. Chapter 8, by Jean Paul Restoule, Sheila Gruner, and Edmund Metatawabin, discusses the relevance of social economy discourse to more traditional Aboriginal views of society.

Aboriginal communities, particularly those with land claim settlements, are creating community-based development companies that invest in for-profit businesses whose net income is channelled in part back into the local community. An excellent example is Makivik Corporation (2008), a nonprofit organization created by the Inuit of Northern Quebec in 1978 to invest the $120 million received from the land settlement. Makivik, governed by an executive committee and board of directors elected by the Inuit of Nunavik, is set up to further the development of the Nunavik region. It owns a group of businesses including regional airlines, a firm that harvests and markets caribou, and a tourism company. It also participates in joint ventures with other Inuit development companies.

The Chapters in This Book

Set within the frameworks of the social economy and social theories of business, the chapters of this book illustrate dimensions of embeddedness and reciprocity of business and society. Within these chapters are stories of harmony and disharmony. From these, we learn lessons for co-operation and collaboration and their relationship with community gain. Some examples discussed in this collection involve the exchange of individual resources only for community gain; other examples bring together community and state resources with individual ones. While chapters 1 to 5 and the first section of chapter 6, on Argentina's worker-recuperated enterprises, provide examples of organizations which facilitate the exchange of individual resources for community gain, the second half of chapter 6, on Venezuela's socialist production units, and chapters 7 and 8 illustrate cases where the state also contributes resources to the mix.

The last three chapters of the book focus on the internal operation of businesses. If businesses that balance social and economic objectives are to advance and achieve harmony with other parts of society, we need to understand the characteristics of those who run them and provide venues to learn from prior successes and failures.

Chapter 1, 'Historic Changes in the Canadian Credit Union Movement,' by Ian MacPherson, explores the development of the credit union movement in English Canada. This chapter emphasizes the nature of their formative periods, the challenges of stabilization, the early process of building larger credit unions and developing central institutions, the challenges that developed, particularly in the 1980s and 1990s, and the restructuring of the movement now underway.

Chapter 2, 'Non-financial Co-operatives in Canada: 1955 to 2005,' by Jack Quarter, Laurie Mook, and Jennifer Hann, uses the data files of the Co-operatives Secretariat to look at historic changes in non-financial co-operatives between 1955 and 2005. The chapter examines issues such as the type of co-operative, memberships, revenues, and assets, and the rural/urban split between non-financial co-operatives. It attempts to understand why co-operatives continue to have their greatest economic strength in rural parts of Canada.

Chapter 3, 'Leaving and Entering the Social Economy: Factors Associated with the Conversion of Organizational Form,' by Jorge Sousa, analyses the impact and circumstances associated with transforming either a market-driven organization or a public service into a co-operative (referred to as mutualization) and converting from a co-operative into an investor-owned enterprise (referred to as demutualization). This chapter is organized around eight case studies, evenly divided between mutualization and demutualization.

Chapter 4, 'The Difference Culture Makes: The Competitive Advantage of Reciprocal, Non-monetary Exchange,' by Ana María Peredo, focuses on ventures undertaken by communities collectively. The ventures may include providing a venue for a regional market for mining, agriculture, community forestry, seafood farming, and the like. The central concept in this research is the contribution made by non-monetary activities and transactions that arise out of tradition and established community relationships, to the operation of community-based enterprises. The research uses the abundant anthropological literature on the gift economy and other forms of reciprocal and non-monetary arrangements.

Chapter 5, 'Community Business Development,' by Greg MacLeod with Mikel Cid, presents the conceptual foundation for understanding community businesses, a subcategory of community economic development. This chapter uses both Canadian and international examples from Spain and Italy to examine the defining characteristics of successful community businesses.

Chapter 6, 'Social Businesses in Twenty-First Century Latin America: The Cases of Argentina and Venezuela,' by Marcelo Vieta, Manuel Larrabure, and Daniel Schugurensky, focuses on two types of social business organizations that have emerged recently in Latin America: worker-recuperated enterprises and socialist production units. The chapter starts with a discussion of the social, economic, and political context that gave rise to these organizations, continues with a presentation of the two case studies, and ends with a comparative analysis of differences and similarities. The authors argue that these organizations are significantly different from the traditional cooperatives and the state-owned enterprises of the twentieth century.

Chapter 7, 'Challenges for Engaging Social Economy Businesses in Rural and Small Town Renewal,' by Laura Ryser and Greg Halseth, draws on examples from the Northern British Columbia towns of McBride and Smithers. This chapter explores how social economic businesses are assisting with the renewal of rural areas and small towns. Despite the success of these social economy groups, research findings indicate more work is needed to improve both bottom-up and top-down policy and program supports to sustain institutional capacities and ensure that communities have a solid foundation for ongoing partnership activities that can broaden community and economic development opportunities.

Chapter 8, 'Land, Self-Determination, and the Social Economy in Fort Albany First Nation,' by Jean-Paul Restoule, Sheila Gruner, and Edmund Metatawabin, discusses the challenges in making concepts such as the social economy relevant to First Nations. The research in this chapter, developed in collaboration and dialogue with the community, shows how for Mushkegowuk people, in Fort Albany at least, social economic relationships are deeply rooted in land, history, identity, and a strong sense of community. They emphasize that to understand the concept of social economy in the North, we must take history, territory, and world-view into account.

Chapter 9, 'Social Entrepreneurship: A Comparative Perspective,' by Roger Spear, begins by discussing the origins of the concept of social entrepreneurship as understood in both the United States and in Europe. The chapter argues that social entrepreneurship often focuses to a great extent on the individual, but has many collective dimensions; it also has often a sponsored characteristic, where organizations sponsor or spin off new social enterprises.

Chapter 10, 'Exploring Social Transformation, Financial Self-Sufficiency, and Innovation in Canadian Social Enterprises,' by Tessa Hebb, Judith Madill, and François Brouard, discusses research designed to investigate social enterprises in Canada along the dimensions of social transformation, financial self-sufficiency, and innovation. One of their findings on the innovation dimension of social enterprises differs markedly from their earlier research. They also suggest several approaches to be taken in future research to achieve more precise operational definitions of the three dimensions studied.

Chapter 11, 'Education for the Social Economy,' by John R. Whitman, reflects on the role of education to improve the competitive performance and sustainability of social businesses. This chapter first examines how social economy businesses are currently being addressed in a small but significant sample of conventional educational institutions that offer the traditional MBA degree – graduate schools of business in Canada, the United States, and, in the case of Spain, Mondragon University. The author reviews a small but important sample of educational programs especially designed to promote the social economy through education on co-operatives, specifically worker co-operatives in Canada and the United States.

REFERENCES

Ben-Ner, A. (1986). Nonprofit organizations: Why do they exist in market
    economies? In S. Rose-Ackerman (Ed.), *The economics of nonprofit institutions:
    Studies in structure and policy* (pp. 161–84). Oxford: Oxford University Press.

Billis, D. (2010). *Towards a theory of hybrid organizations*. In D. Billis (Ed.), *Hybrid organization and the Third Sector: Challenges for practice, theory and policy*. Hampshire: Palgrave MacMillan.

Blue Cross. (2009). *About us*. Retrieved from http://www.bluecross.ca/en/about.html

Bouchard, M. J., Ferraton, C., & Michaud, V. (2006, June). *Database on social economy organizations: The qualification criteria* (Donna Riley, Trans.). Working Papers of the Canada Research Chair on the Social Economy. Research Series no R-2006–3. Montreal: Université du Quebec au Montréal (UQAM).

Canadian Automobile Association (CAA). (2007). *Annual Report, 2008*. Retrieved from http://www.caa.ca

CCEDNet. (2007). *What is CED?* Retrieved from http://www.ccednet-rcdec.ca/?q=en/what_is_ced

Chantier (Le) de l'économie sociale. (2011). *Definition*. Retrieved from http://www.chantier.qc.ca/?module=document&uid=871

Co-operatives Secretariat. (2007). *Co-operatives in Canada, 2005*. Retrieved from http://www.coop.gc.ca/COOP/display-afficher.do?id=1260822374366&lang =eng

Co-operatives Secretariat. (2011). *Top 50 non-financial co-operatives in Canada 2007*. Retrieved from http://www.coop.gc.ca/COOP/display-afficher.do?id=1259243932234&lang=eng

Credit Union Central of Canada. (2010). *System results*. Retrieved from http://www.cucentral.ca/Default.aspx?DN=7ec01257-b591–43eb-a4bd-6fe5ea0ccddc&l=English

Daly, H., & Cobb, J., Jr. (1994). *For the common good: Redirecting the economy toward community, the environment and a sustainable future* (2nd ed.). Boston: Beacon Press.

Desjardins. (2010). *Desjardins figures*. Retrieved from http://www.desjardins.com/en/a_propos/qui-nous-sommes/chiffres.jsp

Ekins, P. (Ed.). (1986). *The living economy: A new economics in the making*. London: Routledge and Kegan Paul.

Ekins, P., Hillman, M., & Hutchinson, R. (1992). *Wealth beyond measure: An atlas of the new economics*. London: Gaia Books.

Evers, A. (1995). Part of the welfare mix: The third sector as an intermediate area. *Voluntas, 6*(2), 159–82.

Favreau, L. (2006). Social economy and public policy: The Quebec experience. *Horizons, 8*(2), 7–15.

Granovetter, M. (1985). Economic action and social structure: The problem of embeddedness. *American Journal of Sociology, 91*(3), 481–510.

Gray, R., Owen, D., & Adams, C. (1996). *Accounting and accountability: Changes and challenges in corporate social and environmental reporting*. London: Prentice-Hall.

Hall, M., de Wit, M.L., Lasby, D., McIver, D., Evers, T., Johnson, C., et al. (2005). *Cornerstones of community: Highlights of the National Survey of Nonprofit and Voluntary Organizations*. (Catalogue No. 61–533-XPE, Rev. Ed.). Ottawa: Statistics Canada.

Hansmann, H. (1980). The role of nonprofit enterprise. *Yale Law Journal, 89*, 835–901.

Henderson, H. (1991). *Paradigms in progress: Life beyond economics*. San Francisco: Berrett-Koehler.

Hoe, S. (1978). *The man who gave his company away: A biography of Ernest Bader founder of the Scott Bader Commonwealth*. London: Heinemann.

Hopwood, A., Burchell, S., & Clubb, C. (1994). *Accounting: A social and institutional practice*. Cambridge: Cambridge University Press.

International Co-operative Alliance (ICA). (2009). *Statistical information on the co-operative movement*. Retrieved from http://guava.xeriom.net/~gmitchell

Makivik Corporation. (2008). *Mandate*. Retrieved from http://www.makivik.org/eng/index.asp

Mathews, M.R. (1997). Twenty-five years of social and environmental accounting research: Is there a silver jubilee to celebrate? *Accounting, Auditing, and Accountability Journal, 10*(4), 481–531.

Mendell, M. (2010). The three pillars of the social economy: The Quebec experience. In A. Amin (Ed.), *The social economy: International perspectives on economic solidarity* (pp. 176–207). London: Zed Press.

Mendell, M., & Neamtan, N. (2010). The social economy in Quebec: Towards a new political economy. In L. Mook, J. Quarter, & S. Ryan (Eds.), *Researching the social economy* (pp. 87–115). Toronto: University of Toronto Press.

Mies, M. (1986). *Patriarchy and accumulation on a world scale: Women in the international division of labour*. London: Zed Books.

Milani, B. (2000). *Designing the green economy*. New York: Roman and Littlefield.

Mook, L., Quarter, J., & Richmond, B.J. (2007). *What counts: Social accounting for nonprofits and cooperatives* (2nd ed.). London: Sigel Press.

Mook, L., Quarter, J., & Ryan, S. (Eds.). (2010). *Researching the social economy*. Toronto: University of Toronto Press.

Pestoff, V.A. (1998). *Beyond the market and state: Social enterprise and civil democracy in a welfare society*. Ashgate: Aldershot.

Polanyi, K. (1957). The economy as instituted process. In K. Polanyi, C. Arensberg, & H. Pearson (Eds.), *Trade and market in the early empires* (pp. 243–70). New York: Free Press.

Putnam, R. (1993). *Making democracy work: Civic traditions in modern Italy*. Princeton: Princeton University Press.

Putnam, R. (1995). Bowling alone: America's declining social capital. *Journal of Democracy, 6*(1), 65–78.

Putnam, R. (1996). *The decline of civil society: How come? So what?* Ottawa: John L. Manion Lecture.

Putnam, R. (2000). *Bowling alone: The collapse and revival of American community.* New York: Simon and Schuster.

Quarter, J., Mook, L., & Armstrong, A. (2009). *Understanding the social economy: A Canadian perspective.* Toronto: University of Toronto Press.

Sachs, W., Loske, R., & Linz, M. (1998). *Greening the North: A postindustrial blueprint for ecology and equity.* London: Zed Books.

Salamon, L. (1987). Partners in public service: The scope and theory of government-nonprofit relations. In W.W. Powell (Ed.), *The nonprofit sector: A research handbook* (pp. 99–117). New Haven: Yale University Press.

Salamon, L. (1995). *Partners in public service: Government-nonprofit relations in the modern welfare state.* Baltimore: Johns Hopkins University Press.

Schumacher, E.F. (1973). *Small is beautiful.* New York: Harper and Row.

Shiva, V. (1989). *Staying alive: Women, ecology, and development.* London: Zed Books.

Shragge, E., & Fontan, J.-M. (Eds.). (2000). Introduction. In E. Shragge & J.-M. Fontan (Eds.), *Social economy: International debates and perspectives* (pp. 1–21). Montreal: Black Rose.

Statistics Canada. (2006). *Canada's nonprofit sector in macro-economic terms.* Satellite account of nonprofit institutions and volunteering. 13–015-XWE.

Tinker, T. (1985). *Paper prophets: A social critique of accounting.* New York: Praeger.

Travel Cuts. (2009). *About: Overview of the federation.* Retrieved from http://www.cfs-fcee.ca/html/english/about/index.php

University of Toronto Press. (2009). *About us.* Retrieved from http://www.utpress.utoronto.ca/about.htm

Waring, M. (1996). *Three masquerades: Essays on equality, work, and human rights.* Toronto: University of Toronto Press.

Waring, M. (1999). *Counting for nothing: What men value and what women are worth.* Toronto: University of Toronto Press.

Webb, S., & Webb, B. (1920). *Problems of modern industry.* New York: Longmans, Green.

Webb, S., & Webb, B. (1921). *The consumers' co-operative movement.* London: Longmans, Green.

Weisbrod, B. (1974). Toward a theory of the voluntary nonprofit sector in a three-sector economy. In E. Phelps (Ed.), *Altruism, morality, and economic theory* (pp. 171–95). New York: Russell Sage.

Weisbrod, B. (1977). *The voluntary nonprofit sector.* Lexington: D.C. Heath & Co.

1 Historic Changes in the Canadian Credit Union Movement

IAN MACPHERSON

The role of credit unions is changing across Canada. It is important to understand recent developments within this sector for three primary reasons. First, the movement today is a significant and dynamic aspect of the Canadian economy, and has the potential to become even more important. The almost 400 credit unions (and a few caisses populaires) associated with Credit Union Central of Canada have over 1,700 locations across the country, many of them in communities not served by banks. They have over five million members and more than $126 billion in assets (Credit Union Central of Canada, 2010c). The Mouvement Desjardins is owned by some 5.8 million members and has assets of over $175 billion (Mouvement Desjardins, 2010). Internationally, the World Council of Credit Unions (WOCCU) represents credit unions in ninety-seven countries with 184 million members and assets of US$605 billion (WOCCU, 2010). The Canadian credit union movement has been an important player in international credit union circles for over fifty years.

Second, the English-Canadian credit union movement, like all co-operative movements with a substantial history, reflects broad social and economic changes over time. Often deeply embedded in the communities they serve and shaped by members who control them through democratic processes, credit unions readily reflect economic transitions and social pressures. To some extent, they are constructed socially; economically, they respond to local pressures as well as large marketing trends, and are particularly sensitive to the views of their most important stakeholders. The study of their history, therefore, not only illuminates some of the key aspects of national, regional, and local history, but can also inform our understanding of the present.

Third, if the full possibilities of credit union and co-operative approaches are to be fully realized in the modern world, there is a clear need for researchers, credit union/co-operative leaders, and policy makers to take them more seriously. They deserve to be considered in light of their own institutional and movement dynamics. They should not be seen as just pale imitations of mainstream banks or as quaint relics from the past. Credit unions are not routinely discussed in the media by business observers, partly because their shares are not traded on the stock market. Nor do their shares rise and fall in response to market speculation, the most common signal business commentators use for identifying important shifts and stimulating discussion. Credit unions are often ignored because they are decentralized institutions: they are not located in impressive office buildings in the financial centres of central Canada, nor are they often the subject of public debate. Credit unions, in short, are just different enough to escape the generalizations commonly made about the Canadian banking industry but not quite big enough to be considered on their own terms.

Background to the Canadian Credit Union Movement

Community-based financial co-operatives began in Germany during the 1850s, largely through the efforts of Hermann Schulze-Delitzsch and Friedrich Raiffeisen (Birchall, 1997; Moody & Fite, 1984; Purden, 1980; Wolff, 1907). They were formed to help meet the saving and borrowing needs of the urban lower-middle classes and rural farm families, though they quickly expanded to meet the needs of other groups as well. As the century progressed, they spread steadily throughout much of western and southern Europe, developing particularly in France and Italy, and, somewhat later, in several eastern European countries as well.

While there were minor differences among the community co-operative financial organizations started in each country, they were all steeped in self-help ideologies and were all organized by membership association, through the bonds of geography or those derived from religion, ethnicity, and workplace affiliations. They were distinct from other financial organizations through their ownership structures, which were based on open and democratic procedures and not on the amount of money individuals or organizations had invested in them. They were not promoted, nor were they attractive as speculative investment vehicles, because they used their surpluses (or profits) to reward 'participation,' either on the deposits members made or, less commonly, for the regular repayment of loans. Early on, they also developed distinctive and independent federations (for example, credit union centrals) to provide themselves with services, to lobby governments on legislative or regulatory matters, and to move funds among member organizations as needed.

Community-based co-operative banking organizations proved to be immensely popular and met the needs of people not being well served by the existing financial industries. Their operations were relatively simple, so leaders could easily learn the skills needed to operate them effectively and members could easily grasp the nature of their business activities. As they grew, they opened up the world of banking to large segments of the working and farming classes. They also helped the lower middle class develop locally based businesses and facilitated access to the market economy for rural households and small urban businesses.

As European immigration expanded overseas, colonists carried varied understandings of community-based co-operative banking to their new homes. Once settled, they typically found themselves in urgent need of financial services: rural settlement regions and ethnic ghettoes in rapidly changing cities typically suffered – and still suffer – from chronically poor credit systems. Within Canada, interest in community-based banking began during the nineteenth century (Armstrong, 1966; MacPherson, 1974). The most important efforts to create such institutions, however, were associated with the development of caisses populaires and credit unions, both of which began in the early twentieth century. Alphonse and Dorimène Desjardins and their neighbours organized the first caisse in 1900 in the community of Lévis, Quebec, across the St Lawrence River from Quebec City (Société historique Alphonse-Desjardins, 1990). Roy Bergengren, an American credit union leader; George Keen, a Canadian co-operative leader; and the employees of Plymouth Cordage Company organized the first credit union in English-speaking Canada in Welland, Ontario, in 1929 (Kenyon, 1976). While Alphonse Desjardins had organized some eighteen caisses populaires previously in the Ottawa area, largely among francophones, they had no direct connection with the Welland credit union. It was an extension northward of the American credit union movement – Plymouth Cordage already housed a credit union in its plant in Massachusetts (Poulin, 2002). From the beginning and until recently, the English-speaking credit union movement regrettably has had limited connections with the Mouvement Desjardins, though they have collaborated over the years in lobbying the federal government about issues of mutual concern (MacPherson, 2007).

In Boston, where large-scale immigration and rapid industrial expansion had created extensive economic, social, and political turmoil, a number of the city's elite also started forming financial co-operatives at the turn of the century. The most prominent of these founders was Edward A. Filene, a member of a leading merchant family. Their work ultimately led to the development of the American credit union movement, which expanded rapidly after World War One, and which would significantly affect parts of the English-Canadian credit union movement over the years.

The Approach of This Chapter

This chapter takes the common view of the English-Canadian credit union movement as being essentially separated from the Mouvement Desjardins. This is a necessary first step before substantial comparisons can be made between the two movements. Making comparisons is an important project, one that is engaging a number of researchers across Canada today. But first, in the tradition of Co-operative Studies, it is important to understand each credit union movement on its own terms.

Co-operative Studies is a field of enquiry that seeks to understand co-operatives primarily on their own terms and not just in comparison with for-profit enterprise. It argues that the values and principles on which co-operative organizations are based create organizations with distinct operation, structure, purpose, and relationship dynamics. The Co-operative Studies approach also invariably involves international perspectives because of the connections between co-operative enterprise around the world. The member organizations of the International Co-operative

Figure 1.1. Co-operative stewardship and its components

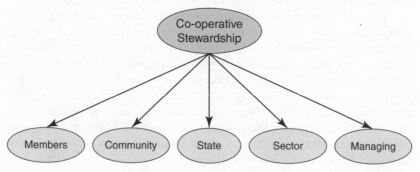

Figure 1.2. Five stages of credit union development

Alliance (ICA), the international organization for co-operatives, estimates that there are over one billion members of co-operatives around the globe (ICA, 2011). The United Nations estimates that three billion people today use co-operatives significantly for their economic and social benefit (ICA, 2011). One of the main challenges of Co-operative Studies is to come to terms with that size and diversity. It can only do so if it pursues its own kinds of questions through appropriate methodologies developed through interdisciplinary enquiry (MacPherson & McLaughlin-Jenkins, 2008).

Using the Co-operative Studies approach, this chapter will argue that credit union development can be divided into five stages related primarily to growth: formative, stabilizing, building, re-examining, and reformulating. In each of these stages, there is change in the key dimensions (see the discussion of dimensions below), such that the dynamics of credit union operations take new directions and relationships are transformed. Credit unions, therefore, are always changing. Because of space limitations, this chapter will consider only in passing the third major theme of Co-operative Studies: the movement's diverse intellectual perspectives and how they apply to credit unions – by those involved directly with them and those who observe them.

Dimensions of Credit Union Activities

Credit unions must maintain a variety of relationships, including with members, communities, co-operative structures, government, and management, in order to support their activities.

First, the relationship between the credit union and its members is an important facet of its activities. While it is possible to perceive contemporary credit union members as essentially customers, that approach undervalues the importance of 'membership,' a range of relationships profoundly important for credit union distinctiveness. When carried to an extreme, making members into mere customers destroys the governance structure basic to effective credit union operation. It throws away the bond of member connections – an important affinity relationship that other organizations would strive to have, which some have called the membership advantage (Webb, 1966).

Credit union membership takes place on three levels: ownership, rewards, and responsibilities. Members elect their leaders and are regularly informed about what is happening in their organization. They have reason to be proud of what they own, and feel a bond to the organization because of what it represents and what it does. Members are entitled to rewards proportionate to how they use their organization through investments and borrowings. In return, they have certain responsibilities: taking an interest in it, patronizing it loyally (as long as service is effective), participating in elections and consultative activities, and, as needed, investing in its future stability.

The most obvious dimension of the member relationship – that of democratic control – is too readily reduced to the elections that take place during annual meetings or through mail-in voting systems. Much more is necessary – trust in the leadership that emerges, effective information systems, high levels of open accountability, and reliable performance. The same generalizations apply to credit unions and other kinds of co-operatives, a challenge for leaders (who need to be well trained for such roles) and an important issue for members. Building credit union democracy requires reflection, resources, and commitment: it is central to credit union distinctiveness and is an important theme in the movement's history.

Second, credit unions relate to the communities with which they are associated. Almost universally, credit unions in English Canada were developed out of community ties, often derived from workplace, religious, and ethnic associations. Notably, more credit unions in English Canada than elsewhere were built on the less binding associations of urban neighbourhoods, small towns, and rural villages. There were important differences between credit unions organized through closed bonds (e.g., religion, ethnicity, and occupation) and through open bonds (open to all kinds of people residing in specific geographic regions). In English Canada, the shift to community-based credit unions has been persistent over the years, and today only a few closed bond credit unions exist.

Third, credit unions have a set of relationships with the co-operative structures that they, like most kinds of co-operatives, create. Credit unions are not just manifestations of localism, even though the reasons for the emergence of specific credit unions may be based on local needs and networks. They are also part of provincial, regional, national, and international organizations, most of them governed through federated structures. Since their beginnings in the mid- and late-nineteenth century, community-based co-operative banks have created central organizations to expand business opportunities, enhance training, lobby governments, and work with other similar organizations (Aschloff & Hennington, 1966; Tucker, 1929; Wolff, 1907). Canadian credit unions have started federated central organizations at provincial and federal levels (e.g., Credit Union Central of Manitoba and Credit Union Central of Canada), and they have joined with credit union organizations internationally to form the World Council of Credit Unions (MacPherson, 1999). These federations provide credit unions with some of the services they need and help ensure financial stability. They have never been intended as the head offices typical of other business forms, especially mainstream banking. There have always been debates over what kinds of activities the central organizations should undertake. They are continuing discussions that change over time within credit union systems, depending on the size of credit unions involved, the nature of the market place, the issues that are being considered, the personalities involved, and the need for greater efficiency.

The unusual structural arrangements of credit unions are also important because they create networks of social capital, opportunities for development, and increased security through both informal and formal arrangements. For example, credit unions have frequently banded together to help other credit unions, such as those in single resource communities needing help when the most important industries decline or disappear. The movement's financial stability is also firmer than is generally recognized because of the ways in which credit unions work together. Central organizations provide support services to help guarantee funds for credit unions encountering difficulties. Moreover, in recent years, both larger and smaller credit unions across Canada have developed arrangements and joint projects to purchase services, syndicate lending, build investment networks, and promote their interests. (For example, the ten largest credit unions in Canada have been meeting regularly since the 1990s and the small credit unions in British Columbia have been doing the same for over a decade.) In addition to formal structures, the credit union world has many informal arrangements and important initiatives undertaken through volunteer efforts and co-operation.

In addition, credit unions, either directly through local organizations or more commonly through their central institutions, have been and are members of general co-operative organizations, also usually structured on a federated basis. Credit unions form webs of co-operative associations (e.g., the Canadian Co-operative Association and its regional affiliates) that are far more important than is commonly recognized, even within the movement.

Fourth, credit unions have an important set of relationships with government. Following the American example, the early English-Canadian credit union movement lobbied provincial governments strongly for effective credit union legislation and practical government regulatory frameworks. This has been an ongoing task that has changed as relationships adapt, as the financial industries evolve, and as the roles of government are altered (Kenyon, 1976; MacPherson, 1996; Pruden, 1980). The state relationship is important because governments determine the kinds of businesses in which credit unions can be engaged, how they report on their businesses, the standards of care their officers must follow, and the deposit insurance programs that are created entirely on their own or jointly with governments.

Most credit union relationships with governments have been at the provincial level, but relationships with the federal government are becoming increasingly important, particularly since the proposed development of federally chartered credit unions (MacPherson, 1979; Poulin, 2002). The Canadian banking industry has attracted considerable positive attention during the recent financial crises triggered by the near collapse of the American banking industries. It was shown that Canadian credit unions have filled important gaps and provided valuable alternatives to traditional banking systems. They could play an even greater role in the future, which is partly why a federal registration process is desired by some within and without government.

Finally, credit unions have relationships associated with their day-to-day management. As in all kinds of co-operatives, the management in credit unions is not essentially the same as that found in conventional businesses. While it includes customary management concerns, such as accumulating and using capital, employing people, undertaking marketing activities, and accounting for expenditures, all of these activities take place within co-operative contexts and need to be shaped by the members' representatives. Direction of credit unions, for example, is much more influenced by elected boards and the surpluses or profits are distributed in unique ways, including the 'sustainable development of their communities' (Credit Union Central of Canada, 2010b). In fact, the leaders and the members of credit unions should be seen as stewards rather than as managers in the conventional sense, with high levels of accountability, based ultimately on values and open-ended commitments to members and communities.

The Formative Period: The 1930s, 1940s, and Early 1950s

Credit unionists today, like many leaders of other successful co-operatives, tend to underestimate the challenges and complexities involved in the formative period of their organizations decades ago. During that time, enthusiastic founding groups envisioned what their credit union could be when a strong, even charismatic, leader (or leaders) emerged, when start-up capital was accumulated, and when incorporation was secured. They made connections with other credit unions and, in many parts of English Canada, forged strong ties with other kinds of co-operatives.

The formative period varied somewhat by region within Canada. Following the formation of the Plymouth Cordage Credit Union in 1929, the first serious stirrings were in Atlantic Canada during the early 1930s, largely because of the work of the Extension Department of St Francis Xavier University (whose program became known as the Antigonish Movement). It was followed by extensive interest within the Prairies, notably in Saskatchewan in the mid-1930s. At the end of the decade, several groups in British Columbia and Ontario showed interest and credit unions began to emerge in both urban and rural areas. In all of these regions, the formative period lasted until effective legislation was in place, significant numbers of credit unions had been formed, resources had been amassed to meet common needs, and effective, sustained leadership had emerged.

Many credit unions were rooted in the Depression. They were essentially populist organizations, geared towards the capacity of ordinary people to be 'masters of their own destiny,' and towards the democratic control of economic activities. Their commitment to democracy resonated with the Canadian war effort from 1939 to 1945, as did their tradition of mutual self-help, including the provision of insurance services to help bereaved families deal with the loss of wage earners.

A noticeable feature of the formative period – and one that helps explain the rapid growth of credit unions from the early 1930s through to the later 1950s – was the credit unions' association with various movements, groups, and classes in Canadian society. Beginning with the interest shown at St Francis Xavier University in 1930, networks within the Roman Catholic Church sparked the formation of numerous credit unions across the country (Laidlaw, 1961; Welton, 1987, 2001). Other churches, especially those influenced by the goal of the Social Gospel to apply Christian values to economic action, encouraged credit union development to a lesser but still significant extent. Occupational groups, notably public servants and transportation workers in nearly all provinces, also organized numerous credit unions. The credit unions within the public service were often immediately successful and important because their members had stable incomes and could help their movement make contact with key politicians (MacPherson, 1995, 2004).

Other groups and organizations, including some unions, also played important roles: for example, auto workers in Windsor, steel workers in Hamilton, transport workers in Winnipeg and Calgary, and fishing unions in British Columbia. In rural areas, farmers' organizations, such as the United Farmers of Ontario and the Prairie wheat pools (particularly the Saskatchewan Wheat Pool) and fruit co-ops on the coasts encouraged the formation of credit unions. Some universities, including those of Toronto, Manitoba, Saskatchewan, Alberta, and British Columbia, as well as St Francis Xavier University, fostered credit union development in their provinces, often through their work in the expanding field of adult education. The importance of associated networks was a central factor in giving life to the movement.

The formative period was also characterized by weak national connections, even as the bonds within communities, regions, and provinces grew stronger. The work of the credit union promoters, especially the Antigonish Movement, did have some national dimensions, but the heritage of the formative period emphasized localism. That would make it difficult, even as the movement stabilized locally and provincially, to create strong national credit unions institutions. The credit union movement grew out of the strengths of localism and regionalism; it did not easily envision – or aspire to – the possibilities of national structures. For many years, a decentralized approach was always viewed more sympathetically than a centralizing mission.

The Stabilizing Period: The Mid-1950s and the 1960s

By the later 1950s, substantial portions of the English-Canadian movement had successfully navigated the formative period. They possessed stable management, usually in the form of one of their early leaders who became, on a part-time or full-time basis, secretary-treasurer – as the managers of credit unions were usually first called. Most of their directors received training through educational programs accessed through the central organizations created by provincial movements or while attending sessions of the American central organization, the Credit Union National Association (CUNA). On a local level, credit unions banded together to form chapters that met regularly for training sessions, discussions of credit union philosophy, and information exchanges. Most provincial movements published newsletters and held conferences as well as regional dialogues to share information, advance training, and make key decisions affecting the movement generally. The annual meetings, which often lasted three to four days in larger cities, were important for many credit union leaders and improved understanding of credit unionism while building movement solidarity. They also reinforced the social relationships so prominent in the formative period.

In the 1950s and 1960s, the movement was still largely guided by the populist ideas of the formative period. Success was measured in terms of the stability of local credit unions and particularly in the creation of new credit unions. Announcements of the formation of new credit unions were highlights of each annual provincial meeting. Individuals who had helped form a credit union received a founder's pin. One, A.B. Macdonald from the Antigonish Movement, received a great number of pins in recognition of his role in organizing more than 200 credit unions. Many others received dozens of such pins. In the flurry of organizational activity, little thought was given to the consequences of creating so many credit unions. The assumption was that they would remain small and would provide their members with only limited deposit and lending services. Most credit unionists at that time were committed to the idea of small credit unions that were friendly, close-knit places where staff and elected leaders would know everyone. There was still a strong emphasis on saving over borrowing. Many credit unions reached out to young people through school credit unions, an economic activity with questionable short-term business wisdom that reaped significant rewards in the decades that followed. They showed young people how a few pennies, nickels, and dimes could be accumulated weekly to create significant sums of money, and helped attract many future credit union directors and employees.

While they complied with the democracy of elections and frequent forms of accountability (newsletters, quarterly meetings, extensive committee structures) during the stabilizing period, credit unions chiefly upheld the 'democracy of familiarity,' a system based in strong bonds of association. The formative period's emphasis on members knowing – and being somewhat responsible for helping – each other was still much in evidence.

As the stabilizing period drew to a close, the business life of many credit unions began to change. The advent of cheque clearing (accepting and transmitting cheques from one organization to another), initially achieved through arrangements with banks, meant members used their credit unions more often. Larger credit unions began to expand their lending activities, at first rather simply to fund the growing demand for automobiles among their members. Then, more controversially, some of the credit unions started to make mortgage loans. This was a significant change that demanded increased sophistication among employees as they evaluated property and prepared the necessary documentation. It required long-term planning for the use of credit union deposits, and sometimes created challenges in managing credit union liquidity. It contributed significantly to the segmentation of employees through increasing specialization and professionalization. Throughout the formative and the early stabilizing periods, most employees could do all the routine tasks required to serve members. That stopped being true once mortgage lending became important.

At the same time, provincial movements began to face some serious structural issues. Most of the provincial movements (except in Nova Scotia) created two types of central institutions. One, usually referred to as credit union leagues (in keeping with American practice), was essentially formed to provide educational and training programs for directors and secretary-treasurers, to organize annual meetings for provincial movements, to support local chapters, and to lobby governments on behalf of the movement. The second kind of provincial organization, which started out much smaller but by the late 1960s had become more important than the leagues, was the co-operative credit societies. They were organized to meet whatever common financial services were required, such as cheque clearing, the movement of funds from credit unions with surplus deposits to others unable to meet member loan demands, the syndication of loans too large for a single credit union, and the development of 'stay-healthy' programs for credit unions encountering difficulties.

In several provinces the existence of these two kinds of organizations encouraged divisions between the philosophers (people deeply committed to credit union ideas and approaches) and the more business-oriented leaders. The philosophers tended to be drawn to the work of the co-operative credit societies (as leagues became known in Canada), while the more business-oriented leaders concentrated on the work of the central credit unions. It was an underlying and divisive situation that became pointed during debates about certain fundamental issues. A frequently contentious point concerned how each type of organization should be funded: should funding be based on maintaining equality among all credit unions, with each one paying the same? Or should credit unions contribute according to the number of members or the size of their asset bases – the larger the organization, the higher the dues? How should services from the central institutions be financed – on a user fee or on flat fee basis? Should membership be compulsory? How should the credit unions react to federal decisions to allow the prime interest rate to rise, thereby contributing to uncertainty in the financial market place over long-term interest rate changes? Should it be on a movement-wide basis or according to the best evaluation of local credit unions?

Some of these important issues, which emerged during the stabilizing period, would perplex all the provincial movements at different times and in different degrees of seriousness for decades. Ultimately, the struggle for a unified way to respond to them led to the amalgamation of the organizations in each province during the mid- to late-1960s, for the most part under the 'central credit union' banner.

It was also during the stabilizing period that the issue of national structuring started to become vitally important. By the early 1950s, the provincial movements were proudly independent and were carriers of the regional attitudes that characterize the Canadian federation. In fact, they were among the most important voices speaking on behalf of provincial and regional economies – not a characteristic that easily leads to national unity.

The search for a national voice was further complicated by the deep entwinement between segments of the English-Canadian movement and the American credit union movement. During the 1940s and 1950s, the credit union movements in the two countries developed an international perspective, reflected in the formation in 1954 of the World Extension Division of CUNA in the United States. Though housed within the national credit union organization of the American movement, it tried to develop an international perspective and to encourage involvement from credit unions in other countries, especially Canada. It was not entirely successful. Increasingly, many leaders within the Canadian movement became committed to a national agenda, especially as concerns grew over the Korean and later wars and Canadian resentments over

American economic domination grew. In 1953, Canadian credit union leaders formed the Canadian Co-operative Credit Society, which also undertook some modest national financial activities. It was the beginning of a struggle to achieve an independent national movement. The resulting division within Canada (and to some extent in the United States as well) would perplex the Canadian movement for over a generation. It was a struggle that was carried to CUNA floor meetings and its World Extension Division, where Canadian leaders led the campaign to create a separate organization to assume leadership for the international movement. It was a struggle that would last at least until 1970, when the World Council of Credit Unions was formed.

The nationalist issue was further complicated within Canada by a significant business struggle. As early as 1935 the American movement had created CUNA Mutual Insurance Society (CUNA Mutual) to provide life and loans insurance for credit union members (Moody & Fite, 1984). This insurance service was widely appreciated in the Great Depression, when the death of an uninsured family member could create long-standing hardship and even bankruptcy. CUNA Mutual spread quickly throughout the American movement and became a very prosperous organization. It also spread northward via some American leaders and Canadian officials attracted to the idea of creating a seamless, united international movement. Some Canadian credit union leaders, however, strongly resisted the expansion of CUNA Mutual. Instead, they wished to create a distinctly Canadian co-operative insurance program that would become a financial hub for co-operative/credit union development. The struggle over insurance – who owned it, what were the connections to co-operatives generally – became the cause célèbre of the Canadian movement from the 1950s through to the 1980s and seriously undermined efforts to create a strong national voice for the movement (MacPherson, 1995). Building effective co-operative structures across a country as large and diverse as Canada is a major challenge for every generation of co-operative leaders, but none has been more challenged by – or more committed to – the possibilities of a national movement than the leadership of the 'building phase' of English-Canadian credit union development.

The Building Period: The 1970s and Early 1980s

Though not as rosy as it is often depicted today, the period between 1945 and the 1980s was generally prosperous for many Canadians. Credit unions participated in, and contributed significantly to, that prosperity. While still popular among many people with lesser incomes, they began to serve a greater portion of the middle class, which led to significant membership and leadership changes. Credit unions became particularly important in providing mortgages on favourable terms through flexible repayment programs and less costly interest charges (for example, by charging interest on diminishing balances). Some of them specialized in automobile and mortgage lending. Some credit unions led the banking industry in welcoming women as member/customers and in lending to them 'on their own right': i.e., in not requiring the guarantee of their spouses or other family members for loans, as was common practice in financial institutions.

The credit unions that did embrace new services and expansion tended to be in the larger locales, such as Vancouver, Calgary, Regina, Saskatoon, Winnipeg, Ottawa, Hamilton, and St John's. In British Columbia, a few credit unions even took advantage of their broad powers under provincial legislation to offer insurance and trust services on their premises – typically through associated co-operative financial organizations. They, became, in effect, the first 'full-service' financial institutions in Canada despite the rigidities of the national financial system with its then sharply separated four pillars – banking, insurance, trust companies, and investment dealers. It was an example of the kind of flexible entrepreneurship one could find within the national movement.

As some credit unions expanded aggressively, size segregation became a challenge. In nearly every province, a few very large credit unions emerged through extensive branching activities, mergers, and acquisitions. These developments created tension around several issues within provincial movements: for example, reshaping central provincial organizations to meet changing needs. Larger credit unions had less need for central services than smaller credit unions; in fact, they often possessed larger and more sophisticated staff complements than the provincial centrals. They invariably competed with each other, especially in larger communities. They sometimes even located branches 'kitty-corner' from each other, with the dual objectives of better service for their members and of competition. That kind of rivalry poisoned many previously harmonious relationships within the movement and helped trigger the merger/acquisition process that became very widespread as the 1980s ended.

In the same period, credit unions were buffeted by extensive marketplace changes, the most drastic being the sharp rise in interest rates during the late 1970s and early 1980s. Rates plateaued in 1984 at just over 20 per cent (MacPherson, 1995). This rapid increase caused a number of problems for credit unions, the most obvious of which was the suddenly widespread mismatching between loan and deposit interest rates, as they forced rates for deposits upward while the rates for long-term loans – the source of much credit union income – remained comparatively low. Financial institutions like credit unions had relied on a difference between deposit and lending rates of about 3 to 5 per cent, a spread that became difficult to sustain. In fact, credit unions were particularly vulnerable because of their narrow asset base and their almost complete reliance on traditional member saving and borrowing business. Credit union leaders were hard-pressed to work their way through the problems of the 1980s, and in British Columbia and Alberta had to turn to guarantee funds (the reserve funds set up to assist credit unions facing difficulties) to weather the storm.

Those struggles magnified a number of earlier trends, including the technological changes that were revolutionizing the banking industry. Procedures that not too long before had been manual became electronic and instantaneous through computerization. Automatic teller machines, costing $8,000 to $10,000, were becoming commonplace and those credit unions that had chosen to move beyond small, contained membership bases had little choice but to place as many of them as they could afford in convenient places. Asset management became increasingly complicated and sophisticated, and credit unions had to hire people with a level of expertise not required only a few years previously.

As the problems in local credit unions increased, management changes became inevitable. Some managers who had risen within the movement were overwhelmed and often poorly prepared for the issues they were facing; a significant number were replaced by people attracted from positions in conventional banks, individuals (including some women) who welcomed the increase in influence and independence that the movement and the local credit unions gave them. Though many became avid supporters of credit unionism, the face and the institutional cultures of many credit unions were transformed. Increasingly, the managerial styles and structures, particularly as they related to size and growth, were influenced by the experiences and practices of the mainstream banking industries. This was the primary reason why mergers and acquisitions seemed to be the natural and best response to the issues confronting the movement.

The Re-examining and Reformulating Stages

Co-operative organizations typically show a remarkable resiliency. Many of them adjust well to altered circumstances and changing internal pressures. It is therefore not difficult to find co-operative organizations, including English-Canadian credit unions, whose roots go back sixty years or more. Their original names may not have survived, usually because in mergers new names are preferred so as to mark a new beginning through the apparent marriages of equals. Frequently, too, as mergers have taken place, the geographic association expanded beyond the original bond: more than one town or neighbourhood was involved and new leadership wished to serve broader, less well-defined areas. Some of the names chosen in recent years, for example, 'Alterna,' 'Innovation,' 'Advantage,' 'Envision,' and 'Prospero,' were selected partly to escape limitations associated with places or communities. They mark a break from the customary naming practices; time will tell how effective this practice is.

Today, there are just under 400 credit unions, a substantial reduction from the 1,500 that existed twenty-five years ago. The decline is almost entirely attributable to mergers and acquisitions, not failure. The merger process stems from internal and external pressures, and the entrepreneurial instincts normal to healthy co-operative enterprise. In fact, the number of branches within the credit union system has been steadily increasing, partly through the course of normal expansion, and more recently through the purchase of branches from the main line banks (Credit Union Central of Canada, 2010a). Credit unions are becoming increasingly visible in the larger cities, even in Ontario, where they have not generally been prominent. They continue to be crucially important financial institutions in smaller communities across the country; in fact, they join with the Mouvement Desjardins in being the only financial institutions in some 900 communities across Canada (Canadian Co-operative Association, 2007).

Credit unions continue to be leaders in technological innovation and in the range of financial services they offer their members, including investment accounts, US funds accounts, and on-line services. Some of them have developed impressive reputations as employers and several are leaders in general community economic development and social responsibility programs, e.g., Vancity, Coast Capital, Affinity, Assiniboine, and Alterna (Credit Union Central of Canada, 2010a; World Council of Credit Unions, 2010; International Co-operative Alliance, 2010). They are significant and responsible players in the Canadian economy.

As they have throughout their history, credit unions today continue to evolve in response to external and internal pressures. They frequently go through the process of re-examining and reformulating, so that institutional cultural change seems to be a constant. This is partly because of the revolutionary communication changes that have altered financial industries around the world, but also because of how those changes affect economic and social relationships. Such change is the most obvious factor in the pace of mergers, which continues unabated. Some believe it will continue until there are only 200 credit unions in English-speaking Canada (Bogarch, personal communication, 16 September 2006).

The merger trend has even started to affect provincial organizations, beginning with the geographically unlikely merger of the central organizations in Ontario and British Columbia. This new two-province central, Central 1 Credit Union, was formed in 2008. More recently, the centrals in both the Prairies and Atlantic Canada have been discussing mergers as well, but so far only those in the Atlantic provinces have decided to go through with them. In some ways technology has had as significant impact on the second-tier organizations as it has had on local credit unions. Few observers ten years ago would have predicted such amalgamations, nor would they have anticipated the common discussions about 'going national.'

Within credit unions, members increasingly demand more and better services, unless members are willing to forgo some services in return for a smaller, more personal institution (for example, CCEC Credit Union in Vancouver), or when credit unions work together to provide enhanced common services (as do several small credit unions in British Columbia). Most credit unions, though, respond to member pressure by expanding assets, services, branches, and electronic banking. They are constantly transformed as personnel change, management systems are revised, members are segmented into groups, and community relations become more formally organized. Associations with other credit unions are based on addressing common issues as well as sharing philosophies.

Many credit unions also struggle with matching business effectiveness with social goals, knowing that they owe part of their success to their community and social contributions. They realize that in the banking crises of today those commitments – along with their niche strengths, high levels of accountability, more conservative investment strategies, and lower but still respectable salary levels – are all advantages they possess in the modern market place.

Conclusion

Credit unions are an important and interesting part of the last eighty years of Canadian history. They have gone through significant changes, and will continue to do so. Their roles and contributions can be evaluated against the measuring stick of market development, but completely understanding them also requires comprehending how they function in keeping with their own stated values and principles. This chapter has briefly explored five dimensions of credit union activity that can be seen as being shaped by those values and principles: membership relationships, co-operative structures, community associations, government relations, and (co-operative) management.

The Canadian credit union movement has gone through a series of periods or stages, particularly over the last eighty years, which can be understood as: formative, stabilizing, building, re-examining, and reformulating. The last two stages, re-examining and reformulating, are cyclical because credit unions are constantly buffeted by internal and external pressures and the need to adapt. The great challenge they face is how, amid those changes, they can retain their commitment to members, co-operative structures, community relations, developing appropriate government relations, and co-operative management.

NOTE

The author is indebted to the two anonymous reviewers for their very helpful comments and suggestions.

REFERENCES

Armstrong, F.H. (1966). *Metropolitanism and Toronto re-examined, 1825–1850*. Historical Papers. Ottawa: Canadian Historical Papers.
Aschoff, G., & Hennington, E. (1986). *The German co-operative system*. Frankfurt am Main: Fritz Knapp Verlag.
Birchall, J. (1997). *The international co-operative movement*. Manchester: Manchester University Press.
Canadian Co-operative Association. (2007). *Credit unions: Banking on our communities*. Ottawa: Author.
Credit Union of Canada. (2010a). *National system review*. Retrieved from http://www.cucentral.ca/Publications07

Credit Union Central of Canada. (2010b). *Community involvement.* Retrieved from http://www.cucentral.ca/CommunityInvolvement

Credit Union Central of Canada. (2010c). *Firsts quick facts.* Retrieved from http://www.cucentral.ca/FirstsQuickFacts

International Co-operative Alliance. (2010). *Co-operative identity statement.* Retrieved from http://www.ica.coop/al-ica

International Co-operative Alliance. (2011). *Homepage.* Retrieved from http://www.ica.coop/al-ica

Kenyon, R. (1976). *To the credit of the people.* Toronto: Ontario Credit Union League.

Laidlaw, A.F. (1961). *Campus and community: The global impact of the Antigonish Movement.* Montreal: Harvest House.

MacPherson, I. (1974). *The story of C.I.S.* Regina: Cooperative Insurance Services.

MacPherson, I. (1979). *Each for all: A history of the co-operative movement in English Canada, 1900–1945.* Toronto: Macmillan.

Macpherson, I. (1995). *Co-operation, conflict and consensus. BC Central and the credit union movement to 1994.* Vancouver: BC Central Credit Union.

MacPherson, I. (1999). *Hands around the globe: A history of the international credit union movement and the role and development of the World Council of Credit Union.* Madison: World Council of Credit Unions.

MacPherson, I. (Ed.). (2004). *It was a great privilege: The co-operative memoirs of B.N. Arnason.* Victoria: British Columbia Institute for Co-operative Studies.

MacPherson, I. (2007). A relationship not easily understood: An historical overview of state/co-operative relations in Canada. In I. MacPherson (Ed.), *One path to co-operative studies: A selection of papers and presentations* (pp. 161–80). Victoria: British Columbia Institute for Co-operative Studies.

MacPherson, I., & McLaughlin-Jenkins, E. (2008). *Integrating diversities within a complex heritage.* Victoria: British Columbia Institute for Co-operative Studies.

Moody, C., & Fite, G. (1984). *The credit union movement: Origins and development 1850 to 1980.* Dubuque: Kendall/Hunt.

Mouvement Desjardins. (2010). *Homepage.* Retrieved from http://www.desjardins.com/fr/bienvenue.jsp

Poulin, P. (2002). The origins of savings and credit co-operatives in North America. In B. Fairbairn, I. MacPherson, & N. Russell (Eds.), *Memory, mutual aid, and the millennium* (pp. 28–39). Saskatoon: University of Saskatchewan.

Purden, C. (1980). *Agents for change: Credit unions in Saskatchewan.* Regina: Credit Union Central.

Société historique Alphonse-Desjardins (1990). *Histoire du Mouvement Desjardins, Tome 1, Desjardins et la naissance des caisses populaires.* Quebec: Author.

Tucker, D.S. (1929). *The evolution of people's banks.* New York: Columbia University Press.

Webb, T. (1966). Marketing our co-operative advantage. *Journal of Co-operative Studies, 87,* 10–15.

Welton, M. (1987). *Knowledge for the people: The struggle for adult learning in English-speaking Canada, 1828–1873.* Toronto: Ontario Institute for Studies in Education.

Welton, M. (2001). *Little Mosie from Margaree: A biography of Moses Michael Coady.* Toronto: Thompson Educational Publishing Co.

Wolff, H.W. (1907). *People's banks: A record of social and economic progress.* London: King and Sons.

World Council of Credit Unions. (2010). *Worldwide credit unions.* Retrieved from http://woccu.org

2 Non-financial Co-operatives in Canada: 1955 to 2005

JACK QUARTER, LAURIE MOOK,
AND JENNIFER HANN

Co-operatives developed out of self-organizing by rural communities in economic need.[1] Beginning in the mid-nineteenth century, farmers, along with fishers and miners, began creating enterprises to help overcome forms of exploitation. These enterprises included co-operatives to market various farm products and stores through which basic consumer goods could be purchased. This chapter explores the changes in the number, type, and size of non-financial co-operatives[2] in the period from 1955 to 2005 and the implications for the co-operative sector as a whole. This chapter also discusses the rise of service co-operatives as a reflection of a shift by co-operatives to an urban environment.

In order to understand the change in co-operatives between 1955 and 2005, we have presented the data on the number of co-operatives and memberships on a per capita basis. Where the data are for a particular type of co-operative relating to farming, we adjusted for the number of farms for each year under consideration. Similarly, we adjusted for inflation in the financial data on revenues and assets. For those figures, we used the adjustment through the Bank of Canada (2011) website (http://www.banqueducanada.ca/en/rates/inflation_calc.html). Additionally, a significant amount of the data concerns Quebec, which reflects the strong investment of the Quebec government in co-operatives and in the social economy more generally.

This chapter is organized as follows. First is an overview of the co-operative sector between 1955 and 2005, focusing on the number of organizations, memberships, revenues, and assets. Following that is a more detailed analysis of various forms of co-operatives, such as agricultural, fishing, consumer, worker, housing, and public service co-operatives. Finally, there is a discussion of trends in the data, particularly the rural tilt among co-operatives and the reasons for it.

General Overview: 1955 to 2005

Although the data gathered by the Co-operative Secretariat are not longitudinal and have not been adjusted for non-response,[3] we can look at general trends to get an idea of the nature of the co-operative sector in Canada from 1955 to 2005.

As shown in figure 2.1, the number of reporting co-operatives declined between 1955 and 1975, but started to increase after that. As will be seen in the following discussion, that increase is due to co-operatives providing public services, particularly housing co-operatives, which multiplied following amendments to the National Housing Act in 1973.

When looking more closely at the number of co-operatives in relation to the degree of urbanization for 1995 to 2005 (see figure 2.2), there are around 2.5 times more co-ops in rural settings per 100,000 population than in urban ones, even including the large number of

Figure 2.1. Number of co-operatives, 1955–2005

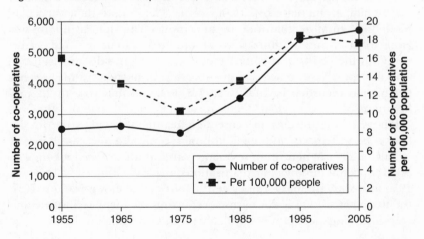

Figure 2.2. Number of co-operatives per 100,000 population, rural and urban, 1995–2005

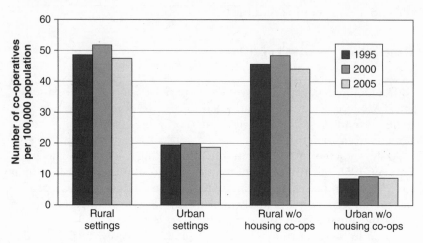

housing co-operatives. Without housing co-operatives, the difference is five-fold.

Taking population change into consideration, the number of memberships (figure 2.3) per 100,000 people in 1955 was 8,983; in 2005, it was 18,307, an increase of 104 per cent. (Please note that some people belong to more than one organization.) The significant rise was largely due to one organization, Mountain Equipment Co-operative (MEC), which had a minimum commitment of a five-dollar surcharge with first purchase to acquire membership in perpetuity. MEC memberships as recorded in 1995 were 775,000, and they rose to 2.2 million by 2005.

Revenues (figure 2.4) increase significantly after adjusting for inflation between 1955 and 2005, although there is a decrease between 1995 and 2005. When revenues using constant dollars are looked at in relation to the number of organizations, there is an increase between 1955 and 2005 by about 70 per cent. However, as shown in figure 2.4, the trend since 1975 is downwards, reflecting the increase in the number of housing co-operatives, which typically have smaller-than-average revenues.

Figure 2.3. Memberships, 1955–2005

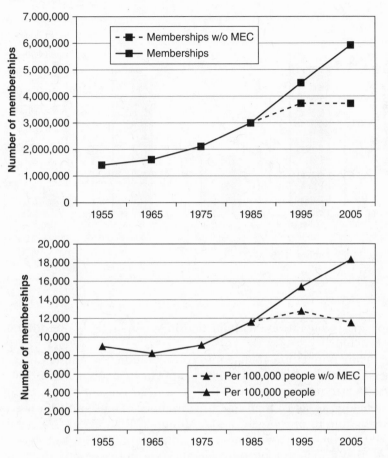

For assets (figure 2.5), the fifty-year increase in constant dollars is just over 4.5 times. The average assets per organization also increased by almost 1.5 times, but there is a significant decline from 1975.

Activity Analysis

To understand the reasons for changes in the sector, we now look at the data by area of activity. We start by analysing data relating to agriculture, fishing, and other rural co-operatives.

Figure 2.4. Revenues, 1955–2005

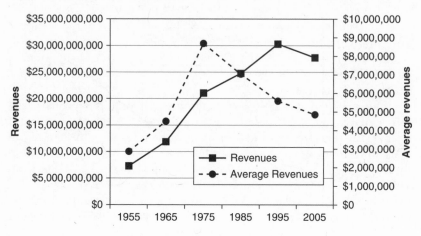

Figure 2.5. Assets, 1955–2005

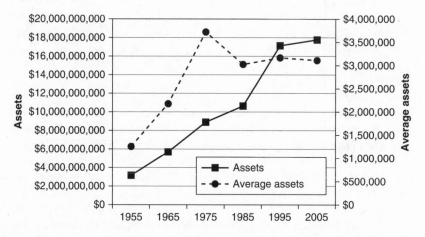

Agricultural Co-operatives

Agricultural co-operatives, which were among the first in Canada, offer a wide array of services to their members, including marketing, distribution, processing, provision of inputs, and the management of small-scale farms. In 1955, agricultural co-operatives dominated the co-operative sector in Canada, both in terms of number of organizations and volume of business. That year, a total of $967 million in revenues was recorded for all reporting co-operatives, of which 73 per cent was from agricultural marketing co-operatives (representing 40 per cent of the organizations in the dataset), 24 per cent was from merchandising co-operatives (of which almost 33 per cent was for farm feed, fertilizer or spray equipment), 1.5 per cent was from fisher co-ops, and the remaining 1.2 per cent was from service co-operatives.

Fifty years later, agricultural co-operatives remained the primary economic player in the co-operative sector; however, there were significant changes in the number and size of the organizations. In 2005, farm marketing co-ops represented only 2.6 per cent of the co-operatives in the dataset but accounted for 24.6 per cent of revenues. When farm supply co-operatives are factored in, revenues in 2005 account for 47.2 per cent of the total. Additional amounts are earned by agricultural co-operatives in such services as feeder finance operations management and grazing management. Without dwelling on the point, agricultural co-operatives were still the economic muscle of Canadian co-operatives in 2005.

However, in terms of the number of organizations, agricultural co-operatives declined significantly, in some cases merging and in other cases demutualizing. This change can also be understood through looking at the data file, Top 50 Co-operatives in Canada, from 1985 to 2005. Of the top ten in 1985, seven – all in agriculture and six specifically in farm marketing – no longer appeared in the top fifty in 2005. These co-operatives were the giants of the sector in 1985: Saskatchewan Wheat Pool (1), Alberta Pool (3), United Grain Growers, Manitoba (5), Manitoba Pool Elevators (7), United Co-operatives of Ontario (8), and Fraser Valley Milk Producers (10). Some of the new players that appeared in the top ten in 1995 also disappeared by 2005, including XCAN Grain Pool (Manitoba), Agrifoods International Cooperative (BC), and Manitoba Pool Elevators. The pattern continued in 2000, with Agricore (Manitoba) and Lillydale Co-operative also disappearing within five years.

All of these organizations either demutualized and became conventional capitalist corporations (see chapter 3 by Jorge Sousa) or were bought out (for example, the purchase of the United Co-operatives of Ontario by the US co-operative Growmark), or merged into new co-operatives. The largest of these new co-operatives were among the *Fortune 100* list of the largest corporations in Canada; for example, the Saskatchewan Wheat Pool had revenues of about $3.3 billion in 2000. In spite of these losses to the co-operative sector, new major players have come to the fore among farm marketing co-operatives. The Co-operatives in Canada 2005 report states, 'A few large co-operatives account for the largest part of total revenues, including Agropur and Gay Lea Foods for dairy, La Coop fédérée for meat and poultry processing and Exceldor for poultry slaughtering and processing' (p. ii). Among the giants in 2005, La Coop fédérée (Quebec) had revenues of $3.2 billion; Agropur Coopérative (Quebec), $2.2 billion; and United Farmers of Alberta Cooperative Limited (Alberta), $1.4 billion. These three were among the five largest co-operatives in Canada for that year. Of the top ten, six were in farm marketing, and of the top fifteen, nine were farm marketing. In other words, the players had new names, but according to Co-operatives in Canada (2005), 'the 151 marketing co-operatives that reported represent a major economic force with a combined business volume of over $8.2 billion and assets of $3.0 billion' (p. ii).

The overall market share of co-operatives by forms of production, according to the 2005 report, is: 'poultry and eggs (38%); dairy (40%); honey and maple (25%); grains and oilseeds (8%); and livestock (18%)' (p. 1). In other words, these organizations are not simply a force within the co-operative sector but also major players within the Canadian economy. Looking back fifty years, the 1955 report states: 'Thirty per cent of all agricultural marketings in 1954–55 were handled by co-operatives. By products, the per cent was as follows: dairy products (23); livestock (15); poultry and eggs (10); wool (89); grains, hay and seed (60); fruit and vegetables (20); maple products (45); tobacco (90); and honey (37)' (p. 7). The product-by-product comparisons are challenging, but overall farm marketing co-operatives still have a significant share of the Canadian economy.[4]

To meet the needs of agricultural producers, co-operatives developed as organizations through which supplies needed to maintain the farm could be purchased. The 1955 report refers to this point and to the fact that it was often problematic to segregate marketing co-operatives from purchasing because 'the associations organized primarily to market produce may purchase supplies as well.' Nevertheless, a class of co-operatives referred to as farm supply has emerged and become major players in support of the farm marketing system. According to the 2005 report:

> In farm supply, co-operatives play an indispensable role in the provision of farm inputs. They provide member co-operatives and producers with a broad range of farm inputs, including fertilizers and chemicals, animal

feed, seed, building materials and petroleum products. The 216 supply co-operatives that reported have a total revenue of $4.8 billion, an increase of 9.5% from 2004. In farm supply market share, the strongest areas are farm petroleum (52%), fertilizers and chemicals (13%), and animal feed (14%). (p. ii)

The 2005 report lists the ten top agricultural co-operatives, and number one, Coopérative fédérée de Québec, and number three, United Farmers of Alberta, are predominantly engaged in farm supplies. These are huge corporations that are ranked second and fourth among all co-operatives in Canada.

It is challenging to look at farm supply co-operatives over time because the categories have changed and their services can be intermixed with farm-marketing co-operatives. From 1985 to 2005, there was a 53 per cent increase in revenues in constant dollars from $3.1 to $4.8 billion; for the same time period, the Canadian population increased by 25 per cent, while farm acreage remained virtually unchanged.

Another class of co-operatives related to agriculture is referred to as production co-operatives. Like supply co-operatives, these are inter-mixed with farm marketing and farm supply, and are also an important part of co-operatives in rural Canada. This form of service first appeared as a category in the 1965 report with constant dollar revenues of 100 million, and the revenues increased quickly so that by 1995 they were 8.4 times that of 1955. After 1995, they started to decline and according to the 2005 report, there are 603 such organizations with revenues of $605.6 million, 65 per cent of which is in Quebec. Feeder finance and of grazing operations management accounted for 45 per cent of these organizations, and a substantial number, particularly in Quebec, were related to forestry – for example, tree farming and reforestation. Animal reproduction was another category. While production co-operatives are not on the same scale as farm marketing and farm supply co-operatives, they are nonetheless significant businesses that provide important services in support of rural Canada.

Fishing Co-operatives

The Antigonish Movement in Atlantic Canada emphasized the development of credit unions and fishing co-operatives (Welton, 2001). The latter emerged in small seaside communities, almost exclusively in Atlantic Canada, with New Brunswick having the largest group.

Only fifty-five fishing co-operatives were part of the 2005 report, twenty-three fewer than in 1955. Their membership of 7,000 was fewer by 3,000 from 1955. Revenues in constant dollars from 1955 to 2005 show an increase of about 2.5 times. In other words, there are fewer fishing co-operatives and fewer members, but the revenues per organization have increased. One major change during this period is the extinction of British Columbia fishing co-operatives. In 1965, they earned about half of total revenues, but subsequently declined.

Badly hurt by the decline of the Atlantic fishing, fishing co-ops were an industry in decline from the late 1980s until 1997, after which revenues starting increasing. This may relate to the 1998 Canadian Fisheries Adjustment and Restructuring Initiative, which provided funding assistance to the industry (Gagne & Roy, 1998).

Other Rural Co-operatives

Natural gas and electrification and water supply co-operatives are also situated exclusively in rural Canada. Rural electrification co-operatives were first reported in 1955. In the 2005 report, '66 reported memberships of 146,647 with assets of $479.9 million and revenues of $272.7 million' (p. iv). The report indicates that most of these utilities deliver natural gas. In Alberta, there are federations representing these forms of enterprise: Alberta Federation of Rural Electrification Associations, the Alberta Federation of Gas Co-ops, and the Alberta Federation of Rural Water Co-operatives. Of these services, only water supply co-operatives have any noteworthy presence beyond Alberta, and are found in significant numbers in Saskatchewan, Manitoba, Quebec, and Nova Scotia.

Other rural co-operatives are in such services as farmers markets, soil conservation, television, cable, and volunteer fire departments, thirteen of which are found in Saskatchewan and Alberta.

The co-operatives that we have described to this point are almost exclusively rural. The next section will discuss co-ops found in both rural and urban settings. These include consumer, worker, housing, and other service co-operatives.

Consumer Co-operatives

This category referred to stores, often small stores in rural communities, in which members purchased food and supplies. The data from the earlier reports combine both food and farm supplies (feed, fertilizer and spray material, machinery, and equipment). All of the revenues of $228.4 million in 1955 (including the sale of farm supplies) amounted to 24 per cent of the total.

Over the next fifty years, the category of consumer co-operatives developed into a major retailing/wholesaling system. The Co-operatives in Canada 2005 report states, 'Revenues from the consumer group totalled $11.8 billion, with food products accounting for 37% of the total and petroleum products, dry goods and home hardware being the other main items sold' (p. iii). If we add supply co-operatives to the consumer group, this total is $16.7 billion. Together, these categories accounted for 60 per cent of the total revenues reported by co-operatives in 2005.

For the period 1985 to 2005, consumer co-operatives are presented as a separate category (which excluded farm supplies). In this period, revenues grew from $2.6 billion in 1985 to $6.4 billion in 1995 to $11.8 billion in 2005. In constant dollars, revenues increased 1.7 times from 1985 to 1995 and increased by 1.5 times between 1995 and 2005. Thus, consumer co-operatives experienced growth in the same period that farm marketing co-operatives declined significantly.

Co-operative stores are organized around three major systems in Western Canada, the Atlantic, and the Far North. In the West, Federated Co-operatives, headquartered in Saskatoon, is the wholesaler for a system of 288 member co-operatives and is the largest non-financial co-operative in Canada with revenues in 2005 of $4.8 billion. One member of the Federated system, the Calgary Co-op Association Ltd. (known as the Calgary Co-op) is the fifth largest co-operative in Canada, with sales of $839.7 million in 2005 and with 405,888 members in a city of about one million people.

Atlantic Canada is structured in a similar manner, with Co-op Atlantic in Moncton serving as the wholesaler of 109 member co-operatives and revenues of $564 million in 2005. The Atlantic system operates on a smaller scale than the Federated system, but it also involves a smaller population base.

Compared with Federated and Co-op Atlantic, Arctic Co-operatives Ltd. (ACL), which has a Winnipeg head office and revenues of $99.1 million in 2005 (Co-operatives Secretariat, 2007), is a minor player; however, in other ways it is a striking example of the power of co-operatives to serve people in small, isolated communities. This federation, founded in 1972, is owned by thirty-one co-operative businesses involving Inuit, Dene, and Métis peoples in Nunavut and the Northwest Territories, covering a vast distance across Canada's north (Quarter, Mook, & Armstrong, 2009). Similarly, the Fédération des coopératives du Nouveau-Québec consists of fourteen co-operatives, with sales of $143 million in 2004, in the Inuit communities of the Hudson and Ungava coasts of Northern Quebec, or Nunavik. This federation is the largest employer in the region (Fédération des coopératives du Nouveau-Québec, 2006).

A major weakness in the consumer co-operative system is representation across Canada. Five-eights of Canada's population is located in Ontario and Quebec, and there is no significant presence in those provinces similar in scope to the Federated, Co-op Atlantic, or Far North systems. The 2005 report of Co-operatives in Canada refers to this point, perhaps too gently: 'Although Québec and Ontario consumer co-operatives are smaller and less influential, they are well-established organizations, however, the vast majority are located outside large urban areas' (p. iii). In Ontario, there are a smattering of food co-operatives and clubs associated with the Ontario Natural Food Co-op, which was organized in 1976 (ONFC, 2009). In Quebec, the 2005 report refers to sixteen 'direct charge' consumer co-operatives in which 'goods are provided to members at cost and a weekly service fee is charged to cover operating costs' (p. ii). In addition, Quebec has a very impressive system of student supply co-operatives in universities and high schools through which about 520,000 members purchase stationery, textbooks, and computer hardware. They also operate cafeterias and some have driver education courses. In 2005, these co-operatives had $154.8 million of income.

Notwithstanding these niches, in Ontario and Quebec, which have most of Canada's sizable urban centres, co-operative retailers of consumer goods have not had the same success in establishing a significant market presence as in the West, Atlantic, and Far North. Moreover, the stores associated with the three systems are predominantly in small communities. For example, 228, or 52 per cent, of the stores listed as part of the Federated Co-operative system are in Saskatchewan with just over one million people and with only ten communities of greater than 10,000 people (Federated Co-operatives, 2010). The Federated stores are predominantly in small town Canada, not just in Saskatchewan but across the West. The same could be said of the network of stores associated with Co-op Atlantic; thirty-eight, for example, are in communities across Nova Scotia, but that province has only three communities with a population of 10,000 or more (Co-op Atlantic, 2010). In other words, the shift among consumer co-operatives away from rural communities must be qualified, as its strength appears to be in relatively small communities in the West (mostly in the three Prairie provinces) and in sparsely populated Atlantic Canada.

The major exception is Mountain Equipment Co-operative (referred to earlier), a retailer of equipment for outdoor activities established in 1971 by a group of students at the University of British Columbia that has become a chain in all of Canada's major centres, including those in Ontario and Quebec. In 2005, MEC had become Canada's fourteenth largest co-operative, with sales of $197 million to 2.26 million members, both within Canada and, internationally, through its catalogue. This is a remarkable success story, but from a business point of view, one that was atypical of consumer co-operative retailers in Canada's major urban centres. While it would be unfair to say that MEC is one of a kind, it certainly does not reflect a pattern.

The three major consumer systems are growing in size, but are still unable to make a significant impact in major urban centres. MEC and the Calgary Co-op are the exceptions.

Worker Co-operatives

Worker co-operatives are a variation on the predominant co-operative model. In worker co-operatives the members are the employees of a firm and not, as is most often the case, the users of the service. They have also proved to be the most difficult of co-operative models to sustain, so much so that early in the twentieth century, the Fabian theorists Beatrice Potter (Webb) and her husband Sidney Webb argued that they were impractical and influenced British co-operatives against them (Potter, 1904; Webb & Webb, 1920, 1921). In Canada, worker co-operatives started forming in the nineteenth century, supported by the Knights of Labour, a very influential union group at that time, and the Iron Moulders International Union in Ontario (Kealey, 1980; Kealey & Palmer, 1987). Among the early experiments were co-operatives in such industries as printing, biscuit and confectionery works, shoe manufacturing, and cigar making.

There was a revival among worker co-operatives in the early 1980s, particularly in Quebec, in part spurred by an investment in the Quebec government in a regional network of co-operative development groups. A summary appeared in Co-operation in Canada 1985 report indicating that there were ninety-eight organizations with 6,577 members and $98.3 million in income, of which $61.6 million was from the sale of lumber and pulpwood. This latter group was from rural Quebec, where forestry co-operatives have had a lengthy history. There was another spike in the growth of worker co-operatives around 2000, when the federal government made available a $1.5 million investment fund to create and expand worker co-operatives.

By 2005, the number of worker co-operatives included in Co-operatives in Canada more than tripled to 341, memberships increased to 13,310 (about double) and revenues reached $527 million, of which $307.1 was from forestry products. As in 1985, 58 per cent of the revenues were from forestry co-operatives in Quebec, another example of the ongoing strength of co-operatives in rural communities. Quebec's forestry co-operatives have their own federation, the Fédération Québecois des Coopératives Forestières, which has 4,200 members and $310 million in revenues (Coopératives Forestières, 2007). The first forestry co-operative in Quebec started in 1938, and there were 167 by 1970. Under government pressure these were consolidated, as the co-operatives were required to enter into a management agreement with the government to have cutting rights to public lands.

Overall, Quebec remains the dominant location for worker co-operatives in Canada. Moreover, the 2005 data include worker shareholder co-operatives, an innovative arrangement in Quebec in which a group of workers employed in a company forms a co-operative that then enters into a shareholder agreement with the company. This usually occurs in companies under financial duress.

While worker co-operatives have exciting potential, they remain marginalized in Canada. Many are in urban centres in such niche industries as organic foods and fair trade products. However, for worker co-operatives other than forestry, the picture that emerges is of very small organizations in which members are eking out a living.

International examples, such as that of the Mondragon Co-operative Corporation in the Basque region of Spain, suggest that worker co-operatives can expand beyond a marginal role as a form of co-operative business. However, that scale of operation has yet to be seen in Canada.

Service Co-operatives

The category of 'service co-operatives' is used in the reports to cover a wide array of services that do not fit anywhere else. Some of these services – such as housing, childcare, healthcare, and homecare – depend on government programs for start-up and ongoing support when their members have low incomes. Therefore, they are a form of public service co-operative with nonprofit characteristics that will be discussed in the section that follows. As a group they represent about half of co-operative organizations in Canada, and they represent some of the best evidence of an urban presence among co-operatives.

Service co-operatives have a lengthy history. The 1955 report refers to 495 organizations within the service category, including 'housing, medical insurance, transportation, recreation facilities, telephone, rural electrification, custom grinding, seed cleaning, co-operative restaurants, and boarding houses' (p. 12). From 1955 to 2005, even when adjusted for population growth, there is a striking increase in service co-operatives (see figure 2.6) by just over 300 per cent to 4,167.

In spite of the flattening out in the 1995 to 2005 period, service co-operatives have the highest number of organizations within the co-operative sector, accounting for 73 per cent of the organizations responding to the Co-operatives Secretariat census of the sector. In 1955 they were 20 per cent of the total, and steadily increased between 1965 (to 25 per cent), 1975 (to 34 per cent), 1985 (to 60 per cent), and 1995 (to 72 per cent). Memberships in service co-operatives increased to 802,000 or 13.5 per cent of the total, by 2005. This is not nearly as high a figure as the total number of organizations, reflecting the fact that many service organizations are relatively small. Their growth was driven largely by one form of organization: housing co-operatives serving low-income communities in cities throughout Canada, to be discussed below under public service co-operatives.

Revenues in service co-operatives in constant dollars follow the same pattern of a sharp increase of twenty-three times over fifty years. Assets of service organizations in constant dollars also increase dramatically by twenty-six times, in part reflecting the increased market value of property in Canada's major urban centres. In 2005, service co-operatives represented 40 per cent of all co-operative assets.

Some service co-operatives are excellent examples of urban businesses. The 2005 report refers to twenty-six taxi co-operatives predominantly in Quebec and sixteen freight co-operatives in British Columbia and Quebec. Car sharing co-operatives have formed in large urban centres, such as Vancouver and Toronto, for members who want to reduce the high cost of car ownership and limit their dependence upon automobiles. Transportation co-operatives as a group reported revenues of $90 million and assets of $60.2 million in 2005.

While many TV/cable co-operatives are rural, other forms of communication co-operatives providing services such as editing and publishing are forming in urban centres. In 2005, there were thirty informatics co-operatives, almost exclusively in Quebec.

Funeral services are another area in which co-operatives have established a niche in a market increasingly dominated by large corporations. In 2005, there were fifty-five locally controlled funeral co-operatives in Canada, mostly in Quebec and the Atlantic.

Public Service Co-operatives

In addition to service co-operatives financed by their members, there is a growing group that provides public services assisted by government programs. While these organizations operate according to the same principles as other co-operatives, they are affected significantly by government policies. Housing co-operatives are the largest group, but childcare co-operatives, healthcare, and homecare are also worthy of attention.

Housing co-operatives are a predominantly urban phenomenon. As housing co-op members, people with lower incomes are able to secure long-term accommodation at a relatively reasonable and predictable cost and to be part of a democratically run community. Although housing co-operatives were referred to in the 1955 report and in subsequent reports on the sector, they had a limited presence until the amendments to the National Housing Act in 1973, with impetus from the New Democratic Party (Rose, 1980; Sousa & Quarter, 2003). The legislation provided for assistance to non-market or nonprofit housing, one form being co-operatives. This government program continued until 1993, when the federal government opted out (except for a small program in Aboriginal housing) and downloaded the responsibility to the provinces (Hulchanski, 2002, 2004, 2005; Prince, 1998; van Dyk, 1995). Some provinces have continued to assist the development of non-market housing (also referred to as social housing), but the decision by the federal government to end its involvement greatly slowed the process. In Ontario, where much of the social housing was being built, eight years of Conservative government, including diverting the program to municipalities who were ill prepared to administer it, ground new development to a near halt.

The essential features of the government program were supply-side subsidies that covered a portion of the building cost through mortgage subsidies or other similar arrangements, thereby making the units affordable to the tenants, as well as rent-geared-to-income subsidies for low-income tenants who qualified. This combination was the stimulus for the growth of non-market housing in general and housing co-operatives in particular.

Housing co-operatives were first noted in the annual report of co-operatives in 1965, when there were only thirty-four. In 1975, just after the government program was enacted, there were 68; by 1985 there were 712; by 1995, 1,946; and in 2005, 2,276. After significant increases until 1998, the number of housing co-operatives to 2005 levelled off. When these figures are adjusted for Canada's population size, there is a remarkable forty-fold increase for that forty-year period. After a high point in 1998 of 124,000 members, by 2005 memberships declined to about 115,000.

By 2005, the assets of housing co-operatives, $5.5 billion, represented 31.1 per cent of the total for all co-operatives, including the giant corporations that market and supply agricultural products. However, unlike these larger co-operatives, housing co-operatives are relatively small associations (averaging about fifty members), and are more dependent upon government as a rule.

Childcare co-operatives, consisting of daycare and nursery schools, were in similar circumstances, and numbered 387 with 34,089 members in 2005. Healthcare co-operatives numbered 101, with 77,469 members, in 2005, while homecare co-operatives, which provide services primarily to elderly people in their homes and which are found mostly in Quebec, numbered 51. Whereas healthcare co-operatives did experience growth from 1995, childcare co-operatives, especially preschools, declined.

Neither childcare, healthcare, nor homecare had the same degree of government stimulus as non-market housing in its period of rapid growth; nevertheless, like housing co-operatives, they too depended on government programs. Had the federal government followed through with the 2004 announcement in the Speech from the Throne for Bilateral Agreements with the Provinces on Early Learning and Child Care starting in 2005, it is possible that there might have been a spurt for childcare co-operatives similar to those in housing between 1975 and 1995. Some provinces, such as Ontario, opted into the national childcare program before the Conservative government cancelled it. It will be interesting to see whether this stimulus increased the number of childcare co-operatives once the data are published for 2006 and beyond.

These public service co-operatives, which make up about half of all non-financial co-operatives, have emerged mostly in urban environments, and predominantly in Quebec and Ontario, where consumer retail co-operatives have been unable make a significant impact. Like consumer retail co-operatives, public service co-operatives address the needs of a membership that benefits from the service. However, there is one fundamental difference: consumer retail co-operatives are self-sufficient businesses functioning in competitive markets. The urban public service co-operatives, growing as a percentage of the sector year by year, have a degree of self-sufficiency but, like other organizations within the public sector, rely in part on government. In the remainder of this chapter, we discuss the patterns in the data and speculate on why urban co-operatives in Canada have taken a much different form than those in rural Canada.

Reflections

Co-operatives are a form of community self-organizing in which a group of people with a mutual interest come together to form a democratically run association that provides a service. Thus co-operatives are often characterized as a form of mutual aid or mutual self-help (Kropotkin, 1989). Co-operatives are not the only form of mutual association – social clubs, professional associations, trade unions, religious congregations, ethno-cultural associations, and self-help groups follow the same philosophy, though often with less economic emphasis than co-operatives.

The data from this research indicate that even though the Canadian population has shifted from 67 per cent urban in 1955 to 80 per cent urban in 2005, only 60 per cent of co-operatives are urban, and excluding housing co-operatives, only 45 per cent are urban. In other words, there is more of a rural tilt among co-operatives than for Canadian society as a whole. Possibly, mutual aid may fit more comfortably within rural communities whose residents are engaged socially with each other and in which relations are more personal.

It is also possible that conventional businesses are less interested in investing in rural communities, leaving a gap that co-operatives can fill. This argument is derived from market-failure theory and has been applied primarily to understanding the circumstances under which non-profits evolve (Ben-Ner, 1986; Hansmann, 1980; Weisbrod, 1974, 1977). This argument may apply to co-operatives in Canada and may help to explain why they have flourished in rural communities but much less so in urban centres. Chapter 6 by Marcelo Vieta, Manuel Larrabure, and Daniel Schugrensky also discusses an example of market failure, the emergence of worker co-operatives in Argentina. Credit unions in Canada, as suggested by Ian MacPherson in chapter 2, also started because conventional businesses were not making consumer loans and credit available to working people.

Market-failure theory could also explain why housing co-operatives and public service co-operatives have evolved, primarily in urban centres. Housing co-operatives, for instance, serve the needs of people who lack the income to purchase equity housing (Hulchanski, 2005; Sousa & Quarter, 2003). As noted above, these forms of co-operatives work with government programs in an arrangement that Salamon (1987) refers to as a partnership. The issue is not simply government programs, as other forms of co-operatives (worker and fishing) have benefited from government programs. However, housing and public service co-operatives more generally differ in that their emergence seems tied to government programs.

The growth of public service co-operatives is also a reflection of the shift in Canada towards a service economy and the growth of government-funded services in particular. If we remove public service co-operatives from the 2005 data, the number of co-operatives is reduced to 2,899 organizations, or by nearly one half of the total reporting in 2005. The total of 2,899 organizations represents an increase from the 2,522 co-operatives that reported in 1955, but when adjusted for population growth, that number is only 56 per cent of the total in 1955. In other words, given the size of Canada's population in 2005 as compared to 1955, we would expect a lot more than 2,899 co-operatives. The growth between 1955 and 2005 is due to the increase in the number of public service co-operatives.

For other forms of co-operatives, predominantly those in rural Canada, smaller organizations are merging and becoming larger, that is, following the patterns of conventional businesses in general. These larger organizations are operated by professional managers who may not have strong backgrounds in co-operatives (a point raised in chapter 3 by Jorge Sousa as an explanation as to why some co-operatives demutualize). Therefore, a dualism has developed among co-operatives in Canada: there are the rural co-operatives of relatively successful businesses that are growing in scale and in such services as farm marketing, farm supply, and consumer retailing, and there are the urban co-operatives, predominantly in public services such as housing, but also in childcare, healthcare, and homecare, which are relatively small organizations focused on lower income groups.

Even though public service co-operatives as a group continue to grow, the development dynamic has slowed since 1998. Public service co-operatives resemble nonprofit organizations, and to groups that are incorporating new organizations the advantage of a co-operative over a nonprofit may not be apparent. This is particularly true for childcare co-operatives, which declined in raw numbers from 1995 to 2005, and for healthcare and homecare co-operatives as well, rather than for co-operative housing. Nevertheless, there is a steady overall growth among public service co-operatives, mostly in central Canada (Quebec and Ontario) and in urban centres, where historically co-operatives have faced the greatest challenge.

There is no reason to believe that these data trends will change in the coming years. Rather, it appears that a duality among co-operatives has developed, with co-operative businesses dominating economically in rural communities and public service co-operatives becoming the main driver for growth in urban centres. This duality could pose a challenge to a sector unified by the principles of the International Co-operative Alliance, as it is unclear whether the members of large co-operative businesses will continue to identify and find common cause with the relatively low-income urban dwellers who are the members of public service co-operatives. This would be ironic, as the co-operative businesses serving rural Canada originated to meet the needs of farmers, miners, fishers, and foresters who were very much on the social margins and, in varying degrees, remain so. Moreover, to the extent that member participation in their governance is a measure, public service co-operatives, particularly in housing, tend to represent strong examples of co-operative culture.

The striking growth of public service co-operatives within Canada represents a departure from the co-operative past. The original Rochdale principles of 1844, as embraced by the International Co-operative Alliance in Geneva, Switzerland, in 1937, listed 'Political and Religious Neutrality' as its fifth principle (ICA, 2009). Although this principle is open to differing interpretations, it reflected the fact that co-operatives were viewed as a 'middle way' that differed from the private market and government. Co-operatives in their early incarnation were collective forms of entrepreneurship or social entrepreneurship (see chapters 4 and 9 by Ana María Peredo and Roger Spear, respectively). This principle was dropped in 1966 when the Rochdale principles were revised by the ICA, perhaps reflecting the new reality of big government and of the importance of government programs. Political neutrality is widely interpreted as meaning that co-operatives have to work with all governments in order to promote the interests of the co-operative sector. That best characterizes the behaviour of the political voices of co-operatives in Canada – the Canadian Co-operative Association and the

Conseil Canadien de la Coopération et de la mutualité. Moreover, it is not only the representatives of public service co-operatives that lobby various levels of government for favourable legislation; co-operatives, like other kinds of business, are guided by government regulations and programs.

We have emphasized the lack of market penetration in Canada's urban centres of co-operatives that have the characteristics of a business, as distinct from public service co-operatives. However, there are exceptions. Among non-financial co-operatives, Mountain Equipment Co-operative is the best example of a business that has successfully penetrated Canada's major urban centres. Interestingly, MEC, which operates both nationally and internationally, invests heavily in online communication as a means of engaging its membership base (Quarter, Mook, & Armstrong, 2009). MEC does this not only as a form of marketing but also as part of its governance. Its annual general meeting attracts only one hundred members on average, but many of its members participate electronically, and to a lesser extent by phone, in elections. In 2008, for example, of 34,308 votes, 31,812 were cast electronically, 2,411 were cast over the telephone, and 55 were cast through the mail. Following the MEC example, the Internet may be a means that co-operatives can use to overcome the decline in face-to-face engagement and reach residents of Canada's cities.

Earlier we speculated on some reasons why co-operatives are over-represented rurally in Canada. In addition to the factors mentioned above one might speculate that tradition is an important consideration. Despite co-operatives' long-standing presence in rural communities across Canada, they are less visible in urban centres. As research by Schugurensky and McCollum (2010) indicates, business and economics textbooks downplay the significance of co-operatives. Without adequate exposure, it is unlikely that persons in large urban centres will consider the co-operative route when starting a business. Nevertheless, this argument does not explain why public service co-operatives have emerged in significant numbers in urban centres that lacked a strong tradition. For those co-operatives, the combination of activism and government funding programs that supported the development of co-operatives seemed critical to their development.

It will be interesting to observe whether government programs continue to stimulate public sector nonprofits. Since the early 1990s in Canada, there has been an increased emphasis on smaller government as part of the neo-liberal agenda. It is uncertain whether anything comparable to the national housing program between 1973 and 1993 that stimulated social housing will re-emerge, or whether a national childcare program will be reintroduced. In spite of the historic emphasis among co-operatives in representing a new form of market enterprise, ironically the growth of co-operatives in Canada, particularly in urban centres, appears very much tied to supportive government programs.

NOTES

1 This chapter uses the reports of Co-operation in Canada between 1955 and 2005. The six reports used for the analysis are in ten-year intervals, with 1955 being the first year and 2005 chosen as the endpoint because it was the most recent file available at the time of analysis. Originally, these reports were compiled by the Department of Agriculture (subsequently changed to Agriculture Canada), and, after 1985, by the Co-operatives Secretariat, who made them available to us for this research. In addition to these data files, we refer to the reports of the Top 50 Co-operatives in Canada from 1985, when it was first produced, 1995, 2000, and 2005. The data in these files are based on co-operatives reporting to the agency undertaking the study. While these reports are viewed as presenting a strong approximation of the sector as a whole, they may miss some co-operatives, particularly smaller ones. We want to thank the staff of the Co-operatives Secretariat for their assistance, in particular, Albert Daoust, Marylene Gagné, and Alain Roy.
2 Henceforth, the term co-operative in this chapter refers to non-financial co-operatives.
3 The response rate ranges from about 70 to 77 per cent. Time series analyses are not possible because of database limitations (Gagne & Roy, 1998).
4 The trend discussed in this chapter has also been noted by Fulton (1999) and Fulton and Gibbings (2000), in research that discusses the changes in the farm marketing sector and the emergence of 'New Generation Co-operatives,' that is, a trend originating in Minnesota and North Dakota by farmers to find market niches for very specific forms of production (bison, tilapia) to which they can add value.

REFERENCES

Agriculture Canada. (1977). *Co-operation in Canada 1975*. Ottawa: np.
Agriculture Canada. (1987). *Co-operation in Canada 1985*. Ottawa: np.
Bank of Canada (2011). *Inflation calculator*. Retrieved from http://www.banqu educanada.ca/en/rates/inflation_calc.html

Ben-Ner, A. (1986). Nonprofit organizations: Why do they exist in market economies? In S. Rose-Ackerman (Ed.), *The economics of nonprofit institutions: Studies in structure an policy* (pp. 94–113). Oxford: Oxford University Press.

Canada Department of Agriculture. (1957). *Co-operation in Canada 1955*. Ottawa: np.

Canada Department of Agriculture. (1967). *Co-operation in Canada 1965*. Ottawa: np.

Coopératives Forestières. (2007). *History*. Retrieved from http://www.ccfq.qc.ca/english.htm#members

Co-op Atlantic. (2010). *Our member co-ops*. Retrieved from http://www.coopatlantic.ca/city.aspx?id=6

Co-operatives Secretariat. (1987). *1985 – Top 50 co-operatives in Canada*. Ottawa: Government of Canada.

Co-operatives Secretariat. (1997a). *Co-operatives in Canada 1995*. Ottawa: Government of Canada.

Co-operatives Secretariat. (1997b). *1995 – Top 50 co-operatives in Canada*. Ottawa: Government of Canada.

Co-operatives Secretariat. (2002). *2000 – Top 50 co-operatives in Canada*. Ottawa: Government of Canada.

Co-operatives Secretariat. (2007). *2005 – Top 50 co-operatives in Canada*. Ottawa: Government of Canada.

Co-operatives Secretariat. (2008). *Co-operatives in Canada 2005*. Ottawa: Government of Canada.

Co-operatives Secretariat. (2010). *Rural and urban co-operatives data file: 1995, 2000, 2005*. Ottawa: np.

Federated Co-operatives. (2010). *About co-op stores*. Retrieved from https://www.coopconnection.ca/wps/portal/fclretail/FCLInternet/CoopStores/AboutCoopStores/!ut/p/c5/04_SB8K8xLLM9MSSzPy8xBz9CP0os3ijkMBQIzdTEwMLT3M3A0_3QD8jjwBfI4NQU_2CbEdFABMA3dk!/?WCM_GLOBAL_CONTEXT =

Fédération des coopératives du Nouveau-Québec. (2006). *Federation*. Retrieved from http://www.fcnq.ca/webconcepteur/web/fcnq/en/nav/federation.html

Fulton, M. (1999). *Traditional versus New Generation co-operatives*. Saskatoon: Centre for the Study of Co-operatives.

Fulton, M., & Gibbings, J. (2000). *Response and adaptation: Canadian agricultural co-operatives in the 21st century*. Saskatoon: Centre for the Study of Co-operatives.

Gagne, S., & Roy, A. (1998) *Geographic distribution of non-fnancial co-operatives in Canada: A rural-urban perspective*. Ottawa: Co-operatives Secretariat, Government of Canada.

Hansmann, H. (1980). *The role of nonprofit enterprise. Yale Law Journal, 89,*
835–901.

Hulchanski, D. (2002). *Housing policy for tomorrow's cities.* Ottawa: Canadian
Policy Research Networks.

Hulchanski, D. (2004). What factors influence Canada's housing policies?
The intergovernmental role of Canada's housing system. In R. Young &
C. Luprecht (Eds.), *Canada: The state of the federation in 2004* (pp. 221–47).
Montreal: McGill-Queen's University Press.

Hulchanski, D. (2005). *Rethinking Canada's housing affordability challenge.* Discussion Paper, Centre for Urban and Community Studies, University of Toronto.
Retrieved from http://www.urbancentre.utoronto.ca/pdfs/elibrary/
Hulchanski-Housing-Affd-pap.pdf

International Co-operative Alliance (ICA). (2009). *Co-operative principles and
values – Revisions.* Retrieved from http://www.ica.coop/coop/principles-
revisions.html#1966

Kealey, G. (1980). *Toronto workers respond to industrial capitalism, 1867–1892.* Toronto: University of Toronto Press.

Kealey, G., & Palmer, B. (1987). *Dreaming of what might be: The Knights of Labour
in Ontario, 1880–1890.* Toronto: New Hogtown Press.

Kropotkin, P. (1989). *Mutual aid: A factor in evolution.* Montreal: Black Rose Books.

MacPherson, I. (1979). *Each for all: A history of the co-operative movement in English
Canada: 1900–1945.* Toronto: Macmillan.

MacPherson, I. (2009). *A century of co-operation.* Ottawa: Canadian Co-operative
Association.

Mook, L., Quarter, J., & Ryan, S. (Eds.). (2010). *Researching the social economy.*
Toronto: University of Toronto Press.

Ontario Natural Food Co-op (ONFC). (2009). *Home.* Retrieved from http://
www.onfc.ca/index.php

Potter, B. (1904). *Co-operative movement in Great Britain.* London: Swan Sonnen-
schein.

Prince, M.J. (1998). Holes in the safety net, leaks in the roof: Changes in Canadian welfare policy and their implications for social housing programs. *Housing Policy Debate 9*(4), 825–48.

Putnam, R. (1995). Bowling alone: America's declining social capital. *Journal of
Democracy 6*(1), 65–78.

Putnam, R. (1996). *The decline of civil society: How come? So what?* Ottawa: John L.
Manion Lecture.

Putnam, R. (2000). *Bowling alone: The collapse and revival of American community.*
New York: Simon and Schuster.

Quarter, J., Mook, L., & Armstrong, A. (2009). *Understanding the social economy: A
Canadian perspective.* Toronto: University of Toronto Press.

Rose, A. (1980). *Canadian housing policies (1935–1980)*. Toronto: Butterworths.

Salamon, L. (1987). Partners in public service: The scope and theory of government-nonprofit relations. In W.W. Powell (Ed.), *The nonprofit sector: A research handbook* (pp. 99–117). New Haven: Yale University Press.

Schugurensky, D., & McCollum, E. (2010). Notes in the margins: The social economy in economics and business textbooks. In L. Mook, J. Quarter, & S. Ryan (Eds.), *Researching the social economy* (pp. 154–75). Toronto: University of Toronto Press.

Sousa, J., & Quarter, J. (2003). The convergence of nonmarket housing models in Canada. *Housing Policy Debate, 14*(4), 569–88.

Statistics Canada. (2009). *Population urban and rural, by province and territory*. Retrieved from http://www40.statcan.ca/l01/cst01/demo62a-eng.htm

van Dyk, N. (1995). Financing social housing in Canada. *Housing Policy Debate 6*(4), 815–48.

Webb, S., & Webb, B. (1920). *Problems of modern industry*. New York: Longmans, Green.

Webb, S., & Webb, B. (1921). *The consumers' co-operative movement*. London: Longmans, Green.

Weisbrod, B. (1974). Toward a theory of the voluntary nonprofit sector in a three-sector economy. In E. Phelps (Ed.), *Altruism, morality and economic theory* (pp. 171–95). New York: Russell Sage.

Weisbrod, B. (1977). *The voluntary nonprofit sector*. Lexington, MA: D.C. Heath & Co.

Welton, M. (2001). *Little Mosie from the Margaree: A biography of Moses Michael Coady*. Toronto: Thompson.

3 Leaving and Entering the Social Economy: Factors Associated with the Conversion of Organizational Form

JORGE SOUSA

The social economy's presence across the different sectors of the Canadian economy demonstrates that there is a real alternative to the alienating and individualistic character of the private sector. However, some organizations have questioned whether the primacy of their social objectives can be sustained when competing with investor-owned firms. As a result, there have been notable cases of social economy organizations selecting to convert their organizational form, referred to as demutualization, in order to compete with market-based organizations. While incidences of demutualization can be perceived to place the social economy at risk, there has also been an opposing trend where organizations have decided to convert into an organizational form compatible with the social economy.

In this chapter, I explore factors and circumstances associated with converting a co-operative into an investor-owned firm (demutualization) and converting business into a co-operative (mutualization). Arguably, the content can be applied to other types of organizations. There are three sections in this chapter: First, I describe two common ways that co-operatives have adopted innovative strategies to address ongoing challenges of membership renewal and accessing different forms of equity. Second, I present overviews of four cases of both demutualization and mutualization drawn from a variety of sectors including agriculture, consumer, and financial. In this section, I describe some of the key factors associated with demutualization and mutualization. Finally, I conclude this chapter with a discussion of some lessons that can be applied to the social economy.

Innovating the Co-operative Business Form

In response to increasing global market pressures, co-operatives have sought to remain competitive in an ever-expanding global economy by altering the traditional co-operative organizational form to resemble private sector corporations. These innovative and at times drastic responses are often intended to address the need for greater access to new equity capital. However, an unintended consequence is that these responses have also changed key features of the co-operative identity (Hogeland, 2004). In this section, I refer to two types of innovation that have resulted in the modification of the co-operative organizational form: the New Generation Co-operative, which is common in Canada and the United States; and the Limited Liability Company, which is a US invention and does not exist in Canada.

The New Generation Co-operative (NGC) is the name given to the over 200 value-added processing co-operatives that have emerged since the 1990s (Herman & Fulton, 2001), first in North Dakota and Minnesota and more recently in other states neighbouring Canada. In many respects the NGC is similar to the traditional co-operative (Stefanson, Fulton, & Harris, 1995), but there are two distinguishing elements. First, membership is restricted to those producers who first purchase delivery rights to the processing facility (Harris, Stefanson, & Fulton, 1996). Second, the NGC will sell delivery shares to raise capital. Each delivery share entitles a member to deliver one unit of farm product (e.g., one bushel of durum, one bison) to the co-operative. Thus, a contract between members and the co-operative is created with respect to the amount the member must deliver and the amount the co-operative must purchase (subject to the product meeting quality requirements).

The NGC concept has attracted attention as a way for farmers to increase their incomes to offset some of the negative impacts of regulatory changes and economic conditions in agriculture (Herman & Fulton, 2001). The impact extends beyond the farm gate, as people in rural communities look to NGCs as a development strategy that will boost rural income, employment opportunities, and population size (James, 1995).

A second innovation of the co-operative form has been the Limited Liability Company (LLC). In recent years, co-operatives have adopted the LLC model in order to obtain new sources of capital (Jorgenson, 2005). Although LLCs do operate as private businesses, each functions as an independent company within a co-operative. The relationship between the two organizations is treated as a partnership, in which there is limited liability for owners in both forms (Brown & Merrett, 2000). According to Brown and Merrett (2000), there are a number of similarities between the two organizational forms. For instance, liability of the LLC's members is usually limited to their level of equity investment in the business, whereas in a conventional co-operative liability is placed on the co-operative corporation and not on individual members. A key difference between the two business forms is that earnings in an LLC are usually allocated according to a member's level of equity investment rather than being based on patronage. An incentive for co-operatives going this route is the potential for introducing additional capital for the co-operative to tackle issues of growth and debt.

The responsibilities and obligations of the partnership are outlined in an operating agreement. For instance, the agreement will detail how business decisions will be made and how voting power (including decision-making) is allocated among the members (Frederick, 1997a; 1997b) of the LLC. There is nothing preventing a member of the co-operative becoming a member of the LLC. An ongoing concern is that a co-operative can potentially implement decisions that benefit the LLC and pose a risk to the co-operative's interests.

While the NGC and LLC options have introduced new sources of capital for co-operatives, some researchers have urged caution in embracing LLCs. Jorgenson (2005) states that the adoption of the LLC model can weaken co-operative structures and create a slippery slope towards shifting decision-making power away from the original members of the co-operative towards new equity partners who are not attached to the organization's social mission.

Exploring the Conversion Option

While the NGC and LLC models have gained some popularity among co-operative developers, increased incidences of conversions through demutualization have raised concerns over the stability of co-operatives (Guadaño, 2005; Jorgenson, 2005). According to Chaddad and Cook (2004b), innovating the co-operative structure has raised an important question of whether 'the co-operative model can survive in an increasingly concentrated, deregulated, privatized and global business environment' (p. 576). As a result, there is the urgent sense that the co-operative model is failing. However, while the trend of conversions either through restructuring or demutualization has gained greater attention since the 1990s, it is being met with a pattern going in the opposite direction – that is, the mutualization of private businesses and public sector services into co-operatives.

Since the early 1990s, several factors have contributed to organizations' decisions to become a co-operative or to convert into an IOF or some other form of private enterprise (Taylor, 2004). A driving force for change has been the coupling of neo-conservativè ideals with neo-liberal practices. These practices are best seen in the reduction of the size of government through cutbacks in social services and a greater reliance on the global marketplace to provide goods and services. In the contexts of co-operatives, these organizations have responded by broadening their presence in new sectors through mergers within the financial sector and aiming for greater market-share among consumer co-operatives (Lee, 2003; Mooney & Gray, 2002). However, there have been conversions of co-operative corporations into investor-owned firms. Chaddad and Cook (2004b), describe the concept in the following way:

> Conversion, increasingly known as demutualization, refers to changes in the ownership structure of user owned and controlled organizations from a mutual to a for-profit, proprietary organization. As a result of demutualization, residual claim and control rights are reassigned among stakeholders with implications to firm behaviour and performance. In particular, co-operative membership rights are converted to unrestricted common stock ownership rights in a corporate organization. (p. 576)

Demutualization among co-operatives has occurred because of economic struggles and an inability to sustain rapid growth. Investigations exploring reasons for the conversions have pointed to the need for increased access to capital (Chaddad & Cook, 2004a), and also have noted that many co-operative organizations no longer function according to their original social mission (Nadeau & Nilsestuen, 2004), a shift referred to as mission drift (Jones, 2007). The inclusion of the conversion option into strategic planning processes demonstrates an increased acceptance of demutualization (Jorgenson, 2005). However, including the option of demutualization has shifted the focus on services to members to the need to seek alternative forms of accessing capital as they aim to compete in an expanding global market (Guadaño, 2005).

For many co-operators, the conversion trend is troubling since co-operatives were founded as a response to limitations to a market economy

(Nadeau & Nilsestuen, 2004); the same conditions are in fact leading to their potential dissolution. Others have claimed that conversions can be considered as a natural part of an organization's life cycle (Jorgenson, 2005). Nadeau & Nilsestuen (2004) provide a sector-by-sector analysis of conversions (including mutual insurance companies and credit unions) within the United States. The authors of the research found that pressure to demutualize came from the organizations' managers and external advisers. Additional factors include financial challenges as well as reduced the emphasis on member education in areas of finance and governance.

Although the trend towards demutualization has become pronounced, this is being met with a move in the opposite direction – that is, towards mutualization. Although there is no standard definition of mutualization, it is commonly defined as involving the transformation of a private business or a public service into a co-operative or into a mutual company – that is, the opposite of demutualization. Mutualization involves transferring assets and developing a membership base rather than a group of shareholders, but members can include the original shareholders. This trend is a response to cuts in social services and fear that private businesses or corporations will close their operations because a specific profit margin is not being achieved. Interestingly, as will be shown later, the formation of new co-operatives occurred in the same sectors where co-operatives have been converted into private enterprises. Research exploring conversions describes a number of factors associated with the decision to either change into a co-operative or convert into an investor-owned firm (Sousa & Herman, 2012):

- A need to acquire new capital
- A wish to promote mergers and acquisitions
- A weak connection to the co-operative's mission
- The role of independent experts
- Professionalized management practices
- A strong attachment to community
- The impact of loss of local economic base

The demutualization of a co-operative can lead to pessimism about the future of the co-operative movement. A concern is whether the trend of increased demutualization implies that the co-operative model is deficient or not resilient to future challenges (Chaddad, 2003).

Transforming Organizational Form: Eight Case Studies

The eight case studies in this section represent a broad variety of organizational structure conversions (Sousa & Herman, 2012). In this section, I provide highlights of the cases as well as an aggregated analysis.

Description of Demutualization Cases

In this section I describe four cases of co-operatives that converted to investor-owned firms. The cases represent the breadth of co-operative ventures, including financial and agricultural.

AUSTRALIAN CREDIT UNIONS

According to Johnston (2012), Australia's credit union sector started to develop in the 1940s but was not fully established until the 1950s. In those early days, the credit unions were thought of as 'thrift associations.' Credit union numbers continued to grow and by the late 1960s were the fastest developing organizations in the financial sector, often workplace-based, and with more than 325,000 members.

Credit unions were not evenly distributed across the financial sector. There was considerable variation in growth and size, with a few large credit unions increasingly dominant in the movement. There were official concerns about the lack of professional management and the financial status of credit unions and other mutual-style organizations. A series of governmental reforms changed the focus of the credit union movement away from the importance of membership towards a greater interest in markets and financial accountability. As such, the focus on member involvement and ownership was diminished as credit unions became more closely aligned with the banking system by being designated into the broad category of authorized deposit-taking institutions (ADIs).

A number of factors came together during the last two decades of the twentieth century that made it easier for demutualization to occur within Australia's credit union sector. First, in 1984 the financial industry was deregulated. While this change allowed for greater technical co-operation among credit unions, this government reform also ensured that there was greater competition within the financial industry at a time when the distinctiveness of credit unions was already being questioned. Second, a number of high profile failures of mutual financial organizations (not credit unions) caused further concern to be expressed at the governmental, public sector, and community level about the accountability and management of these types of institutions, credit unions included. Third, as the management of credit unions became more complex, managers from the traditional banking system were increasingly hired, which further diluted any connection with co-operative principles or philosophy. Finally, in 1997, credit unions lost their tax-exempt status, which meant they were no longer able to compensate for their smaller scale with special benefits for their customers. Inevitably, costs rose, often resulting in the imposition of increased handling fees on accounts, which reduced the competitive advantage of credit unions over banks. These factors opened the door for credit unions to push for demutualization, thereby unravelling any hope of maintaining a strong and cohesive Australian credit union movement.

Demutualization occurred in two ways: either by the choice of the organization to move in that direction or by hostile takeover by another ADTI. Fairbairn (2012) describes the case of Sunstate Credit Union, where demutualization did occur. The case study reveals that the employees and the broader membership were generally unaware of or not committed to the value of mutuality, making them vulnerable to demutualization. Furthermore, the regulator for the industry allows full access to credit unions' membership lists, which can support a concerted effort on the part of an aggressive competitor to convince members that they should demutualize or sanction being taken over.

DAKOTA GROWERS PASTA COMPANY

Dakota Growers Pasta Company (DGPC) of Carrington, North Dakota, was one of the first of many NGCs created by American farmers (Boland, 2012). Formed in 1991 by durum wheat producers, it set the stage for a flurry of subsequent NGC development activity in the upper Midwest. The creation of DGPC was a means for durum growers to become more vertically integrated in the value chain as the owners of the processing facility that would turn their commodity into value-added consumer-ready pasta. Producers thus became processors and were able to reap the benefits from both activities. DGPC quickly became very successful and the owners/members regularly received dividends on their shares.

By 1999, management and the board of directors, in discussing the long-term future of the organization, began to consider the idea of a conversion from a co-operative towards one resembling a private corporation. This consideration was owing in large part to the members' inability to continue to produce quality durum; the motivation, resulting from the introduction of a new farm bill, to grow other crops; and a desire for greater liquidity of member shares. Also, any plans for expansion required greater access to public debt markets.

In late 1999 and early 2000, DGPC's directors considered a report from a large regional investment banking firm on various options for corporate structure and capital sources that might be available to the co-operative. After considering that report, the board recommended to the membership that the co-operative convert to a corporation. The conversion process was not a simple or direct one because a mechanism for converting a North Dakota co-operative into a corporation did not exist. Instead, the organization went through a process of first becoming a Colorado co-operative, then a Colorado corporation, and finally a North Dakota corporation. The process was approved by a member vote and in 2002 DGPC officially became a corporation.

LILYDALE POULTRY CO-OPERATIVE

Lilydale Poultry Co-operative has a long history of processing chickens, turkeys, and eggs in Western Canada (Goddard, Hailu, & Glover, 2012). Established in 1940, Lilydale went through many changes before finally undertaking an equity conversion exercise and becoming a private corporation in 2005. This case provides an interesting perspective, given that Lilydale operates within a supply management environment. Lilydale's management and the board of directors explored alternative means of injecting additional equity into the co-operative for a number of reasons. The company experienced financial strain resulting from operational losses. It needed to service long-term debt and to grow and diversify its operations. It also needed to address the impact of the impending withdrawal of equity as aging members retired.

In principle, the membership supported an initial plan that involved member investment by means of a revolving promotion program, a member loan component, and a voluntary investment program. Unfortunately, only the check-off produced any significant results and management was again faced with considering other options. By the end of 2004, at the insistence of the organization's bank, management began to explore alternative organizational structures that would accommodate external investment. In 2005, member delegates voted in favour of the conversion of Lilydale Poultry Co-operative into Lilydale Inc., a private corporation. Management argued that this move would provide producer members greater flexibility in managing their equity, but would also allow employees to invest in the organization.

SASKATCHEWAN WHEAT POOL

Saskatchewan Wheat Pool (SWP) was a large grain-handling co-operative established by Saskatchewan farmers in 1924 (Fulton & Larson, 2012). SWP typically held a leading market share in the grain handling industry, and with membership at times exceeding 70,000 farmers it also played a significant role as the voice of farmers at a policy level. With extensive networking and education activities, SWP was held up as a model for co-operation.

In the early 1980s, SWP was financially strong, but management and the board of directors argued that in order to remain strong in the future, the organization would need to undergo significant changes. Parts of the proposed changes were in response to external factors, while others reflected the nature of the organization. In terms of the external environment, the grain-handling industry and its operations were evolving rapidly. Subsidies for transporting grain were discontinued, which made a strong case for the value added of processing of grain commodities close to the point of production. Management also argued for the need to diversify the organization's activities at the same time as consolidating its expansive grain-handling facilities. All of these activities required access to significant capital. While the organization had considerable value, it was largely tied up in member equity. Given the SWP's aging membership, the management and board of directors began discussions on how to best deal with the impending retirement of many of its members and the corresponding draw on equity.

An internal financial analysis was conducted and the board of directors and management supported a proposal for the conversion of member equity into two classes of shares: Class A (voting) and Class B (non-voting), with the latter being publicly traded on the stock market. The membership approved the plan and in 1996 Class B shares for the Saskatchewan Wheat Pool began trading on the Toronto Stock Exchange. While the introduction of these new shares did not make large amounts of capital available to the organization, the additional capital meant that the Pool could fund new investments, which could be leveraged to increase borrowing limits from banks.

Management took full advantage of this newly acquired source of debt capital and embarked on a highly ambitious and aggressive investment spree. There was also an accompanying shift in decision-making within the organization from the board of directors to management. While shares in the organization started trading at \$12, they rose to over \$24 in two years, and then began a precipitous slide until they bottomed out at a mere \$0.20 by 2003. SWP was experiencing continuous losses and was unable to service its huge debt load. In 2005, in a last ditch effort to fend off bankruptcy, SWP again restructured its financing. The board of directors, the delegate body, and outside shareholders approved a re-capitalization plan to consolidate the two share classes that had previously existed into a single common share with no ownership limit on the shares. This decision completed the transformation of the Pool from a co-operative to a business corporation.

Analysis of Demutualization Cases

In all the demutualization cases, the leaders of the effort to convert the organizational form were not directly associated with the organization, nor had they experience in the private sector. For instance, the hiring of managers from the private sector influenced the demutualization of Sunstate Credit Union in Australia. Although some organizations considered hiring such individuals a boon, they often brought a change in focus and consolidated decision-making within their office, thereby eroding democratic practices.

At first glance, the Australian case creates the impression that credit unions are unable to compete against banks. However, it could be argued that changes to existing laws that were intended to encourage greater competition caused credit unions to shift their focus from the importance of membership retention and strategic development to simply remaining financially viable in an open market. It is essential for observers from other nations to recognize the importance of having credit unions shape the policies and regulations that can ultimately determine their fate.

The decision to convert was represented as a dramatic way to improve and streamline the business practices. However, a recurring theme from the case studies has been how the lack of member awareness or engagement contributed to demutualization (Johnston, 2012).

The age of the organization was often a consideration in the decision to convert. Generally, the case studies in this chapter involve mature organizations with a mature membership. As in the Lilydale case, an aging membership and an impending draw on equity can affect an organization's financial viability.

A concern expressed in the case studies is the failure to strategically integrate future members in the culture and practices of the co-operative. As older members retire, younger members are not prepared or even interested in maintaining the original co-operative identity. Accordingly, succession planning should be prioritized to ensure that the conditions are in place for younger and future members to be actively involved in the visioning and direction of the organization.

The agriculture cases reveal an enormous turbulence in a sector in which mergers and acquisitions are commonplace. In the case of the North Dakota farmers, a key to the conversion to a private sector firm was the availability of external capital that encouraged expansion. As a result, DGPC became well positioned as a private investor-owned firm to take advantage of the changes occurring in the US pasta industry.

An additional issue was waning growth, which caused these organizations to seek alternative ways to gain new revenue or build equity. In the cases where demutualization occurred, managers often demonstrated a tendency to prefer demutualization, largely because they lacked experience and understanding of a co-operative identity. As shown in the Dakota Growers Pasta Company case, management chose demutualization to the model with which they were most familiar and were thus able to champion to an uninvolved membership. There was additional liquidity since the conversion, as well as newly favourable conditions for external investors.

In the case of Lilydale, the co-operative was faced with serious financial burdens, including accumulating unmanageable debt and loss of market share. Although the members initially supported the continuation of the co-operative structure, continued losses influenced the members to vote to demutualize in June 2005. The restructuring plan helped the company by encouraging investment from existing shareholders, outside investors, and employees.

Description of Mutualization Cases

In this section I describe four cases of investor-owned firms or public service organizations that have converted into a co-operative. The cases represent the breadth of co-operative ventures, including financial and health.

COOP SANTÉ AYLMER HEALTH CO-OP
In 2002, Aylmer merged with four other municipalities to form the new city of Gatineau. Although Aylmer has more than 35,000 inhabitants, the locality has suffered over time from a lack of medical resources in comparison to other cities (Girard, 2012). In 2001, no new medical clinics were expected, in spite of the need of at least thirty additional

doctors and a lack of hospital facilities. More importantly, it was anticipated that some doctors were going to leave the area.

Two doctors practising in Aylmer's Centre Medical Aylmer-Lucerne
organized an informal meeting in order to explore ways to improve the
health services situation in the locality. A group of forty citizens participated in the gathering. With collaboration from the regional development co-operative, several community leaders visited an established
healthcare co-operative in another region of Quebec. They were im-
pressed with the facilities and organization, which led to the creation of
a temporary committee whose mandate was to study the implementation
of a similar project in Aylmer.

Over time, the objective became clear: to create a co-operative; to buy
an existing medical clinic to provide the services; and then to capital-
ize on a strong membership in order to improve existing services and
develop additional ones. In 2002, a solidarity co-operative was created
to serve these purposes. Solidarity co-operatives include three categories
of members: the workers, the users, and the supporting members. Individuals from any of these member categories can take part in the annual
general meeting. In addition, each category of members should have at
least one representative on the board of directors. This legal status was
officially recognized in June 1997.

The first board of the health co-operative was composed of individuals
with a solid background in policy and governance, including a former executive director of the regional school board and a former federal deputy
minister. Most members of the board had participated in the temporary
committee. A pre-feasibility study demonstrated the relevance of buying
the Centre Medical Aylmer-Lucerne. In the spring and summer of 2003,
independent consultants prepared a business plan. During the following
months, a series of intense discussions took place between co-operative
board members and a group of doctors before an agreement was reached.

The doctors agreed to finance the sale to the co-operative over a period of fifteen years. This was an innovative way to secure the presence of
doctors in the clinic over that time. In January 2004, the Aylmer Health
Co-op became the official owner of the medical clinic with three goals
in mind: to improve working conditions, including the recruitment of
doctors; to offer the best possible equipment; and to ensure public representation. The co-operative offers the following services in both official languages: a medical clinic, including eight doctors and one nurse;
medical laboratory and radiology services; dental care, psychology, and
audiology services; and a pharmacy.

This is the first instance in Canada of a solitary co-operative buying a medical clinic, and this case provides some useful observations. The role of an existing development agency, the Outaouais-Laurentides Regional Development Co-op, and the involvement of other co-operatives (including the caisse populaire Desjardins, a funerary co-operative, and a housing co-op) were critical to the success of this venture. It is important to note that the board of directors was composed of members with various skills, good reputations, and large networks of contacts. Finally, the organization's success was the result of careful timing and planning.

DAKOTA CARRIER NETWORK

The 1990s saw the United States leading a wave of deregulation in a number of industries, including telecommunications (Davis & Patrie, 2012). Organizations such as US West, which operated in many countries, believed that reorganization was necessary and shifted their focus and resources to only the most profitable areas of activity. Too often this meant a shift away from interest in serving rural or remote areas. This case study documents a complex transaction that involved fifteen distinct legal entities in North Dakota that acquired assets (exchanges) from US West in the mid-1990s. The company, now known as Quest, decided to exit large portions of rural North Dakota by selling sixty-eight exchanges or service territories and assets to other telephone service providers. In 1991, fifteen organizations (mostly co-operatives) agreed to meet and produce one common bid for an extremely diverse array of properties.

The ability of co-operatives to co-operate was severely tested, since there was a large appetite for acquisition on the part of some of the telephone co-operatives, one or two of which were interested in most of the properties that were for sale. The bid preparation process took two years to formalize. There was no common method of determining the value of a given US West property and each of the fifteen companies had to determine the price they were individually willing to pay. They also had to develop an internal method of determining which one was entitled to bid on a particular property.

The $1.36 million transaction was completed in 1996. The eventual owners of these properties created a jigsaw puzzle of glass fibre lines that together formed the backbone for an interstate and intrastate voice and data network. Buoyed by their recent success, the telephone co-operatives and independent companies formed a new company called Dakota Carrier Network (DCN) and built the few missing pieces to create a seamless system. Finally, because these service territories were added to existing co-operatives that were already providing a similar service, thousands of North Dakotans became members of the new co-operative that created the Dakota Carrier Network.

SOUTH INTERLAKE CREDIT UNION

Conversions occurred in significant numbers in parts of Western Canada in recent years. As chartered banks orient their business towards global markets, they have shown a willingness to divest local retail-banking services and sell branches to credit unions. A key consideration when exploring the development of a co-operative from an investor-owned firm is what the local clients/members and staff perceive as being different. Typically in these cases, the location, building, specific services, and clientele begin as identical to those operated by the bank; some staff may even remain.

One successful credit union that has acquired several bank branches within its territory is South Interlake Credit Union[1], located in the Interlake region just north of Winnipeg. South Interlake is an aggressive, economically focused, regional community credit union that competes directly with bank branches in many of its locations. Hostility to the disinvestment policies, labour policies, and loan-authorization procedures of the chartered banks contribute to a positive view of the credit union. Banks were seen as having demonstrated lack of support for local communities and employees. Members and employees who thought rates and services were the most important aspects of the credit union were not disappointed. The South Interlake Credit Union was viewed positively because decision-making was locally based and there was a stronger orientation towards personal service. Furthermore, there was greater teamwork and opportunity for personal and professional development among employees. Bank customers were asked to purchase hundreds of dollars in membership shares and overwhelmingly accepted this new financial arrangement. The new credit union did not lose many bank customers. Interestingly, participants do not necessarily attribute the co-operative advantages to co-operative philosophy, although some advantages they identify are clearly linked to local ownership and to related management approaches.

Overall, this case shows that a credit union can achieve greater satisfaction than a bank among clients/members and employees in a rural, retail-banking environment that is likely marginal to the bank's strategic objectives. As a case study of a success story, this research does not prove that all co-operatives will necessarily succeed in these ways, but rather illuminates the dynamics and the key factors that enabled this one co-operative to do so.

VIRGINIA POULTRY GROWERS CO-OPERATIVE

This case study involves the mutualization of assets of a for-profit, investor-owned firm. Pilgrim's Pride Corporation into an agricultural co-operative called the Virginia Poultry Growers Co-operative (Wadsworth & Brockhouse, 2012). The Virginia Poultry Growers Co-operative is unique in that it reflects a reversal of a demutualization that had occurred eighteen years earlier, when Rockingham Poultry Marketing Co-operative consolidated with two private companies to become WLR Foods Inc., which was subsequently purchased by Pilgrim's Pride Corporation.

The conversion project began with the announcement of the closure of a major processing plant in Virginia's Shenandoah Valley, which would have adversely affected the region's turkey producers and meant the loss of numerous jobs. Almost immediately, turkey growers met and charted a course to create a co-operative and subsequent ownership in the closing processing plant. The conversion process was complicated and risky, but was completed in only six months through the perseverance of leadership, involved producers, with the co-ordinated aid and guidance of outside professionals and agencies. Factors that led to this successful conversion were:

- A sound business idea
- Strong leadership from producers and trust among them
- Effective communications among partners
- A clear unwavering focus on the goal
- Financial and psychological commitment from potential members
- Co-operation among numerous professionals, private and governmental
- The availability of financing on favourable terms

Analysis of Mutualization Cases

For the cases involving mutualization, the outcome was really a convergence of circumstances. In general the motivation to form a co-operative organization was a response to companies threatening to exit the market and therefore leaving customers without a service. In the case of Dakota

Carriers Network, Quest decided to exit a large portion of rural North Dakota in favour of cherry-picking more lucrative markets. A consortium of telephone co-operatives worked together to purchase the assets for those rural exchanges and continue and even improve service to those high-cost service areas. While not a conversion in the usual sense, the acquisition of former bank branches by the South Interlake Credit Union resulted in customers becoming members of the co-operative and of former bank employees working for the credit union. Most important, financial services continued even after banks that formerly owned these branches decided to move out of the area.

As shown in the acquisition of credit union branches in the South Interlake case study, a strong sense of community involvement and commitment to the new branches made it likely that the acquisition would have a membership base. The acquisition of bank branches is remarkable primarily because local co-operatives demonstrated their ability to make significant investment in rural communications technology pay off. The credit union conversions were framed as offering a prospect for community revitalization, with a commitment to maintain strong community connection. It was vital to get a critical core of dedicated individuals and supporters in order to maintain strong leadership from producers and establish trust.

The Aylmer Health Co-op is an excellent example of how the co-operative model is used to accommodate the succession of an existing enterprise. In this case, the physicians who owned and operated a health clinic worked with clients and other community citizens to turn over ownership and control of the clinic to the members. At the same time, it allowed the physicians to focus on the provision of healthcare over administration in the short term, while providing for their retirement in the longer term. In the case of the Aylmer Health Co-op, the project had many important influences, and although it is still in its infancy, its impact on the community has been significant. It also illustrates the importance of support from other co-operatives. In the Virginia Poultry Growers case, turkey producers selected the co-operative model as the best response to a decision by an investor-owned firm to close a local plant. In rescuing the processing firm, the producers ensured a continued market for the poultry.

Lessons for the Social Economy

While there is variation in the fundamental reasons behind the decision to convert organizational form, there are some general patterns that can be gleaned from the case studies. Although the factors that contribute to co-operatives converting to investor-owned firms are at times a taboo subject, the reality is that conversions have become a realistic alternative for many co-operative organizations. The reported rationales behind most demutualizations include better access to capital required for growth, addressing membership disengagement, a desire to have greater control over the future of the organization, and a wish to rescue failing ventures. The frequent involvement of third parties in both forms of conversion demonstrate a lack of capacity within the organization to manage internally. In the cases of mutualization, the reasons predominately focus on community-based issues including the value of membership and saving the local economy.

It is important to note that the underlying reasons for a conversion to occur may reflect a greater problem that plagues many organizations, not merely co-operatives. Even where a conversion has taken the form of mutualization, a group may not be ready for the responsibility of member control (Sousa, 2006). Therefore, I conclude this chapter with several key lessons from the case studies that can inform an organization's decision to seek the conversion option.

Investigate Creative Approaches to Accessing Sources of Capital

A recurring factor that contributed to the demutualization of co-operatives was their limited access to new sources of capital. Many organizations, for example the Saskatchewan Wheat Pool, felt that the constraints associated with raising capital while operating as a co-operative prevented expansion and limited their growth potential, as global markets have become increasingly competitive. However, as found in the Lilydale case, organizations seeking to convert to an investor-owned firm need to be aware that market conditions for their product or service may not be favourable during a period of change. Moreover, although demutualization has been one option pursued by co-operatives, greater consideration could be given to seeking alternative access to sources of capital within a co-operative framework. Therefore, prior to any conversion for the purpose of accessing sources of capital, there should be a thorough investigation of what creative approaches to accessing sources of capital are available. Alternatives may involve different approaches for capitalization, such as developing new capital-seeking entities or ventures. The intention should be to preserve the organization's original identity while allowing for an infusion of new capital. However, caution is urged with respect to agreements made with external investors.

Make it Simpler to Convert Organizational Forms

The decision to convert organizational forms is never an easy one. In some instances, the organizations did not have appropriate guidelines related to undertaking a conversion process. In others, legislative hurdles introduced delays into the processes. Government bodies were unaware of how to proceed, which had a negative effect on the organization's already limited resources. Additionally, significant reliance on third-party groups or managers unfamiliar with the co-operative identity resulted in an uneven influence on member opinion towards demutualization.

The case studies consistently highlight an apparent lack of an accountable, transparent conversion process, a key problem in the development of the Dakota Pasta Growers Company and the Dakota Carrier Network. These conversions were often a reaction to adverse circumstances, and in many instances the membership was unaware of fiscal problems or of whether there were consequences of converting organizational form. In organizations that went through either of the two conversions, members felt somewhat confused and disenfranchised. Some members even expressed suspicion towards the managers and the board of directors. In one case, for instance, individuals promoting the demutualization option were accused of benefiting financially from the change.

Creating a simpler and streamlined process would ensure that co-operative organizations are aware of conversion alternatives, which can include remaining as a co-operative, by receiving information that is accessible, accountable, and transparent. A streamlined process can be legislated to include government guidelines that rely on the resilience of the co-operative identity rather than its limitations. Such legislation does exist in different jurisdictions in the United States, and across different sectors. However, there is a notable lack of guidelines consistently applied in the Canadian context. Ultimately, co-operatives are responsible for ensuring that the members are completely informed when the conversion option is introduced as a solution to addressing fiscal challenges and limitations to service delivery. However, legislative changes can have the effect of encouraging greater flexibility of the co-operative model and protecting the membership in order to ensure that due diligence has been followed.

Building Capacity for Social Economy Organizations

The challenges the members faced when having to switch roles from producers/users to managers was a recurring theme across the cases that pursued demutualization. As shown in Girard's description of the Coop santé Aylmer Health Co-op, members in leadership roles must understand business principles, be willing to devote time to frequent meetings, be willing and able to engage outside professionals for assistance, and be willing to make tough decisions in a timely fashion. Most of all, these individuals must work well together. The challenge associated with switching roles often leaves organizations relying on external managers and advisers to make decisions that are integral for the future of the co-operative. Furthermore, they may be unfamiliar with the significance that maintaining a co-operative identity has for the membership.

Capacity-building initiatives should be implemented to support the current and the new organization. Relying on sweat equity and the good will of individuals introduces numerous obstacles, as these individuals may not possess the adequate knowledge required to operate a business, such as the ability to understand a financial statement. Capacity building can be supported and achieved by reinforcing core principles of community development associated with co-operatives. Effective communications, unwavering dedication, and hard work on the part of co-operative leaders are essential. To ensure success, members require training grounded in practical knowledge as well as strategic planning.

The importance of education of current and future members was also a gap highlighted by organizations that have undertaken either type of conversion. Education in this context refers to making sure potential members are knowledgeable about what co-operatives are, how they work, and their potential benefits to members in order to keep a positive focus on the conversion process as it relates to co-operative development. An education plan should be developed, approved and implemented by the members throughout the conversion process. The education plan would highlight important pieces of information regarding the new organizational form, objectives of the conversion, and collaboration with similar organizations, including other co-operatives.

Involve Apex and Sector Organizations during and after Conversion

A consistent finding across the case studies was the benefit of an apex or sector organization during and after a conversion process. An apex organization can serve as a voice of member organization (e.g., the Canadian Co-operative Association) whereas sector organizations can both support and represent co-operatives that are part of the same sector (e.g., the co-operative housing federations). Since there are still not a large number of examples of conversions, organizations rely on a limited number of developers that have both experience in conversions and strong ties to government. In the conversion to co-operative scenarios, these organizations provided key support and training to the emerging membership; however, their presence was significantly reduced during the post-conversion period. For instance, the conversion of the Virginia Poultry Growers Co-operative was only possible through the collaborative efforts of an engaged membership and resource persons familiar with the sector and government bureaucracies. Organizations that followed a route towards demutualization were often composed of an uninvolved membership and management who vigorously pursued the private option. Oppositional voice by co-operative sector organizations was notably absent.

Apex and sector organizations need to be involved when both types of conversions are being considered. They can express opposition during the demutualization process or serve as an independent observer to ensure that the membership's desires are followed. In conversions resulting in a new co-operative, sector organizations should continue to be involved with the new co-operative for a period of time after the conversion has been completed. Support from specialized professional resources in managing co-operatives should continue to be provided in the interim. Specific training concerning co-operative administration should be offered regularly to the members. Such training can be much more than providing information: it can help to ensure that the new co-operative is functioning from proper financial and community development perspectives.

NOTE

1 South Interlake Credit Union became known as Sunova Credit Union as of 2008 (Sunova Credit Union, 2011).

REFERENCES

Boland, M. (2012). When you need to expand: Dakota Growers Pasta Company. In J. Sousa & R. Herman (Eds.), *A co-operative dilemma: Converting organizational form* (pp. 40–52). Saskatoon Centre for the Study of Co-operatives, University of Saskatchewan.

Brown, R., & Merrett, C. (2000). The limited liability company vs. the new generation co-op: Alternative business forms for rural economic development.

84   Jorge Sousa

Rural Research Report. Illinois Institute of Rural Affairs, Western Illinois University. Retrieved from http://plantsforhumanhealth.ncsu.edu/extension/mar ketready/cooperative-development/pdfs/llcs-vs-new-generation-coops.pdf

Chaddad, F., (2003). *Waves of demutualization: An analysis of the economic literature.* Paper presented at the congress, Mapping Co-operative Studies in the New Millennium.

Chaddad, F., & Cook, M. (2004a). Understanding new co-operative models: An ownership-control rights typology. *Review of Agricultural Economics, 26*(3), 348–60.

Chaddad, F., & Cook, M. (2004b). The economics of organization structure changes: A US perspective on demutualization. *Annals of Public and Co-operative Economics, 75*(4), 575–94.

Cobia, D. (1989). *Cooperatives in agriculture.* Englewood Cliffs, NJ: Prentice-Hall Inc.

Coleman, W. (2006). Globalization and co-operatives. Retrieved 15 August 2006, from http://www.usaskstudies.coop/pdf-files/Coleman.pdf

Davis, S., & Patrie, W. (2012). Co-ordination among co-operatives: Dakota Carrier Network. In J. Sousa & R. Herman (Eds.), *A co-operative dilemma: Converting organizational form* (pp. 171–89). Saskatoon Centre for the Study of Co-operatives, University of Saskatchewan.

Department of Finance, Canada. (2000). *Canada's credit unions and caisses populaires: The Canadian financial system.* Retrieved from http://www.fin.gc.ca/toce/2000/ccu_e.html

Fairbairn, B. (2006). *Cohesion, adhesion, and identities in co-operatives.* Retrieved from http://www.usaskstudies.coop/pdf-files/Fairbairn.pdf

Fairbairn, B. (2012). The "new" credit union: Sunova Credit Union. In J. Sousa & R. Herman (Eds.), *A co-operative dilemma: Converting organizational form* (pp 200–21). Saskatoon Centre for the Study of Co-operatives, University of Saskatchewan.

Frederick, D. (1997a). The ABCs of LLCs Limited Liability Companies offer new option for rural businesses. *Rural Co-operatives, July/August,* 36–9.

Frederick, D. (1997b). *Co-operatives 101: An introduction to co-operatives.* Report. Retrieved from http://www.rurdev.usda.gov/rbs/pub/cir55/cir55rpt.htm

Fulton, M., & Larson, K. (2012). Failing Members and Investors: Saskatchewan Wheat Pool. In J. Sousa & R. Herman (Eds.), *A co-operative dilemma: Converting organizational form* (pp. 94–124). Saskatoon: Centre for the Study of Co-operatives, University of Saskatchewan.

Girard, J.P. (2012). More than just a band-aid solution: Coop Santé Aylmer Health Co-op. In J. Sousa & R. Herman (Eds.), *A co-operative dilemma: Converting organizational form* (pp. 157–170). Saskatoon: Centre for the Study of Co-operatives, University of Saskatchewan.

Goddard, E., Hailu, H., & Glover, F. (2012). Striking a balance: Lilydale Poultry Co-operative. In J. Sousa & R. Herman (Eds.), *A co-operative dilemma: Converting organizational form* (pp. 53–72). Saskatoon: Centre for the Study of Co-operatives, University of Saskatchewan.

Guadaño, J. (2005). *The demutualization process of European co-operative societies.* Retrieved from http://www.uv.es/iudescoop/abstracts/Fernandez_ Guadanno.doc

Harris, A., Stefanson, B., & Fulton, M. (1996). New generation co-operatives and co-operative theory. *Journal of Co-operatives, 11,* 15–28.

Herman, R., & Fulton, M. (2001). New generation co-operatives: Part of a revitalization strategy for rural economies. *Making Waves, 12* (1), 37–40.

Hogeland, J. (2004). How culture drives economic behavior in co-operatives. *Journal of Rural Co-operation, 32*(1), 19–36.

International Co-operative Alliance. (2007). *Statement on the co-operative identity.* Retrieved from http://www.ica.coop/coop/principles.html

James, C.L. (1995). *Spanning boundaries: Rethinking community, competitiveness, and cooperation.* Work in process. National Rural Co-operative Development Task Force and the Co-operative Development Foundation, April.

Johnston, J. (2012). Credit co-operative to credit corporate: Australian credit unions. In J. Sousa & R. Herman (Eds.), *A co-operative dilemma: Converting organizational form* (pp.25–39). Saskatoon: Centre for the Study of Co-operatives, University of Saskatchewan

Jones, M.B. (2007). The multiple sources of mission drift. *Nonprofit and Voluntary Sector Quarterly, 36*(2), 299–307.

Jorgensen, N. (2005). Leaving home? Reasons vary for co-operative conversions: Critics remain wary of producers losing control. *Rural Co-operatives, 7*(1), 8–11.

Lee, R. (2003). *Changing market structures: Demutualization and the future of securities trading.* Retrieved from http://www.oecd.org/dataoecd/5/15/18450470. pdf

Mooney, P., & Gray, T. (2002). *Co-operative conversion and restructuring in theory and practice.* Retrieved from http://www.rurdev.usda.gov/RBS/pub/rr185.pdf

Nadeau, E.G., & Nilsestuen, R. (2004). *Strengthening co-operative business structures: Lessons learned from demutualization and co-operative conversions.* Study commissioned by National Co-operative Business Association. Retrieved from http://www.ncba.coop/pubs.cfm

Quarter, J., Mook, L., & Armstrong, A. (2009). *Understanding the social economy: A Canadian perspective.* Toronto: University of Toronto Press.

Paradis, G. (2000). *Capital needs and co-operatives.* Retrieved from http://www.did. qc.ca/documents/GPA_RIO_DEC00_ang.pdf

Sousa, J, & Herman, R. (2012). Converting organizational form: An introductory discussion. In J. Sousa & R. Herman (Eds.), *A co-operative dilemma: Converting organizational form* (pp. 1–22). Saskatoon: Centre for the Study of Co-operatives, University of Saskatchewan.

Sousa, J. (2006). *Building a co-operative community: The conversion of Alexandra Park to Atkinson Housing Co-operative.* Unpublished dissertation.

Stanford, L., & Hogeland, J.A. (2004). Designing organizations for a globalized world: Calavo's transition from co-operative to corporation. *American Journal of Agricultural Economics, 86*(5), 1269–75.

Stefanson, B., Fulton, M., & Harris, A. (1995). *New generation cooperatives: Rebuilding rural economies.* Saskatoon: Centre for the Study of Co-operatives.

Sunova Credit Union. (2011). *Introducing Sunova.* Retrieved from https://www.sunovacu.ca/news/introducing_sunova/

Taylor, M.P. (2004). *Co-operative conversions: Demutualizations still rare but pressures growing, study finds.* Retrieved from http://www.coopscanada.coop/pdf/Resources/articles/CBJ-Conversions-CenterSpread.pdf

Wadsworth, J.J., & Brockhouse, J.W., Jr. (2012). An unexpectedly quick conversion: Virginia Poultry Growers co-operative. In J. Sousa & R. Herman (Eds.), *A co-operative dilemma: Converting organizational form* (pp. 222–33). Saskatoon: Centre for the Study of Co-operatives, University of Saskatchewan.

4 The Difference Culture Makes: The Competitive Advantage of Reciprocal, Non-monetary Exchange

ANA MARÍA PEREDO

Increasingly, the relationship of business to the communities in which it operates is the focus of attention among management scholars. In this chapter, I wish to go beyond the view that communities should be seen as stakeholders and/or as the target of corporate social responsibility. I will argue that certain cultural endowments in certain communities may in fact contribute a sustained advantage to enterprises embedded in those communities. I will focus on a concentrated form of this embeddedness: 'community-based enterprises' (CBEs), or ventures in which communities act collectively as both entrepreneur and enterprise. An outline of the conditions in which they typically arise, the features they characteristically display – especially their blend of social and economic goals – and their participation in the global economy demonstrate the way that their cultural endowments contribute a rich supply of non-monetary resources to their operations. These resources constitute an important and sustained competitive advantage.

In this chapter, I will focus on CBEs as a concentrated example of a more general force in many business operations: the contribution of culturally derived, reciprocal, and non-monetary exchanges to sustained competitive advantage. I will argue that an essential element of this contribution is the way in which these forms of enterprise include social aims, often predominantly, in their goal structure. I begin by defining CBEs more precisely. I continue by outlining the conditions in which they arise and their characteristic features, and mention some of the many examples of this form of enterprise that exist around the world. I then discuss CBEs' participation in the globalizing economy, including an interpretation of their operations that takes account of theoretical constructs such as embeddedness, gift economies, and social capital.

There are significant challenges to this kind of enterprise, as recognized the next section of the chapter. I make no attempt to predict the outcome of these challenges. I end the chapter with some summary conclusions and suggestions for future research.

What Is Happening in Canada?

In early 1988, as a newly-minted graduate student, I began my first fieldwork in an isolated community called Canaca, in the southern province of Puno, in my native country of Peru. I was there to study how a recently-introduced program of agricultural loans to communities was developing on the ground. Canaca, a community at 4,500 metres above sea level, was the first recipient of such a loan. Villagers' houses were scattered through thick, brown hills, and ever-present and excitable dogs made them hard to approach. I knew it was harvest season, so I did not take anything to eat. When I became hungry, I approached people I encountered returning from their harvesting and asked if they could sell me something. They were invariably polite, but just as invariably replied, 'I am sorry. I do not have anything. Maybe the next person has.' The next person never did. It appeared no one could sell me anything, even if I offered a high price for their products. I knew food was being harvested. I was baffled by this apparent breakdown of the system of supply and demand.

A month later my relationship to the villagers was quite different. I was now working with them in the fields in the potato harvest, and their response to my nutritional needs had also changed. I was regularly and generously supplied with chuno (dried potato) and cheese, though no one would accept any cash in exchange. I realized that I was being introduced to a vital concept in understanding how Andean rural people survive. I called it 'the Andean insurance,' in which resources are circulated in keeping with deep and diverse cultural traditions of reciprocity. My expectation that the production and distribution of necessities would be governed by some version of market forces was simply an alien import.

My initial research on credit evolved into research on social networks and rituals as I came to understand that the credit resources I was studying were entangled with the social and cultural life of the community and its emphasis on reciprocity. Loans had become 'diverted' into looking after responsibilities that came from community membership, such as 'first haircut' ceremonies, weddings, funerals, or other events that benefited others in the community. From the perspective of financial or government institutions, the program had failed. People were not taking capitalistic advantage of their loans.

Field work often presents the researcher with phenomena that are deeply puzzling, given an outsider's point of view. It was years later, many of them spent in remote communities in the Andes, that I began to understand the full potential of that network of reciprocity as the basis for the creation and maintenance of CBEs functioning in this community as well as in many others. Recognizing this kind of provisioning activity, deeply rooted in traditions of reciprocity, solidarity, and collective undertaking, changed my simplistic assumptions about the ways that economies could work, and the ways that business venturing could fit into them.

What Is a 'Community-Based Enterprise'?

The theoretical notion of the CBE is based on research in a number of Andean communities, and was shaped by an interdisciplinary literature concerning such topics as economic anthropology, network theory, and entrepreneurship. I define it as a community acting corporately as both entrepreneur and enterprise in pursuit of the common good. 'Entrepreneurship' itself is a keenly contested concept (Venkataraman, 1997), however, let us suppose that entrepreneurship is the linking of an inadequately met need or want with an under-used source of supply. The way in which this link may be forged varies according to circumstances, for example:

> an alertness to profit opportunities (Kirzner); the exploitation of a new technological possibility (Schumpeter); a bet, gamble, or chance on some new idea (Brenner); the exercise of control over means of production (McClelland); a management discipline (Drucker); the creation and ownership of a small business or new business (Drucker; Reynolds, Hay & Camp); a purposeful task or practice (Drucker); and the acceptance of risk and/ or uncertainty in the pursuit of profit opportunities (Cantillon). (Brenkert, 2002, p. 9)

No doubt there are more. For our purposes, it will be sufficient to say that the community acts as an entrepreneur when its members, acting as planners, owners, managers, and employees, collaboratively create or identify an opportunity to bring together some need or want with some way of supplying it, and organize themselves in order to respond to that opportunity.

'Enterprise' is a less contentious concept, though there is a degree of ambiguity about it. Generally, enterprise may be understood as 'an undertaking, especially a bold or difficult one' (Barber, 1998, p. 466). More narrowly, it may simply be taken to refer to 'a business' (p. 466). For our purposes, it is best to mingle these two definitions, while broadening the definition of business to include activities that are not confined to profit-making for some individual or collective. That is, a community acts as an enterprise when its members work together to jointly produce and exchange goods and/or services using its existing social structure as a means of organizing those activities. In sum, CBEs represent both the entrepreneurial process of venture creation and the venture created through that process.

What delineates the communities in this discussion is geographical location, perhaps combined with culture and ethnicity and other shared relational characteristics (Molinary, Ahern & Hendryx, 1998). This distinguishes them from 'communities' that are formed on the basis of shared goals or participation in some productive activity. The communities in CBEs exist before they become CBEs.

The idea that members act 'together,' 'corporately,' or 'collaboratively' must allow for some differences in involvement. Some members may be more active than others, but most or all will have some role in developing and implementing the entrepreneurial initiative. Governance is corporate in the sense that most if not all members will take some part in overseeing the enterprise's activities. These operations are typically governed by the community assembly, of which all community participants are members. Decisions are made at assemblies concerning policy directions, and often with respect to more detailed matters concerning the community enterprise. Sometimes, there are sub-committees of the assembly with specific responsibility for monitoring and directing the operations of the enterprise, or for specific elements in the enterprise if its activities are complex. Some members of the community will also be directly involved in carrying out the work of the enterprise. But fundamentally, it is understood that community members will be more or less united in their commitment to their collective undertaking, and to taking some significant role in deciding upon its direction and in reflecting on its actual operations.

An essential feature of these undertakings is that while they must return some profit in order to be sustainable, profit is typically seen as a means to achieving other community goals, such as health or educational services. Lower profits may be acceptable if that is the price for achieving other community purposes, such as wider employment. In CBEs, therefore, profitability is generally a means to serving other community objectives.

CBEs are not the same as organizations set up by government to operate in the interests of a community, or operations that may be put in place by a sub-group to benefit the community. However important enterprises like these may be, their dynamic is quite different from CBEs, which are owned, managed, and governed by community members themselves, and not by others on their behalf. CBEs are also distinct from co-operatives, though they can share similarities. The membership of a co-operative is a voluntary association of people who may or may not share community membership but decide to unite in co-operative pursuit of some goal. As mentioned above, CBEs begin in a shared community, and evolve from there into a collective undertaking. In certain circumstances, there may be co-operatives that are so linked with communities that they are hard to distinguish from CBEs, but 'The world is not perfectly tidy with respect to what is and what is not a CBE' (Peredo & Chrisman, 2006, p. 316), and that is not a bad thing.

What Gives Rise to Community-Based Enterprises?

The emergence of CBEs are favoured by a fertile combination of at least five community characteristics: (1) some condition or event of stressful disequilibrium, (2) cultural traditions of reciprocity and generous deposits of social capital, (3) previous experience of collective, concerted action, (4) a repertoire of skills in the community, either traditional or acquired more recently, and (5) an appropriate size. Each of these deserves a brief explanation.

First, CBEs are typically rooted in the attempts of a community to respond to serious economic and social stresses. These stresses may be material, such as a gathering crisis in food production or economic circumstances; or they may be social and even political, such as the alienation of a community from mainstream society or political life. They may in turn be brought on by critical or accumulated environmental forces, such as drought or flood, soil erosion, or climate change. Or they may result from armed conflict, social marginalization, or political oppression. These factors are often, but not always, a reflection of macro conditions, such as large-scale environmental changes, national economic crisis, or shifts in political ideology. At the community level, the aggravating factors are often multiple and inter-related. The main point is that a major factor in the emergence of CBEs appears to be an experience of community disequilibrium that threatens its sense of survival. The result is a drive to find new resources and new social arrangements.

Second, a factor that seems to focus this drive to gain or regain an acceptable way of life is a cultural deposit of co-operative social organization. In the Andean highlands, traditions of co-operative interaction are vital instruments of survival in an environment where the agricultural production that forms the backbone of the economy is precarious and government safety-nets are non-existent. The traditions of *ayni* (reciprocal work among two families), *minga* (among a group of families), and *faena* (involving activities for the benefit of the entire community) (Alberti & Mayer, 1974; de la Cadena, 1989) represent ingrained patterns of interdependence and reciprocity that are fertile ground for CBEs.

Third, and related to these traditions, CBEs arise in part out of an experience of collective action (Helmsing, 2002). The communities in which CBEs emerge have frequently had past involvement in combined political action, such as demanding access to basic services from the government, contesting government reforms, or protesting against such conditions as counterinsurgency or large-scale landownership. The experience of these activities results in the development of collective tacit knowledge related to marshalling and organizing collective energy to pursue community goals (Nahapiet & Ghoshal, 1998; Spender, 1994). It is easy to see how communities may draw on this resource and channel their motivation for community activism towards enterprise creation.

A fourth and crucial factor in CBE development is the existence of an endowment of skills that can be exploited in enterprising activity. As with any entrepreneurial venture, the start-up and success of a CBE require that the community possess, or have access to, sufficient resources (Chrisman, Bauerschmidt, & Hofer, 1998; Gartner, 1985; Katz & Gartner, 1988). The repository of skills and experience in the community is available as a resource that can be used in developing a CBE. Some of those skills are collective ancestral knowledge, assembled over generations of engagement in endeavours such as textiles, pottery, forestry, and agriculture. Others have been developed more recently, such as when community members are employed in industries such as mining or manufacturing, either when those industries enter the community or when members find employment elsewhere. The collection of these skills and experience provide the raw material from which CBEs may be constructed.

Finally, size is a factor. As with any entrepreneurial start-up (Chrisman, Bauerschmidt, & Hofer, 1998), CBEs require a certain level of resource endowment (including skills, capital, and extended social networks) to support their launch and potential for success. Especially in relatively poor communities, the per capita endowment of these resources is not great, and so up to a certain point, an increase in size increases the likelihood of launch and the potential for success. At the same time, many of the factors mentioned above depend on the functioning of developed social networks and the exploitation of 'social capital.' As networks increase in size, they also become more fragmented, and the contacts on which they depend become less frequent. Kranton (1996) argues that reciprocal nonmarket exchanges are more likely and provide greater benefits in smaller markets owing to the likelihood of frequent future contacts. In general, the frequency and quality of contacts is a potent factor in establishing and maintaining the networks that undergird CBEs. So, as communities grow larger and surpass the levels that increase available resources, they reduce the support for factors that encourage the formation of CBEs. The outcome is that successful CBEs fall into a moderate size range – large enough to supply requisite resources, but small enough to encourage and maintain social networks. There are many external factors that influence what the viable range will be, but there is a general range within which CBEs fall.

That is not to suggest that each of these factors is necessary for CBEs to emerge, nor is it to propose that they are jointly sufficient. All I am suggesting is that these are events or conditions that are highly relevant to the emergence of CBEs as defined above. But however complete or accurate the list may be, it offers only a preliminary idea of what CBEs are like in operation.

What are CBEs Like?

One fundamental feature of CBEs is their commitment to a configuration of goals in which profit-making is a means to other ends. Communities forming CBEs typically emphasize the need to achieve social, economic, environmental, and cultural goals simultaneously, for several reasons. To begin with, such communities are often poor or disadvantaged, with little or no access to the social and economic resources of a government or large industry that could provide aid. Frequently, they must find ways of providing or supplementing a variety of things: health and educational services; seed resources for small, family-sized enterprises that form a web of local production; infrastructure such as roads and agricultural implements; the means of addressing soil degradation or other environmental challenges; the preservation of traditional arts or crafts that define their culture and way of life; local employment opportunities for young people; and more. Any or all these and more may urgently require attention, and they are often combined in a complex and dynamic way. Different sectors of the community will have different priorities in the cluster of needs that are evident, and so maintaining a variety of goals, with a flexible balance between them, is part of the operation of the CBE. This balancing act means that CBE goals tend to be holistic and multifaceted, and take into account the particular cluster of economic, cultural, social, and environmental needs that a community faces. Like any entrepreneurial undertaking, CBEs are aimed at economic gain. But that gain is meant to support the array of social, cultural, and material goals that the community has identified as requiring its collective action.

Second, the kind of economic activities adopted by CBEs generally draw on the local repertoire of skills and experience that pre-date the CBE. As indicated above, this repertoire is an important factor in fostering the creation of CBEs. Not surprisingly, then, CBEs are characteristically formed out of that repertoire, whether based on collective knowledge such as crafts or agriculture, or arising out of recent experience in industries of one kind or another. In general, the skills and resources acquired before undertaking a venture are important factors that both improve the chances of success (Bygrave & Minniti, 2000; Harvey & Evans, 1995) and provide a framework for seeking opportunity (Ardichvili, Cardoze, & Ray, 2003). Given that the community in this case is the entrepreneur, the creation and performance of a CBE is a function of the community's ability to combine and adapt in an innovative way its variety of ancestral and new skills, experiences, co-operative practices, and values. CBE undertakings are characteristically an inventive combining of the experience and aptitudes available in the community in relation to the needs and opportunities around them. Indeed, that stock of experience and aptitudes helps the entrepreneurial community identify what opportunities exist.

Third, the governance structure of CBEs has a characteristic form that emerges from the cultural traditions of co-operation and reciprocity noted above. Members of CBEs typically see their ventures as a naturally evolved social and economic form, adapted to the realities and pressures of the market economy while integrating their own cultural traditions (Anderson, 2002; Peredo, 2001). Traditional community management and decision-making are frequently revitalized to play an important part in the communal life into which the enterprise is woven. In general, the governance structure of a CBE can be expected to be consistent with the structure of decision-making in its community, typically involving communal assemblies of stakeholders. Indeed traditional communal assemblies – the governance form for the community itself – are frequently the same body that governs the community enterprise. These bodies are collective in two related senses: all community members (called 'commoners' in the Andean communities that began this story) are members of the assembly/governing body and are expected to take their membership responsibilities seriously; and the decision-making process is highly democratic, with all members having a right, in fact a responsibility, to speak to decisions under consideration, and to vote in determining the resolution. There are several advantages to this arrangement. Community assemblies provide a vital mechanism for achieving that dynamic balance of goals referred to earlier, and in the course of that, dealing with power imbalances and conflict. Collective governance enhances members' sense of ownership (Bendick & Egan, 1995; Hadi, 2001; Hodson, 2002), in contrast with 'development' projects that import solutions and resources or manage them on the community's behalf. Community-based decision-making, with its pooling of experience and expertise, has been shown to improve planning perspective, including anticipation of ecological outcomes (King, 1995), which is crucial in these settings. It also provides a well-accepted and effective means of maintaining accountability in those executing the enterprise. Furthermore, it is important to recognize that while cultural tradition can become the launching pad for new enterprise, there is frequently a significant reciprocal action: the presence of collective enterprise can strengthen or create local social and cultural systems. The active involvement of local members not only reflects the sense of community that exists, but reinforces and recreates it (Bowen, Martin, Mancini, & Nelson, 2000).

Where Are CBEs Found?

This chapter began in communities in the Peruvian sierra, and branched out to communities up and down the Andean backbone of Latin America. However, CBEs and their close relatives are found in communities around the world. These community-based ventures, where community is both collective entrepreneur and enterprise, display variations on the relation to a set of favourable conditions and characteristic features outlined above – and they exist on almost every continent.

In Peru, the self-managed community enterprise of Llapampa and the Community of Chaquicocha Trade Fair are paradigmatic cases of CBE (Peredo, 2003). Moving along the Andes, the communal enterprises of Salinacocha in Ecuador (Peredo, 2001) continue the pattern. The Walkerswood Community in Jamaica launched a community-constituted venture in the 1970s producing traditional cooking sauces, spices, seasonings, preserves, and canned vegetables for world-wide sales and using the proceeds to supply local water, schooling, and employment (Lean, 1995). The Nuevo San Juan Community Forest is community-based organization established in the early 1980s with the aim of promoting development through the use and management of forest and non-forest resources (Quintero, 2006). The database of the UNDP's 'Equatorial Initiative' contains numerous examples of communities organizing around traditional forms and expertise to initiate collective ventures based on environmentally respectful production aimed at enhancing community well-being (Berkes & Adhikari, 2006; Equator Initiative, 2009). The indigenous population of Bali sustains itself while maintaining its distinctive culture through an inventive form of CBE that depends on a dual monetary system, one part entirely non-cash and built out of ancient traditions of co-operation and reciprocity (Lietaer & De Meulenaere, 2003). The declining town of Amagase, Japan, decided as a community in the late 1970s to switch from uncompetitive rice production to co-operative floriculture, using its hot springs as a low-cost source of energy (OECD, 1995a). Community forest projects in Gambia feature an element of government initiative, but build in the CBE manner on existing co-operative traditions to create community-based ventures built on tradition connections with the forest (Dampha & Camera, 2005). The village of Ralegan Siddhi in India used its community traditions and resources to work collectively on projects that led to an abundant water supply, improved services in education and health, and co-operative agricultural production that fuelled development (Hazare, 1997). The highly successful Mondragon Co-operative Corporation in Spain bears all the marks of a complex CBE (Greenwood, 1992; Morrison, 1997). Even relatively prosperous parts of the world produce CBEs. MacLeod (1986) has documented the ways in which communities in

Maritime Canada, acting collectively, have advanced their well-being through communal ventures building on a co-operative culture and a shared store of skills (see Chapter 5 in this book). Elliot Lake in Canada, a community suffering from the collapse of its uranium mine, constituted itself in 1987 as a community corporation aimed at community betterment through the establishment of 'Retirement Living in Elliot Lake' (OECD, 1995b).

It is safe to assume that this is the tip of a very large iceberg. The phenomenon of communities building on their traditions to act corporately in pursuing community well-being is widespread, and in many cases has impressive results, at least in the short run. But how can we understand their participation in the complex, globalizing economies in which they are increasingly immersed? Can they survive, let alone prosper, in that environment? Do they have any hope of maintaining and building the traditions and ways of living that are precious to them?

CBEs in the Global Economy

In what follows, I will argue that CBEs possess certain features that may, given other factors in the business and economic climate, equip them to survive and perhaps even prosper in this heated environment. In order to suggest this, I will appeal to arguments based on theoretical constructs that contribute to my case. An important result of that appeal is that organizational forms that are not necessarily CBEs, but share some significant features with them, and may well have the resources for a particular kind of competitive advantage. In short, I will conclude that resources in the form of traditions of reciprocal, non-monetary exchange often confer an advantage on CBEs and relevantly similar competitors in the global market-place.

In the globalizing economy, participants are exposed to intense price competition, and the ways most frequently adopted to compete in that environment are (a) to increase firm size, so as to take advantage of various kinds of scale, (b) to keep firms mobile, so that they may take advantage of shifts in factor costs, especially labour, and (c) to fragment production, to take advantage of differential deposits of production factors in different locations. These strategies together entail delocalizing enterprises. They tend to lower prices and intensify competition, but they also disconnect ventures from a particular place and community.

Sustained Competitive Advantage (SCA)

What we are considering is whether, in this environment, CBEs might be said to have any potential advantage that would allow them to acquire and maintain a share of the markets they enter that provides them with the return they aim at. The business term for this is 'sustained competitive advantage' (SCA), classically explicated by Barney (1991):

> A firm is said to have a sustained competitive advantage when it is implementing a value creating strategy not simultaneously being implemented by any current or potential competitors and when these other firms are unable to duplicate the benefits of this strategy. (p. 102)

Barney underlines two elements in this definition. First, it refers not only to existing competitors but to potential rivals. Second, the kind of sustainability referred to is not for a temporal period, but represents a kind of equilibrium position where the advantage persists beyond the closure of attempts to replicate it. While a SCA will not last forever, and may be overcome by other changes in economic or other relevant factors in the business environment, it is not lost by other ventures duplicating it.

It is worth emphasizing that this advantage need not enable an enterprise to eliminate all competitors. For our purposes, a venture possesses an SCA if its advantage enables it to achieve and maintain a market share that it finds satisfactory. An SCA need only be sufficient for the enterprise's purposes, however grand or limited those might be. An SCA is therefore relative to the aspirations of a particular venture.

The basis for developing an SCA is an enterprise's resources of various kinds. 'Resources' may be identified and categorized in a variety of ways (Hoffman, 2000), but Barney (1991) provides a useful and concise classification into three categories: physical, human, and organizational capital. Physical resources include technology, plant and equipment, geographical location, and access to raw materials. Human resources comprise the training, skills, personal capacities, and relationships of individuals in the enterprise. Organizational resources encompass the myriad aspects of organizational structure: methods of planning and execution, monitoring, and informal relations both among groups in the enterprise and between the enterprise and people in its environment. These are the potential sources of an SCA.

If any of these kinds of resources are to be the raw material of an SCA, they must not be accessible to competing enterprises (they are 'heterogeneous'), and not easily acquired by any venture that wants to lay hands on them (they are relatively 'immobile') (Barney, 1991). This means that whatever the sources of an SCA are, they may not be purchased on an open market. If they could be, any competitor with the purchase price could duplicate the advantage and it could not be sustained.

Barney (1991) has argued, convincingly, that a resource must possess four characteristics in order to be a potential source of an SCA. To begin with, it must be 'valuable,' or useful, in the sense that it takes advantage of some opening, or at least counteracts some hazard, in the business environment of the venture. Further, it must be 'rare' in the sense that few if any competitors have access to that resource, or at least to the same extent or quantity of that resource. Further still – and this turns out to be crucial – the resource must difficult to replicate, 'imperfectly imitable.' What might make resources 'imperfectly imitable'?

The answer, according to Barney (1991), is some combination of at least two factors strikingly relevant to the forms of enterprise at the centre of our enquiry. Unique historical circumstances are one potent source of inimitability. The particular historical path followed by an enterprise may furnish ways of acquiring and exploiting resources that are simply not available to others with a different history. Second, 'social complexity' – the degree of intricacy and density that exists at all levels of an enterprise, may be a resource that rivals cannot replicate. Relations among those involved in the historical development, direction, management or conduct of the enterprise, or the relationship of the enterprise to its business, social, cultural, and political surroundings, may be and frequently are sufficiently complicated that attempting to reproduce them is futile. Even if competitors knew what it was about the enterprise's 'culture,' its relationship to its community of suppliers consumers and so on, that gives it an advantage, in many cases it is not clear how that connection could be replicated.

Finally, the resource must not lend itself to 'substitutionability,' i.e., it must not be possible to replace the resource with some other that is not rare and can be used to implement the same strategy. Obviously, if a competitor replaces a valuable resource with a different resource that is readily accessible, that resource cannot generate an SCA.

Next, I will argue that the circumstances and backgrounds of CBEs provide them with a rich source of potential SCA. In a nutshell, CBEs are typically supported and enabled by a deeply and tightly woven web of reciprocal exchanges that is extremely valuable, rare, and hard to replicate.

Non-monetary Exchanges and CBEs

Consider the example of Llapampa, a community in the Andean highlands of Peru. The region has been occupied for more than a millennium by a people known as *Wankas*. Today's community members are fiercely proud of their lineage and of having both survived centuries of attempted domination by Incas and Spaniards. These are the people who in 1975 launched and today operate the self-managed community enterprise (SMCE), a CBE under whose umbrella a range of productive activities are conducted, ranging from agriculture to tourism to marble quarrying and silica mining. The history of the SMCE's foundation and the methods of its governance illustrate the above account of favouring circumstances in history and tradition, and characteristic forms of complex goal structure and democratic governance. The mining operation is the most profitable, but agriculture and other operations have played their part in providing the community with a level of social, medical, and educational services, as well as an infrastructure of roads and public buildings that are quite remarkable in the area. At the centre of this network of activity is the tradition of *faena*: unpaid work contributed by all community members to community projects as a matter of regular obligation. *Faenas* built the school and the health centre, are fundamental to the agricultural operations, and their role in reducing costs has been essential to the productivity of the SMCE.

It is important to recognize that *faena* is a part of a complex network of reciprocal exchanges that undergirds life in these communities. These are grounded in an understanding of mutual responsibilities that exist between pairs of families, groups of families, and families and community at large. These reflect the interdependence and reciprocity that are the basis for countless transfers of products and services without a financial basis for exchange. There is a comparatively strong sense of 'community-orientation,' in which members experience their membership as resembling the life of parts of an organism; they tend to feel their status and well-being is a function of the reciprocated contributions they make to their community (Peredo & Chrisman, 2006, p. 313). Alongside this is the sense that members have a right to certain societal benefits, such as health, education, and safety. Individual rights, even to such things as private property and private use of time, are to some extent subordinated to this. This brings with it the impression that the community is not only a provider of benefits but itself has needs, and is a party to these reciprocal, non-monetary exchanges of valuable goods and services. The practice of *faena* is continuous with the pattern of community involvement with their enterprise, including their active participation in governance.

Economic systems based on reciprocity and redistribution are neither archaic nor rare. This elaborate arrangement of reciprocal exchanges regulates the mobility of labour, work, and services in many communities worldwide. They are currently prominent in the economic life of not only the Aymara and Quechua people of South America, but also of the peoples of Papua New Guinea, the communities of Tristan de Cunha in South Africa, the Lio and Maneo of Eastern Indonesia, the Guarani of the Amazon in South America, the Salish and other First Nations people of North America, the Inuit of Rankin Inlet, the indigenous people of Bali, and many others. These networks of non-monetary contribution and exchange are a resource with potential basis for sustained competitive advantage that many CBEs have already seized upon, and other communities would do well to consider.

Non-monetary forms of contribution are a resource, and there can be no doubt they are 'valuable' in the sense outlined above. They are a powerful instrument in opening up and exploiting opportunities that communities identify in considering how to provision and sustain themselves.

Though these arrangements are not rare in the sense that they are found throughout the world, they are 'rare' in the sense that the competition CBEs face as they are confronted by the globalizing economy seldom if ever have access to the same resource, nor can they easily imitate or replace it. To see how 'rare' they are, let us employ the conceptual lenses of 'social capital,' 'embeddedness,' and 'the gift economy.'

The Rarity of Reciprocal, Non-monetary Exchange

It is well-recognized that what is called 'social capital' is an extremely valuable resource in enterprise activity (Flora & Flora, 1993; Flora, 1998; Flora, Sharp, Flora, & Newlon, 1997). Among those who made the concept popular, Pierre Bourdieu defined social capital as 'the aggregate of the actual or potential resources which are linked to possession of a durable network of more or less institutionalized relationships of mutual acquaintance and recognition' (1983, p. 249). Scholars found this a fertile way of identifying a resource, providing the avenues and lubricants of interaction available to those who wished to engage in transactions of various kinds. Interestingly for our purposes, J.L. Flora (1998) expands this notion to include what he calls equality, inclusion and a sense of agency, to constitute 'entrepreneurial social infrastructure': a powerful resource for competitive advantage. There can be no doubt that these added features are among those that typically characterise the communities described here. Social capital, then, especially when it is understood as 'entrepreneurial social infrastructure,' is a resource; and CBE communities possess it in abundance. ·

But seeing social capital simply as a resource fails to recognize the factors that make it rare and inimitable. It was noted above that unique historical origins are a way of furnishing resources that cannot be accessed, and cannot be imitated, by those without that history. Social capital, or 'entrepreneurial social infrastructure,' is generally the outcome of generations of communal experience laid down in dynamic cultural traditions. One way of underlining the profundity of that accumulation is to add the concepts of 'embeddedness' and 'the gift economy.'

One important use of embeddedness is as a tool to understanding the way that economic transactions are affected by the location of transacting individuals and organizations in networks of personal relationships. Granovetter (1985) highlights the degree to which economic transactions are, contrary to standard economic analysis, shaped not just by impersonal calculations of personal benefit but also by immersion in networks of personal relationship. Granovetter's work has been hugely influential in bringing attention to the way that these transactions are the outcome, in part, of social interaction with others in our communities of significant contact.

A related but deeper sense of embeddedness (Krippner & Alvarez, 2007) was advanced earlier by Karl Polanyi (1977, 2001 [1944]), who argued that 'economy' is a broad term that includes various ways of providing for the needs of societies, and that exchanges are governed by a variety of prevailing institutions in the society. Markets are recent as a governing institution, Polanyi argues, but alternative institutions of reciprocity and redistribution are long-lived and deeply-rooted. From the viewpoint of an economic historian, Polanyi suggests transactions were generally undertaken in the context of a web of reciprocal obligations and understandings, and/or acceptance of redistributive rights of community authority. They were not determined by market prices or expectations of individual gain, but by notions of community benefit and one's place in realizing that.

It is arguable that Polanyi's view represents many of the communities engaging in CBE. They are, in this view, not fossils or historical oddities, but fully viable alternatives for conducting an economy. In practice, they constitute the marshalling of resources from an alternative economy as it engages with the forces of a market economy in the process of globalization.

My argument is that these roots of the resource we are discussing, non-monetary exchange, run very deep. Their history and their depth are fundamental in rendering them rare and inimitable. The rivals of CBEs in the globalizing economy are not other CBEs. CBEs are, by nature, relatively small, local, and specific in their operations and resource consumption. What impinges on them in the globalizing economy are enterprises that are enlarging, de-localizing, and broadening in their scope. In that context, the resource of CBEs in non-monetary exchange, deeply understood, will not constitute a sustained competitive advantage no matter what other market conditions are. But it is, potentially, a powerful source of sustained competitive advantage in certain identifiable circumstances. In that role, CBEs are a counter-example to the standard views of what is needed for 'business success.' The sustained competitive advantage related to traditions of reciprocal exchange point to a promise that other forms of enterprise that are not exactly CBEs may build upon.

Challenges in the Globalizing Environment

I have argued that the CBEs typically have access to a resource with high potential for conferring a sustained competitive advantage in their attempts to survive in the globalizing environment. As discussed above, however, a sustained competitive advantage is not guaranteed to last forever. It is worth noting some of the challenges that CBEs and similar ventures face in their contact with an evolving market scene.

To begin with, increased emphasis on cash crops and migration, especially as a result of increasingly export-orientated national economies, characterize the realities of many villages in poor countries. Both have disruptive effects on the fabric of reciprocal exchanges as agriculture becomes more intensely monetized. For example, many households headed by women as a result of outward migration by males in search of employment find it difficult to engage in non-monetary exchange of labour on behalf of their reduced households. Major emphasis on cash crops led to increased wage labour. One Quechua woman, in talking to me about her changing circumstances, referred to cash as 'the devil.' Similar patterns are found throughout Latin America, Asia, and Africa. Netting, Stone, and Stone's study (1989) in Africa documents the way in which patterns of abandoning traditional reciprocal co-operative behaviour leads to inequality and poverty among the Kofyar peoples. Their detailed investigation led them to contest the assumption that rural wage labour is cheaper than co-operative labour. However, labour scarcity gives young men an incentive to make demands and break customs concerning reciprocal work, which depletes the store of social capital that provides potential competitive advantage.

Not only have relationships within communities been transformed and weakened, but relationships among communities have as well. Historical records demonstrate local trade systems among communities based on reciprocal relations. However, many of those been broken in the struggle for accessing cash and by large migrations into shantytowns in the outskirts of large cities.

Second, cultures do not remain static. They evolve and adapt to changing circumstances, and CBEs are one example of that evolution. One change seen in many communities, however, is that younger members, especially those educated at universities outside the community, frequently return with views that create tension with the cultural traditions on which the CBEs rest. It is remarkable to observe young people, particularly those studying business or economics, openly questioning the prominence of social and cultural goals in the structure of the enterprise, and the traditional management by community. At the conclusion of a general meeting in one community, I had the opportunity to meet with a number of students and hear their ideas. Their approach was reflected in the comments of various like-minded young management students from the community: 'We need to become professionals and we should not and cannot carry social expenses in this community,' said one. Another said, 'We have to run this as a private business.' Yet another said, 'Yes, we have to privatize, maybe through commoners' groups that can buy shares, and enter into joint ventures with other companies. To do things right means: community is one thing, enterprise another.' Or: 'We have to hire a manager here.'

No doubt there is a need for increased management skills in the communities, but it seems that management education, perhaps among other things, has the effect of cultural attenuation and disconnecting younger members from the values and cultural traditions of their communities.

Third, 'development' initiatives undertaken by nations or regions in which CBEs are located frequently ignore culture as a resource and fail to appreciate cultural and economic diversity. Discussing one tribal group in Nigeria, Bohannan (1955) writes:

Tiv pride themselves on their family abilities and their subsistence wealth. Today however their ideas of economic exchange and their traditional methods of investment and economic aggrandizement are being undermined by a new economic system which demands different actions, motives and ideas. (p. 60)

Unfortunately, similar things can still be said about other traditional peoples, including the Inuit and the First Nations people of North, Central, and South America. Ethnic groups and communities worldwide are under intense pressure to abandon their cultural and economic way of life in the name of economic development. An Inuit elder leader narrated to me the conflict and divisions that development programs created in his community of Rankin Inlet in the Canadian Arctic. He reported pressure to adopt and engage in 'entrepreneurial' behaviour, explaining that values such as personal gain and individualism being encouraged as part of the drive for economic development contradicted their traditional way of provisioning based on collective undertaking and sharing. Young people, he said, are no longer attracted to learning traditional skills; and if they do, it is only for leisure. The Inuit community of Rankin Inlet indeed are making efforts to build community-based commercial activities based on customary skills. However, there as elsewhere their efforts often go under-appreciated. There is frequently a clash between officials in charge of economic development offices and educational institutions on the one hand, and community leaders on the other.

As result of misunderstandings like these, CBEs' efforts are often constrained and even discouraged. Most of them, in many different countries, are not well supported by financial and legal institutions in their struggle to overcome other productive challenges such as under-capitalization and reduced access to technology. What lies behind the clash are different understandings of development and entrepreneurial activity.

Finally, CBEs not only have to manage in a global environment dominated by giant MNCs that have the advantages of mobility, outsourcing, and scale to cut costs, but they also have to deal with the ideology created by them. Globalization is not just about a set of business ideas and practices, as it also embodies 'a set of political ideas and beliefs coherent enough to warrant the status of a new ideology, but also constitutes the dominant ideology of our time' (Steger, 2005, p. 11). In fact, this ideology promotes values and norms of consumerism as constituting identity around world. MNCs with well-built marketing budgets decide what is produced and consumed everywhere. They define what is 'normal' and 'authentic' (Guliz, 1999). The products of TNCs are regarded in poor countries as modern, fashionable and consequently highly desirable, and as status symbols (Friedman, 2000). In this way, global competition can have the effect of threatening the survival of any local firms, including CBEs. A simple example is a CBE that produces local soft drinks while the young people prefer to buy Coca Cola.

Conclusions and Further Research

I have shown that with their rich endowments of non-monetary exchange embedded in a tradition of reciprocity, CBEs possess a resource well-equipped to provide sustained competitive advantage. Three primary conclusions may be drawn from this.

First, CBEs, with their access to this resource, have strong potential as instruments of provisioning and improved well-being in communities that may be relatively disadvantaged with respect to other resources. They should be searched out, encouraged, and supported by appropriate financial and legal arrangements.

Second, CBEs have great potential, and we should recognize and take advantage of the diversity of economic logics that exists in different regions and locales. Too often, CBEs are seen as instances of one basic economic form in various stages of development, and in need of re-direction when they stray too far from the standard form.

Third, the arguments given above should underline for us the potential of culture as a resource, and not – as often argued, an impediment – in improving well-being for disadvantaged peoples.

There needs to be significant research in locating other forms of enterprise that exploit this same resource of reciprocity and solidarity as a non-monetary contribution to the common good. It is grossly under-recognized the extent to which the functioning of many contemporary societies and economies depends in elements of co-operation, trust, reciprocity, and the 'gift economy' (Offer, 2006). Features of reciprocity and gift economy are the basis for the functioning of families and communities in every society.

For example, rural families in North America as well as in the former Soviet Union engage in a wide range of alternative economic activities that exploit reciprocal exchange as protection from poverty. Alternative market arrangements, such as local currencies, community support agriculture initiatives and micro-credit create a context for the co-existence of monetary and non-monetary relations (Hinrichs, 2000; Pratt, 2007). Even open source software is often cited as an outstanding example of the reciprocity-based gift economy, creating openness and relationships among people sharing and developing the software, while challenging digital commodification (Best, 2003).

The above are just a few examples of the role of non-monetary reciprocity in contemporary life. The volunteer element is also significant in the not-for-profit sector in Canada or in global institutions such as Habitat for Humanity. In business, research on immigrant ethnic enclaves in the last fifteen years has contributed to our understanding of the role that personal networks have for starting a venture (e.g. Fadahunsi, Smallbone, & Supri, 2000). What needs further consideration, however, is the extent to which communities, as collective units, may function as entrepreneurs and enterprises and may benefit from the gift economy and social capital at their disposal.

REFERENCES

Alberti, G., & Mayer, E. (1974). Reciprocidad andina: Ayer y hoy. In G. Alberti & E. Mayer (Eds.), *Reciprocidad e intercambio en los Andes peruanos* (pp. 13–37). Lima, Peru: Instituto de Estudios Peruanos.

Anderson, R. (2002). Entrepreneurship and Aboriginal Canadians: A case study in economic development. *Journal of Development Entrepreneurship, 7*(1), 45–66.

Ardichvili, A., Cardoza, R., & Ray, S. (2003). A theory of entrepreneurial opportunity identification and development. *Journal of Business Venturing, 18*(105–23).

Barber, K. (Ed.). (1998). *The Canadian Oxford dictionary.* Toronto: Oxford University Press.

Barney, J. (1991). Firm resources and sustained competitive advantage. *Journal of Management, 17*(1), 99–120.

Bendick, M., & Egan, M.L. (1995). Worker ownership and participation enhances economic development in low-opportunity communities. *Journal of Community Practice, 2*(1), 61–86.

Berkes, F., & Adhikari, T. (2006). Development and conservation: Indigenous businesses and UNDP Equator Initiative. *International Journal of Entrepreneurship and Small Business, 3*(6), 671–90.

Best, K. (2003). Beating them at their own game: The cultural politics of the open software movement and the gift economy. *International Journal of Cultural Studies, 6*(4), 449–70.

Bohannan, P. (1955). Some principles of exchange and investment among the tiv. *American Anthropologist, 57*(1), 60–70.

Bourdieu, P. (1983). Ökonomisches kapital, kulturelles kapital, soziales kapita. In R. Kreckel (Ed.), *Soziale Ungleichheiten (Soziale Welt, Sonderheft 2)* (pp. 183–98). Goettingen: Otto Schartz & Co.

Bowen, G.L., Martin, J.A., Mancini, J.A., & Nelson, J.P. (2000). Community capacity: Antecedents and consequences. *Journal of Community Practice, 8*(2), 1–21.

Brenkert, G.G. (2002). Entrepreneurship, ethics, and the good society. In R.E. Freeman & S. Venkataraman (Eds.), *Ruffin series in business ethics #3, ethics and the entrepreneur* (pp. 5–43). Charlottesville, VA: Ruffin Publishing.

Bygrave, W., & Minniti, M. (2000). The social dynamics of entrepreneurship. *Entrepreneurship Theory and Practice, 24*(3), 25–36.

Chrisman, J.J., Bauerschmidt, A., & Hofer, C.W. (1998). The determinants of new venture performance: An extended model. *Entrepreneurship Theory and Practice, 23*(1), 5–29.

Dampha, A., & Camera, K. (2005). *Empowering communities through forestry: Community-based enterprise development in the Gambia. Working Paper No. 8.* Rome: Food and Agriculture Organization of the United Nations.

de la Cadena. (1989). *Cooperacion y conflict en la comunidad Andina: Zonas de producción y organización socia.* Lima, Peru: Instituto de Estudios Peruanos.

Equator Initiative. (2009). *Equator knowledge zone.* Retrieved from http://www.equatorinitiative.org/knowledgebase/index.php

Fadahunsi, A., Smallbone, D., & Supri, S. (2000). Networking and ethnic minority enterprise development: Insights from a North London study. *Journal of Small Business and Enterprise Development, 7*(3), 228–40.

Flora, C.B., & Flora, J.L. (1993). Entrepreneurial social infrastructure: A necessary ingredient. *The Annals of the American Academy of Political and Social Science, 529,* 48–58.

Flora, J.L. (1998). Social capital and communities of place. *Rural Sociology, 63*(4), 481–506.

Flora, J.L., Sharp, J., Flora, C., & Newlon, B. (1997). Entrepreneurial social infrastructure and locally initiated economic development in the nonmetropolitan United States. *The Sociology Quarterly, 38*(4), 623–45.

Friedman, T.L. (2000). *The Lexus and the olive tree* (Rev. ed.). New York: Anchor Books.

Granovetter, M. (1985). Economic action and social structure: The problem of embeddedness. *The American Journal of Sociology, 91*(3), 481–510.

Greenwood, D.J. (1992). Labor-managed systems and industrial redevelopment: Lessons from the Fagor Cooperative Group of Mondragon. In F.A. Rothstein & M.L. Blim (Eds.), *Anthropology and the global factory: Studies of the new industrialization in the late twentieth century* (pp. 177–90). New York: Bergin & Garvey.

Guliz, G. (1999). Localizing in the global village: Local firms competing in global markets. *California Management Review, 41*(4), 64–83.

Hadi, A. (2001). Health knowledge through micro-credit programmes: Experience of BRAC in Bangladesh. *Health Promotion International, 16*(3), 219–27.

Harvey, M., & Evans, R. (1995). Strategic windows in the entrepreneurial process. *Journal of Business Venturing, 10*(5), 331–48.

Hazare, A. (1997). *Ralegan Siddhi: A veritable transformation* (B.S. Pendse, Trans.). Ralegan Siddhi, India: Ralegan Siddhi Pariwar Publications.

Helmsing, A. (2002). Perspectives on economic localized development. *Eure-Revista Latino Americana de Estudios Urbano Regionales, 27*(84), 33–61.

Hinrichs, C. (2000). Embeddedness and local food systems: Notes on two types of direct agricultural market. *Journal of Rural Studies, 16*(3), 295–303.

Hodson, R. (2002). Worker participation and teams: New evidence from analyzing organizational ethnographies. *Economic and Industrial Democracy, 23*(4), 491–528.

Hoffman, N.P. (2000). An examination of the 'Sustainable Competitive Advantage' concept: Past, present, and future. *Academy of Marketing Science Review, 2000*(4). Retrieved from http://www.amsreview.org/articles/hoffman04–2000.pdf

King, A. (1995). Avoiding ecological surprise: Lessons from long-standing communities. *Academy of Management Review, 20*(4), 961–86.

Kranton, R. (1996). Reciprocal exchange: A self sustaining system. *American Economic Review, 86*, 830–51.

Lean, M. (1995). *Bread, bricks, and belief: communities in charge of their future.* West Hartford, CT: Kumarian Press.

Lietaer, B., & De Meulenaere, S. (2003). Sustaining cultural vitality in a globalizing world: The Balinese example. *International Journal of Social Economics, 30*(9), 967–84.

MacLeod, G. (1986). *New age business: Community corporations that work.* Ottawa: Canadian Council on Social Development.

Morrison, R. (1997). *We build the road as we travel.* Philadelphia: New Society Press.

Nahapiet, J., & Ghoshal, S. (1998). Social capital, intellectual capital, and the organizational advantage. *Academy of Management Review, 23*(2), 242–67.

Netting, R.M., Stone, M.P., & Stone, G.D. (1989). Kofyar cash-cropping: Choice and change in indigenous agricultural development. *Human Ecology, 17*(3), 299–319.

OECD. (1995a). Floriculture using local energy in Japan. In *Niche markets as a rural development strategy* (pp. 16–31). Washington, DC: Author.

OECD. (1995b). Retirement living in Elliot Lake, Canada. In *Niche markets as a rural development strategy* (pp. 75–87). Washington, DC: Author.

Offer, A. (2006). *The challenge of affluence: Self-control and well-being in the United States and Britain since 1950.* New York: Oxford University Press.

Peredo, A.M. (2001). *Communal enterprises, sustainable development and the alleviation of poverty in rural Andean communities.* Unpublished doctoral dissertation, University of Calgary, Calgary.

Peredo, A.M. (2003). Emerging strategies against poverty: The road less traveled. *Journal of Management Inquiry, 12*(2), 155–66.

Peredo, A.M., & Chrisman, J.J. (2006). Toward a theory of community-based enterprise. *Academy of Management Review, 31*(2), 309–28.

Polanyi, K., & Pearson, H.W. (1977). *The livelihood of man.* New York: Academic Press.

Polanyi, K. (2001 [1944]). *The great transformation: The political and economic origins of our time* (2nd Beacon Paperback ed.). Boston: Beacon Press.

Pratt, J. (2007). Food values: The local and the authentic. *Critique of Anthropology, 27*(3), 285–300.

Quintero, A.O. (2006). *Lessons from the Equator Initiative: The Community-Based Enterprise of Nuevo San Juan, Mexico.* Winnipeg: Natural Resources Institute, University of Manitoba.

Spender, J.-C. (1994). Knowing, managing, and learning: A dynamic managerial epistemology. *Management Learning, 25,* 387–412.

Steger, M.B. (2005). Ideologies of globalization. *Journal of Political Ideologies, 10*(1), 11–30.

Venkataraman, S. (1997). The distinctive domain of entrepreneurship research: An editor's perspective. In J. Katz & R. Brockhaus (Eds.), *Advances in entrepreneurship, firm emergence, and growth: Vol. 3* (pp. 119–38). Greenwich: JAI Press.

5 Community Business Development

GREG MACLEOD WITH MIKEL CID

This chapter focuses on community business development as a subset of community economic development. Community economic development has been an important movement for over forty years in the United States. It covers a range of developmental activities, but its core is usually job creation for the marginalized. A number of federal government agencies are involved in community economic development. They provide grants to local community groups to build museums, to establish nature trails, to support the arts and so on. They contribute to local economic development, but they tend not to result in self-sustaining, wealth-creating businesses. Governments tend to reduce all economic activities to either profit-making business or charity. Nonprofit businesses that generate a profit or a positive net income and create community wealth seem to be a contradiction in the eyes of most government agencies.

Advocacy groups, while important, differ from community businesses. Advocacy groups require broad community support, and the grassroots approach is relevant because there is power in numbers and an advocacy group must exert enough power to change a political reality. In contrast, a community business organization must ultimately generate a profit; hence the recruitment of people with business skills is more important than building a large number base.

Some community groups engage in commercial activities for community improvement, but they are not businesses. One well-known example is Habitat for Humanity, a group that builds houses for underprivileged people. However, their services are provided by volunteers, in order to reduce the eventual costs of its homes. Similarly, many church groups run low-cost clothing centres as nonprofit organizations, and are sustainable because of donations and volunteers. It is not a community business per se, but rather a market-oriented activity that uses the conventional tools and techniques of business for social purposes.

This chapter is organized as follows. First, we discuss the three defining characteristics of community businesses through the use of examples. Second, we discuss the requirements for a community business strategy that draws on the examples in the chapter. Finally, we conclude with a section on the kind of infrastructure that community groups should strive to establish for the development of job-creating community businesses. Several themes run through this chapter, including the difficulty of conciliating practice with theory, and of balancing business efficiency with social goals. These are age-old concerns for practitioners familiar with the history of social-economic reform movements, and they have not yet been resolved. This chapter is written from the point of view of a practitioner.

Characteristics of Community Business

The following three characteristics differentiate community businesses from other types of economic development:

1 Intention – The business must have local social improvement as its primary intention.
2 Balancing imperatives – The business must balance social imperatives and business imperatives.
3 The social – The business must be person centred and place based, i.e., local people must take priority over capital.

Intention

In characterizing a community business, the intentions of the leaders are critical, and the 'why' becomes just as important as the 'how.' A business is not a 'thing'; it is a group of people working together to produce goods or services for exchange. Thus participants can be held socially responsible as part of a corporation (Gower, 1979).

Our notion of community business or community development corporations grew out of the thinking of Dr Alex Laidlaw. He worked closely with Moses Coady and Jimmy Tompkins of St Francis Xavier University in the 1940s but had a much stronger background in economics and history than his colleagues. Laidlaw served as the executive director of the

Co-operative Union of Canada and sought to introduce innovative ways of reforming the economy. At a community development workshop at Acadia University in 1975, Laidlaw called for 'the creation of clusters of specialized co-operatives or a single multi-purpose society especially in urban areas in such a way as to provide a wide range of economic and social services: housing, credit, banking, insurance, restaurants, industrial enterprises, medical services, tourism, recreation, etc., within the scope of a single neighbourhood co-operative complex' (Laidlaw, 1975, p. 12). Like Tompkins, Laidlaw feared that the institutionalization of great ideas and great movements would stultify change. He said that the great innovations in social economic reform were not the results of new thinking, but rather of discovering or rediscovering the deeper nature of society itself. Classically educated, Laidlaw believed in basing one's actions on higher universal truths and principles. He understood very well the importance of clarifying an organization's intentions.

Human action is human in sofar as it is intentional (Anscombe, 1957). For instance, from the outside, some production activities at the Mondragon Corporation look like operations at General Motors, but there are different motives and intentions behind them. For example, that different intention is the reason that during the 1980s economic crisis, Mondragon accepted lower profits rather than laying off workers (MacLeod, 1997; Whyte & Whyte, 1991).

Intentionality fundamentally defines community business. Some community business leaders intend to create a new world order, a 'co-operative commonwealth.' Others intend to respond to local needs. In all cases, the intent is to improve the quality of life and allow people to develop their full human capacities. Historically, most social movements were inspired by either religion or Marxism. In the twentieth century, these universal movements were dampened by the force and power of global economic systems. Yet, even though the goals have become more modest, the ideals and principles of these movements provide the real force behind community business development.

Commitment to the well-being of the local community implies responsiveness to local needs. This intention clearly differentiates community businesses from conventional corporations. In community business, a clear improvement in community well-being is the measure of success. This can include a lower unemployment rate, increased affordable housing, or greater environmental sustainability. Community business development begins with an analysis of the needs of the community and a commitment to fulfil those needs. Don José María, the moral founder of Mondragon, often said, 'Ideas divide us but necessity unites us' (Azurmendi, 1984, p. 318). We say: needs unite us.

New Dawn Enterprises in Cape Breton is a clear example of a community business intended to respond to local needs. In the early 1970s, New Dawn was founded by several professors from Cape Breton University (one of whom is an author of this chapter) who were concerned about local economic decline. The beginning was simple. The original board members each lent some money to the organization and then guaranteed a loan at the credit union to gather funds to purchase a building. They rented the first floor to the Cape Breton School of Crafts and built small apartments on the second floor to generate income to pay off the debts. Building affordable housing was one of New Dawn's first projects because many people in the area lived in dilapidated company houses. While other co-operative housing was common in the area, members would often receive support to finance and build their own homes co-operatively, but were not interested in helping other projects once their debts were paid. The resulting self-enclosed system helped only current owners in an approach suggestive of Kropotkin's 'co-operative egoism' (Buber, 1996, p. 42). Just as an individual can focus only on personal needs and forget the needs of others, a co-operative organization can focus on the needs of its members and forget the needs of the larger community. New Dawn organizers found that the early housing co-operative model had no element of growth and extension to the rest of society. Because of this, New Dawn used an alternative approach by retaining ownership as an equity base for borrowing and developing more apartment buildings. The rent paid down the mortgages and created an asset base intended for further development.

New Dawn used that asset base to both improve the community and generate further income. For instance, as in many small Canadian communities in the early 1970s, there was a dentist shortage in Cape Breton. Some communities hoped to attract dentists by building clinics, which were funded through bazaars or other charity events. New Dawn, however, opted to build a clinic first, and then offer an attractive rental rate to attract recent dental graduates. Through this arrangement, New Dawn generated income to pay off the debts. In 2009, New Dawn had approximately 200 employees, $5 million in revenues and $10 million in assets, with enterprises in four divisions: real estate (with 160 residential units and three commercial properties), healthcare (with mobile home services and a nursing home), job training (with programs in homecare, welding, and management), and community services (which include

Meals on Wheels and a Volunteer Resource Centre) (New Dawn, 2010). New Dawn intended to improve the well-being of the community instead of simply profiting, and so it changed the pattern of service provision for marginalized populations by creating community businesses.

The distinction between a co-operative and a community business is not always clear, and depends on the intention. Some co-operatives are community businesses and some are not. For instance, a large dairy marketing co-operative may intend only to benefit the worker shareholders, some of whom might be quite wealthy by virtue of the national quota system. If the marketing co-operative also sets aside funds to expand and diversify in order to create jobs and improve the community, then it could be called a community business.

Just Us! Coffee Roasters is a worker co-operative based in Wolfville, Nova Scotia, that has a different intention than conventional coffee houses. Founded by Jeff Moore in 1995, it aims to address the exploitation of coffee growers in developing countries with the mission 'people and the planet before profits.' It buys coffee, tea, and chocolate that is 100 per cent certified as fair trade and organic, and operates nationally and internationally. In addition to aiding those in developing countries, it raises funds in the local community and sets aside a portion of its earnings in order to diversify with projects such as coffee houses across Nova Scotia. Just Us! has created over one hundred jobs in Nova Scotia and its employees have the right to become worker owners after two years with the company. It is an excellent example of a community business that has gone international.

Balancing Imperatives

The challenge of balancing social intentions and imperatives with the requirements of managing a financially sustainable business (or the business imperative) characterizes the community business experience. One of the main institutions that has promoted the business imperative is the Chicago School of Economics, which has long held that the principal goal of business should be wealth creation through maximizing profits. This group considers social goals an impediment to efficiency and wealth in business (Klein, 2007). For example, the dominant concern of General Motors management over the years has been increasing shareholder value regardless of environmental impact or job reductions. In contrast, in the past, many co-operative stores in Atlantic Canada were overly focused on their social goals, and refused to amalgamate for fear of losing local autonomy and weakening democratic member control. As a result, most of them went bankrupt.

This tension between social and business goals is especially evident in the history of the co-operative movement, which started in France, Britain, and Germany in the first half of the nineteenth century (Yuichiro, 2000). Early leaders of the movement, prompted by a sense of moral responsibility, wanted to negate the suffering and poverty that resulted from the industrial revolution. There were two different approaches: on one side were the idealistic visionaries who wanted to bring about lasting change towards a just society in the form of the Co-operative Commonwealth; on the other side were the pragmatists who carved out smaller projects that could be implemented in a successful fashion. The pragmatists experimented with forms of alternative business based on humanitarian principles, which carry on to this day. Today, millions of people belong to the co-operative movement, which in Canada has a substantial economic presence (Co-operatives Secretariat, 2009). Most Canadian cities have credit unions and co-operative stores with roots in this history (see chapters 2 and 3 in this collection for a discussion of credit unions and non-financial co-operatives, and chapter 1 for a discussion of their role in the broader social economy).

However, the co-operative movement never achieved the results the original pioneers desired. While there are many multimillion dollar co-operative businesses, they pale in comparison with large multinational publicly traded corporations, and the co-operative movement is not the major economic force in any country. Walmart, for example, is the largest corporation in the world, and had annual sales of over $404.4 billion in 2009 (Walmart, 2009). In comparison, Canadian government revenue was forecast to be $224.9 billion dollars (Government of Canada, 2009). Thus, sales at Walmart were almost double Canadian government revenue in 2009. The revenue of co-operative businesses does not compare.

While the vision held by the social economic reformers still has merit, in practice it has fallen short of expectations, and a critical re-appraisal is needed. The key problem lies with the apparent conflict between social logic and business logic. While equality and democracy are enduring social values, the requirements for business success change according to context. The world has changed significantly since the founding of the co-operative movement, and it has impacted how we do business.

In the nineteenth and early twentieth centuries, it was possible for community leaders to organize local citizens into businesses such as credit unions and co-operative retail stores. The locals could own and manage their own businesses for their own benefit. The contemporary business world makes this extremely difficult. Massification has occurred in two domains: economic and demographic. The dominance of global corporations has changed the way everyone does business, and the very survival of small town and rural economies is in question. Many planners think that small scale communities will not likely be sustainable in the future (Williamson, Imbroscio, & Alperovitz, 2002).

The opposition between social values and business efficiency is deep and historic but must be faced by those in community economic development. In general, academic experts in the field do not believe that socially oriented businesses can be serious economic options. Their case studies and examples are drawn primarily from profit-oriented businesses. Rarely would an honours student in business be presented with in-depth analyses of co-operatives and nonprofit businesses. Also, most government agencies seem to share that view as indicated by the proportionate share of government support granted to profit making business as compared to that given to co-operatives and community businesses.

It is fair to criticize leaders who organize businesses motivated solely by profits. However, the reality of business is that a surplus of income can serve many important functions for a socially motivated group. It allows management to establish a reserve for the years with deficits; it provides capital for reinvestment and expansion; and it allows a business to contribute to local community development. The issue is not having a positive net income or profit; it is what the business intends to do with it.

Many of us would argue that companies have a moral obligation to expand and create jobs when they are located in an area with a high unemployment rate, even when it means restructuring the business. For example, during the economic crisis of the 1980s, the Mondragon Corporation began to lose money. Rather than lay off workers, it reorganized. Its bank lowered interest rates and workers accepted a reduction in wages. Other workers were retrained to work in newly created businesses (MacLeod, 1997; Whyte & Whyte, 1991).

In reality, the tension between social and business imperatives can be a creative dialectic. Profits – the business imperative – are important; using them to benefit communities – the social imperative – is equally important. Both are complementary aspects of business. The problem arises when profit is emphasized to the detriment of the social or vice versa. Mikel Cid (2005), a graduate of Cape Breton University and Mondragon University, focused on this very problem as a doctoral thesis. He sought to prove that businesses incorporating social goals were not necessarily less efficient or less profitable than businesses based simply on profit maximization. He used standard empirical measurements such as found in Dun and Bradstreet (2003) to determine business efficiency and measures such as the Kaplan Balanced Scorecard (Kaplan & Norton, 1996) to determine social commitment. He chose at least two businesses in each of three countries and surveyed them. The criteria for selection included that the companies be engaged in industrial production, that they exported on the world market and that they clearly express a social orientation.

Other Examples of Balancing the Business and Social Imperative

QUEBEC

In Quebec, Cid chose two co-operatives: Promo Plastik, a worker co-operative, and Poulies Maska, a worker-shareholder co-operative. Each had started as a conventional capitalist business, but later added a new social dimension through worker participation. The data show that these companies are financially successful and that their social dimension does not interfere with their financial success. Indeed it seems that the social dimension does enhance their productivity. The latter is difficult to prove empirically, so the topic was limited to the simple disproof of the Chicago School argument that social concerns are an impediment to efficiency.

Whereas Promo Plastik is a simple worker co-operative, Poulies Maska is a more complex worker shareholder co-operative formed through a shareholders' agreement between a workers' co-operative and other shareholders. Innovative frameworks such as Poulies Maska help Quebec to be the leader in social economic development in Canada. In such a case, when a manager-owner has difficulty maintaining operations, either because of obsolescence or lack of capital, an agreement can help the business survive. The employees form a co-operative and purchase a percentage (which can vary) of the shares of the company that employs them. Often, when workers fully take over a business, they do not have management experience. In this approach, the workers can participate in both profit and control and still have the benefit of an experienced manager. In the case of Poulies Maska, the worker co-operative had 12 per cent of the votes and 8 per cent of the capital.

Since 1964, Pulleys Maska has established itself both in Canada and the United States as a leader in designing, producing, and distributing commercial and industrial pulleys. Socially, workers participate in management decisions and share in profits. Today, they export to three continents and employ 160 people. For two consecutive years, Maska was among the fifty best-managed private-capital firms in Canada, as ranked by the award established by Arthur Andersen, Mallete & Maheu and the Canadian Imperial Bank of Commerce (Conseil de la Cooperation du Québec, 2003). Eventually, Pulleys Maska reverted to a standard capitalistic company, as usually occurs when a structural innovation in a business is not part of a strong network of like-minded businesses. With success, shares increase in value and sometimes the workers cannot resist the temptation to sell their shares which may be ten times worth the original value.

EMILIA ROMAGNA

In Italy, Cid picked three socially oriented worker co-operatives located in Imola, Emilia-Romagna: Cefla, Società Anonima Cooperativa Meccanici Imola (SACMI), and Ceramica d'Imola. SACMI was created in 1919 by nine workers who, supported by a loan from a local co-operative bank, started to produce ceramics in a gymnasium of a local school. The social values of the founders are illustrated in their by-laws which govern profit distribution: 25 per cent of profit goes to suppport the local labour union movements, 50 per cent is reinvested in reserves, 20 per cent is divided among members, and 5 per cent is used to promote co-operative values. They avoided co-operative egoism. The nine members, who agreed initially to be paid less than the minimum wage, started by repairing and maintaining machinery.

SACMI developed into a modern international business enterprise during Italy's economic boom in the early 1960s. The co-operative hired excellent managers and engineers from elsewhere, and, in the late 1970s, subsidiaries were started in countries such as Spain, West Germany, Portugal, Argentina, Mexico, Brazil, and Singapore (Earle, 1986). One of the criteria to be hired as a manager has been a commitment to co-operative principles.

In 1947, Ceramica d'Imola, a neighbouring worker co-operative, was seriously damaged and needed machines to start its tile production. As a gesture of solidarity, SACMI produced several machines for La Ceramica at a lower cost. In the 1970s, when the price of oil rose dramatically, many industries in the Italian economy suffered losses and closures. However, SACMI and other local co-operatives were able to deal with all those difficulties much better than other firms. SACMI has been a leader in its sector and exports 80 per cent of its production to more than one hundred countries. In 1989, SACMI set up the Research and Development Centre to support all areas of activity of the Sacmi Group.

The region of Emilia Romagna has one of the highest concentrations of co-operative business in the world and has one of the lowest unemployment rates in Italy. The region contains many companies that have retained their co-operative principles and also have become became internationally successful.

BASQUE REGION OF SPAIN

The Mondragon Co-operative Corporation (MCC) is the most famous worker co-operative in the world. Founded in the 1950s by five young engineering graduates, it has expanded to include over 125 business enterprises with subsidiaries in seventeen countries. It has over 95,000 employees, annual sales over $24 billion, and assets of approximately $58.2 billion (Mondragon, 2010). Much has been written about Mondragon (MacLeod, 1997; Whyte & Whyte, 1991) and MCC has received a United Nations award as one of the best fifty social economic experiments in the world.

Irizar is the oldest co-operative enterprise in the Mondragon system, although initially it was not part of the worker co-operative network. Irizar was founded in 1889 in a small Basque town called Ormaiztegi, as a family-owned company called Irizar Brothers Bodywork. In its early days, it produced wheels and wagons, and by 1962 it was manufacturing metal bus bodies. In 1962, the Irizar brothers met Don Jose Maria from Mondragon and invited him to speak to their workers about his new ideas. Following his lecture, Miguel Irizar wanted to convert their company into a worker co-operative. This was a challenge, since the value of a share would have been approximately $5,000 (US), a rather large sum for workers to invest. After many discussions and a visit to the ULGOR Co-operative Ltd, a decision was made in 1963 to become a co-operative and join the Mondragon group. The Irizar brothers, as the original owners, guaranteed loans for the workers.

During this reorganization, it was necessary to reduce staff by 22 per cent. In the Mondragon system, this did not mean job losses – rather, it meant transfers to another Mondragon enterprise, with retraining. The remaining workers were asked to accept a 15 per cent pay reduction, and overtime pay was also eliminated. The hope was that with improved efficiency, both income and worker pay would increase over time (Forcadell & Guadañillas, 2002).

Irizar then focused on luxury buses as its main product, with an emphasis on quality and service. It established service centres in various countries that could rapidly respond if a bus developed a problem. Sales increased quickly. There were three basic components to their success: a focus on customers, the organization of work based on teamwork and a model of leadership based on shared responsibility (Forcadell & Guadañillas, 2002). This plan resulted in profits increasing by 20 per cent within a year and the workforce expanding to 263 workers. Other indications of success included Irizar becoming the first European firm in the industry to be awarded ISO-9001 Business Quality Certification. It was also the recipient of and receiving the UK Coach of the Year Award in 1994 (Forcadell & Guadañillas, 2002).

Cid found that Irizar was very successful from a business point of view, and that it outsold Volvo in some markets. He also found that the company maintained a high level of attention to social values such as shared leadership. It should be noted that in all of these selected cases, the companies did not go to foreign countries because of cheap labour or lax environmental standards. In most cases when a capital-intensive industry becomes successful, it must increase the volume of production in order to pay for technology. Often, the domestic market is too small and foreign markets must be sought, as a natural consequence of modern manufacturing. In studying the expansion of the Mondragon system, Luzarraga (2007) argued that MCC subsidiaries maintained the highest level of social principles as possible in all operations. All of the businesses in this section strike a balance between business performance and maintaining the social values necessary for community businesses. These common features are:

1 They were recognized for excellence in business.
2 They were able to compete in the global economy successfully and still maintain their social values.
3 They established important research and development programmes.
4 They showed a willingness to change and adapt as economic circumstances changed.
5 Their workers were willing to share losses as well as profits, through wage cuts.
6 They had first-class managers.

The Social

The social dimension means that priority is given both to the people involved in the business and to the community in which they live. There is an old argument about whether capital or labour should dominate in business. Mondragon clearly states in its guiding principles that the human element must take priority over capital, one example of its commitment being that its workers are effectively guaranteed lifetime employment. Personal relationships are fundamental to any approach in community business development (MacLeod, 2004). The best-known community businesses often begin with a group of friends deciding to develop a business based on shared human values. In other words, they are based on personal relationships.

In *Bowling Alone*, Robert Putnam (2000) brought to light a fact that most American economists have largely ignored: that human relationships underpin all economic activity. In traditional economic theory, there has been scant recognition of human purpose as being economically significant in relationships within an enterprise, or in the relationship of the enterprise with the community. Anonymity characterizes the world economic system, particularly with respect to publicly traded corporations, in which investors operate remotely with little to no interaction with the factories and employees supporting their stock market shares. In English, a business corporation is simply a 'corporation,' as in General Motors Corporation. In French, a business corporation is called a 'societé anonyme,' while in Spanish it is 'sociedad anonima,' as in Renault, S.A. In English, language masks the lack of transparency and secrecy of corporations, while the French and Spanish terms are more descriptive, as they suggest a faceless, anonymous decision-making system.

In contrast, enhancing human relationships is central to community business. Instead of business being a matter of numbers and data, it becomes a question of humans relating to each other through producing and selling goods and services.

The German sociologist and philosopher Jürgen Habermas (1987) distinguishes between the 'life world' and the 'systems world.' Usually the systems world, or technocracy, dominates. Institutions in business, health, and government have become a complex technocratic system over which individuals have little influence. Schools develop courses that respond to the needs of the system, and ask students to adapt to the needs of impersonal structures instead of learning to reflect on who they are and where they want to go. They become outer-driven instead of being inner-driven. The outer-driven person is guided by manuals and rules imposed by the organization for which he or she works. Rewards and advancement depend on how well one follows external system guidelines. The inner-driven person reflects on personal values and makes decisions based on internal guidelines, even when it means clashing with institutional guidelines. The outer-driven person may advance in the system and receive a higher salary. The inner-driven person will suffer exclusion at times, but will grow as a person. It is the choice between having more or being more.

Large contemporary corporate systems are often technocratic and impersonal and control is usually more powerful than that of the systems of the nineteenth century (MacIntyre, 1984). In contrast, in community business, relationships can be humanized, and a worker is not simply a tool controlled by someone else to generate profit. Internal relationships become humanized when workers can participate in both capital and in management. In the Mondragon system, each enterprise has a social council to assure that social needs are attended to and a board of management where workers have input. Relationships to society are expressed through profit sharing with outside entities, for job creation or cultural development. In Emilia Romagna, co-operatives contribute to a central fund for new enterprise development. Linkages between enterprises are organized in both Mondragon and Emilia Romagna through joint marketing and sharing of common facilities such as research centres. In Quebec, there are regional development co-operatives to encourage collaboration rather than competition.

Workers relate to the enterprise itself as owners in most of the above cases. They play an active part in maintaining a healthy community. Instead of the worker being a tool, the enterprise itself becomes a tool for workers to contribute to the needs of society.

Another approach to community business is place-based development (Hudson, 2001; Lionais & Johnstone, 2010; Williamson et al., 2002). It is a reaction to corporate globalism in which large corporations spread from country to country with little commitment to local populations. Corporations become self-enclosed systems driven by a need to expand and grow, and self-survival dominates. It is now very difficult for any government to influence these huge corporations. In contrast, in all of the cases examined in this chapter, the community business's relationship to a particular place, and to the people who live in it, was the key to success. It is a real problem when a community based business expands to another country. The local and the global are in seeming contradiction; but when the system is based on a social philosophy, creative compromises and solutions can be found (Luzarraga, Dionosio, & Etxebarria, 2007).

In the community business approach, the location becomes the foundation of development. The basic difference between conventional economic development and place-based economic development is the motive or purpose. In conventional economic development, the motive is individual gain. In business terms, success is measured by the increase in shareholder value. The shares are privately owned and can be traded on an open market to increase value. In place-based development, the purpose is the good of the local community. The measure is an increase in community well-being, not individual gain. This can take the form of job creation for the unemployed, development of affordable housing, establishment of a more sustainable environment and so on. The result is an improvement in the quality of life for the local population.

Drawing on the discussion of community businesses and their defining characteristics, we turn to a development strategy for them. What does it consist of?

Community Business Development Strategy

Many communities lack the infrastructure for business development. Launching new businesses therefore requires establishing new infrastructure. Our analysis is based on three cases: local experience in Atlantic Canada, Mondragon, Valencia, and Emilia Romagna. Our focus here is place-based development. Rather than trying to change the world or a whole nation, we concentrate our efforts on the local context in the hope that eventually the larger context will change.

Community business development depends on five pillars: formation, finance, research, technology, and governmental policy. Each relates to the others, and each is a necessary – but not sufficient – component of success. It is important to understand what it means to be necessary but not sufficient. For example, in business, finance is necessary but not sufficient. You may have a great deal of money, but if you have no understanding of modern technology, you will fail. It is also possible to have the five pillars in one place, but if they are not connected the business will experience difficulties. Business development occurs when there is a dynamic relationship between these pillars. We will examine briefly each of these pillars.

Formation

Personal formation has several interpretations. One is moral formation. This implies personal commitment and dedication to the community. It means that one is willing to put special effort into community development projects. In the community economic development sector, this kind of formation is evident. Leaders are expected to make personal sacrifices and work hard. The other kind of formation concerns technical skills.

Fifty years ago, it was possible for fishers in a small community to form a self-managed co-operative, as only very basic business skills were needed. However, in the global economy all business is affected by international competition, and is regulated in a way that did not exist fifty years ago. The manager of even a small business today must possess a wider range skills and knowledge. We use the term 'information economy' to indicate the importance of information in business. If a business manager does not have the information to understand government regulations and tax laws, then that business will fail. Science and technology are another part of the information economy, and always changing, which affects every business. Large corporations have special departments for research and development, but smaller businesses must also be able to keep up. Managing a business therefore requires special talent, training, and education. This training is often fulfilled by local schools, colleges, or universities. Usually, community business groups cannot afford expensive consultants, so it is important that they become partners with local colleges and universities. Many faculty members are happy to help community groups develop new skills. Student workers can also become an important human resource for community groups. It is important that local organizers recognize the necessity of skills and specialization. Early in its development, the Mondragon Co-operative Corporation established a technical school emphasizing both theory and practice. The factory was set up so that students could work four hours a day and study four hours a day. They learned both practice and theory, both of which are essential for community business managers.

Finance

Modern nations have capital located in large financial institutions. It is a general experience of activists in community business that most investment companies are not interested in community-based business initiatives. Hence Mondragon created its own investment bank within the local community (MacLeod, 1997). Emilia Romagna formed several joint funds for the establishment of new co-operative businesses. On a much smaller scale in Cape Breton, the Tompkins Institute at Cape Breton University organized the BCA Group (Banking Community Assets) to raise money in the community for local investment. BCA started simply. A committee was formed and local people were invited to invest in local business projects. Interest was paid annually. The government provided an interest-free loan to match the money raised locally, and BCA's success meant the loan was soon paid back. BCA purchased dilapidated buildings and replaced them with commercial centres as part of a downtown renewal strategy. BCA also achieved considerable success in buying bankrupt companies and reorganizing them. Eventually BCA formed a number of companies to take advantage of government tax credits. BCA will soon form a foundation in order to provide charitable receipts.

In finance it is important to have good legal advice about risk management. No matter how poor a community is, there is always capital present, though the amount depends on motivation and organization. The Carrot Common in Toronto is an example of innovative financing by community activists who joined forces with David Walsh, a prominent real estate broker, and launched a multimillion dollar organic food business (Quarter, Mook, & Armstrong, 2009).

Research

There are business opportunities wherever a group of people live together, but research is important to help discover and develop them. A locally established action research centre not only publishes articles, but also encourages new business developments. To understand the local context, it is important that the research centre be situated in the area under examination and be clearly directed to benefit the local community. A business research centre in New York is not going to be geared towards the specific requirements of Mondragon or Newfoundland. But while the local context is extremely important, so is the global context. It is pointless to develop a new product in one place if someone on the other side of the world has developed the same product using better technology and for a lower price. In the Mondragon Corporation, several important technical research centres were formed and each enterprise dedicated a percentage of its revenue to research. In Emilia Romagna, joint centres for design helped the shoe manufacturing cooperative become worldclass.

Technology

In the early days of Mondragon and Emilia Romagna, organizers decided to seek out the best technology in the world for their new businesses. This became a major source of their success. However, it is important to remember that technology includes not only physical machines, but also the means of organization. How a business is organized, and how it relates to other businesses and to support systems, is called 'organizational technology.' In Mondragon, the co-operative includes over one hundred enterprises, but they linked them together in one marketing system, in one research system, and in one financial system. In the Mondragon co-operative bank, the associated client companies are monitored and must present a five-year budget and monthly profit and loss statements. A central program indicates deviation and then an inspector will be authorized to suggest solutions to prevent further losses. This kind of technology prevents financial problems from getting out of control. If the client does not agree to the system, the loan is refused.

Government

Government plays a role in any business. It is extremely difficult to develop any kind of business if the government is hostile. Often governments have programs to assist small business and, in theory, community businesses can apply. Positive government support often varies from region to region. It is usually easier for social activists to obtain grants for study and social purposes, but with a bit of ingenuity a social grant can sometimes be parlayed into the creation of a business. New Dawn received an important boost in the early 1970s though a federal program called Innovation. Today, less than 5 per cent of the New Dawn budget comes from government grants. The BCA Group is also now completely independent of government. During its first thirty years, Mondragon received no government help. However, it pays to establish good relationships with all levels of government. It does not pay to become identified with any partisan political party. It is also useful for community-based business groups to make policy presentations to government. Tax and other regulations can make the difference between success and failure. In general, governments are happy to see citizen volunteers taking responsibility for job creation and business development. It is particularly important to place a priority on a good relationship with the municipal governments.

GNP Development Corporation, a very dynamic community business, is based in Newfoundland's Great Northern Peninsula (MacLeod, 1991). It established an aquaculture project, a fish plant, and a lumber mill in an area with a population under 30,000. Local participation was strong and the businesses were well run. However, eventually they needed more capital to buy new technology for the lumber business and requested a government loan. The government refused, because the GNP still owed money to the government for the fish plant. Instead of lending to the GNP, the government eventually agreed to lend money to a large mainland company to buy out the community-based business. If the government had been supportive of community business, GNP would have continued to grow and create jobs. Instead, the large mainland company eventually went bankrupt.

Conclusion

These five elements become effective only if they are linked together in a dynamic way. This brings us back to the need for that elusive human element, 'leadership.' Leadership involves personal commitment, energy, and talent. Every community includes people with energy and talent. The Friedmanites in the Chicago School have claimed that greed is the best motivator, however, those who are motivated mainly by profit will usually move to the major successful economies and to large global corporations. In distressed economies, however, a moral commitment to the community is the most successful source of motivation. This personal commitment to one's fellow human beings energized leaders such as Mohammad Yunus in Bangladesh and Don José María in Mondragon. While few can aspire to their kind of leadership, every distressed community has potential leaders who only need to be sought out and encouraged. Creative people often like to be invited to share their talents. Organizers should not hesitate to invite and recruit prospective leaders. If we analyse how each of the five factors actually functions in practice, we will see that dedicated leadership is fundamental to all of them.

REFERENCES

Alcelay, P. (2006). Análisis de una experiencia de filiales productivas en varios continentes: El Caso Irizar. In I. Irizar (Ed.), *Cooperativas, globalización, y deslocalización* (pp. 69–82). Mondragon: Mondragon University Press.

Anscombe, E. (1957). *Intention*. London: Oxford University Press.

Buber, M. (1996). *Paths in utopia*. Syracuse: Syracuse University Press.

Azurmendi, J. (1984). *El hombre cooperativo*. Mondragon: Caja Laboral Popular.

Berle, A., & Means, G. (1932). *The modern corporation and private property*. New York: MacMillan.

Cancelo, A. (2006). Particularidades cooperativas de los procesos de globalización. In I. Irizar (Ed.), *Cooperativas, globalización y deslocalización* (pp. 135–40). Mondragon: Mondragon University Press.

Casadesus-Masanell, R., & Jordan, M. (2006). Irizar in 2005. *Harvard Business Review, 15*(March), 1–26.

Chassagne, M. (1988). L'Europe rurale a l'heure des choix. *La revue Pour,* 115/116, 133–8.

Cid, M. (2005). Making the social economy work within the global economy: An empirical study of worker co-operatives in Quebec, Emilia Romagna, and Mondragon. Unpublished thesis. Cape Breton University.

Conseil de la Cooperation du Québec. (2003). Annual Report, 2003.

Co-operatives Secretariat. (2009). Co-operatives Secretariat Annual Report, 2009. Ottawa.

Dun & Bradstreet. (2003). *Industry norms and key business ratios: One year desktop edition*. Bethlehem, PA: Dun & Bradstreet Industry & Financial Consulting Services.

Earle, J. (1986). *The Italian cooperative movement: A portrait of the Lega Nazionale delle Cooperative e Mutue*. London: Allen & Unwin.

Forcadell, F. (2005). Democracy, co-operation and business success: The case of Mondragon Corporacion Cooperativa. *Journal of Business Ethics, 56*(3), 255–74.

Forcadell, F.J., & Guadañillas, F. (2002). A case study on the implementation of a knowledge management strategy oriented to innovation. *Knowledge and Process Management, 9*(3), 162–71.

Friedman, M. (1980). *Free to choose*. New York: Harcourt Brace.

Government of Canada. (2009). *Federal budget 2009*. Retrieved from http://www.budget.gc.ca/2009/pdf/budget-planbugetaire-eng.pdf

Gower, L.C.B. (1979). *The principles of modern company law*. London: Stevens & Sons.

Greenspan, A. (2008). *The age of turbulence.* New York: Penguin Books.

Habermas, J. (1971). *Knowledge and human interests.* Boston: Beacon Press.

Habermas, J. (1987). *The theory of communicative action.* Boston: Beacon Hill.

Hudson, R. (2000). *Production, places and environment: Changing perspectives in economic geography.* Harlow: Prentice Hall.

Hudson, R. (2001). *Producing places.* London: Guildford.

Irizar, I. (2006). La globalización y la deslocalización: Estrategias de futuro. In I. Irizar (Ed.), *Cooperativas, globalizacion, y deslocalizacion.* Mondragon: Mondragon University Press.

Kaplan, R.S., & Norton, D.P. (1996). *The balanced scorecard: Translating strategy into action.* Boston: Harvard Business School Press.

Klein, N. (2007). *The shock doctrine.* Toronto: Knopf, Canada.

Laidlaw, A. (1975). *Outline of an address presented to a community development workshop for the Atlantic provinces* (January 29). Wolfville, NS.

Lionais, D., & Johnstone, H. (2010). Building the social economy using the innovative potential of place. In J.J. McMurtry (Ed.), *Living economics, perspectives on Canada's social economy* (pp. 105–28). Toronto: Emond Montgomery.

Luzarraga, J., Dionosio, A., & Etxebarria, I. (2007, October). *Understanding the Mondragon globalization process: Local job creation through multi-localization.* Paper presented at the First World Congress of CIRIEC, Victoria, BC.

MacIntyre, A. (1984). *After virtue.* Notre Dame: University of Notre Dame Press.

MacLeod, G. (1991). *The Great Northern Peninsula development corporation.* Sydney: Tompkins Institute.

MacLeod, G. (1997). *From Mondragon to America: Experiments in community economic development.* Sydney: Cape Breton University Press.

MacLeod, G. (2004). The business of relationships. In C.D. Merrett & N. Walzer, (Eds.), *Cooperatives and local development* (pp. 290–315). New York: M.E. Sharpe.

McMurtry, J.J. (2010). *Living economics: Canadian perspectives in the social economy, cooperatives and community economic development.* Toronto: Edmond Montgomery Publications.

MacPherson, I. (1979). *Each for all: A history of the cooperative movement in English Canada, 1900–1945.* Toronto: MacMillan.

Marcuse, H. (1964). *One dimensional man.* Boston: Beacon Press.

Mondragon. (2010). *Economics data.* Retrieved from http://www.mondragon.mcc.es

Morrison, R. (1991). *We build the road as we travel: Mondragon, a co-operative social system.* Santa Cruz, CA: New Society.

New Dawn. (2010). *Annual statement.* Retrieved from http://www.newdawn.ca

Perry, S. (1987). *Communities on the way: Rebuilding local economies in the United States and Canada.* Albany: State University of New York Press.

Quarter, J., Mook, L., & Armstrong, A. (2009). *Understanding the social economy: A Canadian perspective*. Toronto: University of Toronto Press.

Putnam, R. (2000). *Bowling alone: The collapse and revival of American community*. New York: Simon and Schuster.

SACMI. (2010). *History*. Retrieved from http://www.sacmi.com/en-US/About-us/The-History-of-the-Company.aspx?idC=899&LN=en-US

Walmart. (2009). *Wal-Mart Stores Inc: Financial statement*. Retrieved from http://ca.moneycentral.msn.com/investor/invsub/results/statemnt.aspx?Symbol=us%3Awmt

Whyte, W.F., & Whyte, K. (1991). *Making Mondragon: The growth and dynamics of the worker cooperative complex*. Ithaca: ILR Press.

Williamson T., Imbroscio D., & Alperovitz G. (2002). *Making a place for community, local democracy in a global era*. New York: Routledge.

Yuichiro, N. (2000). Development of French co-operative thought in Britain. *Bulletin of the Institute of Social Sciences, 22*(4), 15–30.

Yunus, M. (1999). *Banker to the poor*. New York: Purseus Books Group.

6 Social Businesses in Twenty-First Century Latin America: The Cases of Argentina and Venezuela

MARCELO VIETA, MANUEL LARRABURE, AND DANIEL SCHUGURENSKY

In the first decade of the twenty-first century, Latin America became an exciting laboratory of alternatives to neoliberalism. This was no small feat, because during the last decades of the twentieth century neoliberalism was the only game in town. The rise of neoliberalism in the region can be traced back to 1973 in Chile, when General Pinochet took over the country through a bloody coup d'état. Chile soon thereafter became the first widespread test of free-market oriented economic policies proposed by the Chicago School of Economics. These policies, which recommended privatization of public companies, trade liberalization, deregulation of services, reduction of public budgets, and labour flexibility, among other strategies, were introduced by the Chicago Boys, a group of Chilean economists trained at the University of Chicago. In the following years, in a context of military coups and strict conditions imposed by international agencies (often related to the dismantlement of the welfare state), neoliberalism became the dominant model in other Latin American countries as well.

This dominance became even more hegemonic after the fall of the Berlin Wall in 1989 and the rise of economic globalization. The absence of viable options led British Prime Minister Margaret Thatcher to boast that 'there is no alternative' to neoliberalism. However, by the end of the twentieth century, it became clear that the neoliberal experiment had not solved Latin American societies' economic difficulties. The expected 'trickle down' effect of the 'invisible hand of the market' on wealth redistribution became a 'vacuum up' effect instead. In several countries, neoliberalism promoted corporate welfare at the expense of social welfare, widened the gap between rich and poor regions and people, deteriorated labour conditions, dismantled domestic industries though cheap imports, favoured transnational capital, monopolies and oligopolies, and generated massive unemployment and underemploy-ment (Harris, 2000; Portes & Hoffman, 2003). Consequently, during the first decade of the twenty-first century, efforts to create viable alternatives to neoliberalism began to flourish in different parts of the region. This can be attributed to at least three factors.

First, the economic and political crises that resulted from the failure of neoliberalism – the socio-economic collapse that was most strongly felt by the region's working and marginalized classes – gave birth to a variety of community groups, grassroots movements, and social economy organizations, including neighbourhood assemblies, bankrupted facto-ries recovered by their workers, community kitchens, co-operatives, bar-tering networks, and trade unions that included the unemployed and the retired.

Second, the ideological dominance of neoliberalism was challenged by the World Social Forum, launched in Porto Alegre, Brazil, in 2001 as a response to the World Economic Forum held annually in Davos, Swit-zerland. Since then, the World Social Forum and its regional and local forums have congregated thousands of people under the banner 'an-other world is possible.' In line with this slogan, Susan George (2008), a prominent critic of neoliberal policies and a participant of the World Social Forum, contrasted Thatcher's 'there is no alternative' thesis with the idea that 'there are thousands of alternatives.'

Third, electoral politics in many Latin American countries shifted drastically, as the political parties that challenged neoliberalism moved from opposition to government. Election after election, a chain of left and centre-left governments (known as the 'pink tide') expanded throughout the region, promoting wealth redistribution and innova-tive experiments with power decentralization, such as participatory bud-geting or communal councils. Some of these governments proposed a paradigmatic shift in development models, using as foundation the indigenous philosophy of 'living well,' which includes the principles of nurturing life (recognizing the rights of all living species), communitarianism, complementarity, reciprocity, solidarity, and partici-pation.[1]

It was in this historical context that the social economy expanded in Latin America during the first decade of the twenty-first century, some-times due to grassroots initiatives responding to an economic crisis, some-times due to projects promoted by government agencies, and sometimes due to a combination of both factors. This expansion included attempts to replace a 'social economy of the poor' (downloading social programs to community organizations) with a new kind of solidarity economy in which alternative economies are prefigured by grassroots and community groups, with varying levels of government support.[2]

In this chapter, we present two case studies of social businesses that attempt to balance their social and economic missions: Argentina's worker-recuperated enterprises (empresas recuperadas por sus trabajadores, or ERTs)[3] and Venezuela's socialist production units (SPUs).[4] In Argentina, the case study included twenty-six participants in four ERTs in different sectors (print shop, waste disposal and parks maintenance, newspaper publishing, and health provisioning) located in the cities of Córdoba, Buenos Aires, and Avellaneda. In Venezuela, it included eighteen participants who belong to three SPUs located in the states of Lara and Barinas: a tomato processing plant, a coffee processing plant, and an agricultural equipment service centre. In both countries, we interviewed other key figures such as researchers, government officials, and social movement leaders.

The transformative potential of the social economy and its myriad organizations and practices span a continuum, with reformist designs for a kinder capitalist market system on one end, and more ambitious visions for a radical economic and political democracy on the other (Amin, 2009; De la Barra & Dello Buono, 2009; Fontan & Shragge, 2000). Both ERTs and SPUs are social economy organizations that tend to fall towards the latter end of the spectrum. That is, when compared with strictly capitalist firms, they engage in substantively different economic practices under the auspices of self-management, such as worker-led decision-making processes, worker-run or worker-reorganized labour processes, community development, and involvement in solidarity economies. At the same time, they both face the challenge of operating within capitalist markets while prefiguring paths beyond those markets in the economies of solidarity they are helping to forge. Although ERTs and SPUs have different origins – ERTs were started by workers trying to recuperate failing private firms with little state support, while SPUs were born as state-sponsored, co-managed productive entities – both types of social businesses result in similar outcomes for their workers and the communities they engage with. As suggested in chapters 1 and 7 in particular, like many social economy organizations, ERTs and SPUs incorporate values of mutual aid, community well-being, social objectives, and democratic self-determination, and aim at overcoming gaps and social inequalities brought on by markets and economic crises (Amin, 2009; McMurtry, 2010; Pearce, 2009; Quarter, Mook, & Armstrong, 2009; Vaillancourt, 2010).

In our research, we explored five questions:

1 What is the history of the new kinds of social businesses that emerged as reactions to neoliberalism?
2 What are their relationships with the state and the market?
3 How are they organized internally?
4 How do they fullfill their social mission?
5 What are their main commonalities and differences?

In the following pages, we address the first four questions, first in relation to Argentina's ERTs, and then in relation to Venezuela's SPUs. After presenting the findings from the two case studies, we examine the fifth question and discuss the main similarities and differences between these two types of social businesses. Finally, we argue that these two experiments prefigure a new phenomenon within Latin American social economy businesses that is somewhat different from the traditional cooperatives and the state-run enterprises of the twentieth century.

ERTs as Social Economy Businesses

Historical Background and Current Situation

Argentina's empresas recuperadas por sus trabajadores (ERTs), while all unique, tend to follow a similar pattern. After years of suffering under the economic hardships of neoliberalism faced by small- and medium-sized enterprises (SMEs) throughout the country, broken institutional promises, the threat or outright closure of the firm due to legal or illegal declarations of bankruptcy by owners, and the ineptitude or greed of business owners reflected in unpaid benefits and salaries, workers at a particular firm were pushed into carrying out risky workspace takeovers. Founding an ERT sometimes entails long periods of round-the-clock occupation and resistance against violent attempts at eviction. The slogan of the National Movement of Recuperated Enterprises (Movimiento Nacional de Empresas Recuperadas, or MNER), borrowed from Brazil's landless movement, captures the typical ERT's three-staged struggle towards self-management: 'ocupar, resistir, producir.'

Argentina's ERTs can be found in many sectors, including printing and publishing, metallurgy, foodstuffs, waste management, textiles, tourism, health, shipbuilding, mining, and oil refining (Fajn, 2003; Lavaca, 2004; Rebón, 2007; Ruggeri, Martinez, & Trinchero, 2005; Vieta & Ruggeri, 2009). Currently, there are over 200 ERTs that are self-managed by roughly 10,000 workers (Palomino, Bleynat, Garro, & Giacomuzzi, 2010; Ruggeri et al., 2010). While ERTs represent a small fraction of Argentina's worker co-operatives,[5] and their workers represent a tiny percentage of Argentina's fifteen to sixteen million active participants in the urban economy (Ministerio de Trabajo, 2009), they have nevertheless inspired social change (Palomino, 2003). These firms not only show workers' innovative capacities for saving jobs and avoiding the fate of precarious welfare plans or structural unemployment, but also highlight their ability to self-manage their own work environment.

There are two distinct phases in the development of ERTs. The first phase, from 1998 to 2003, took place in the context of a deep political and economic crisis that led to record levels of business bankruptcies, underemployment and unemployment, and a proliferation of ERTs. During this period, strategies and tactics of workplace takeovers and business conversions into worker co-operatives started to be articulated and formalized. ERT associations, leaders, and lobby groups prioritized political mobilization, solidarity work with social justice groups, and struggles to legitimate workplace takeovers and conversions with the political-judicial system and the Argentine public. The second phase, from 2004 to 2010, took place during a period of economic recovery and political stability. ERTs continued to emerge, but at a slower pace. They developed specifically as worker responses to micro-economic crises within particular economic sectors or workplaces and were not as etched with the anti-systemic discourses that brought first-phase ERTs in close affinity with organizations of the unemployed (piqueteros), neighbourhood assemblies, barter clubs, and land- and housing-rights movements that swelled Argentina's social and solidarity economies around the turn of the millennium (Palomino et al., 2010; Vieta & Ruggeri, 2009).[6]

As social economy businesses, ERTs face several challenges as they consolidate production processes: securing organizational stability, gaining market share, fixing or replacing depreciated machinery, retraining workers, recovering social security benefits, educating ERT workers in the values of co-operativism, forging economic networks of solidarity with other ERTs and traditional co-operatives, and lobbying for laws that would improve their labour conditions and competitive advantage. By the end of the first decade of the twenty-first century, ERTs had secured considerable legitimacy in the eyes of Argentina's public and some members of the political and judiciary establishments. Furthermore, the pioneering strategies, practices, and initiatives derived from ERTs have taken hold in Argentina's working class sectors. National and regional governments have yet to implement coherent policies and procedures for assisting ERTs, mainly due to the state's continued acquiescence to the capitalist economic model and its continued privileging of private property. However, the process of starting a worker co-operative from the ashes of a failed owner-managed firm is now, together with traditional business strategies of declaring bankruptcy or 'restructuring,' one more option available for failing enterprises. As such, ERTs' legitimacy is rooted in their positive influence.on the communities they work within, and their value extends far beyond their numerical size.

Considering ERTs' long struggles for self-management, the deteriorated technological infrastructure recovered by workers from failing capitalist firms, the reduced size of an individual ERT's workforce in contrast to the firm under owner management, the limited access to credit, and the scarce government assistance, it is not surprising that most ERTs produce below their potential capacity when compared with their production runs under owner management. Most ERTs have a workforce that is about 80 per cent smaller than it was under private ownership and average from twenty to fifty workers. Workers who continue in the ERT are often older than those who leave, and tend to be over age forty. Moreover, the younger workers who leave tend to be professionals, administrators, or in possession of more transferable technical skills, which results in a paucity of professional, technical, and administrative staff by the time the remaining worker collective decides to take over a failing firm. This is because it is easier for administrative or professionalized workers than for blue-collar or service sector workers to find jobs elsewhere. Argentina's job market has also traditionally favoured younger workers. Rather than risk the problems and insecurity of self-managing a firm in trouble, most of these younger and more technical and administrative workers – who could help immensely in the reorganization of an ERT's labour process – decide to leave for more secure positions in other owner-managed private firms (Ruggeri et al., 2005; Vieta & Ruggeri, 2009).

For some ERT workers in our study, political engagement emerged from the personal and economic crisis they found themselves in. For almost all of these workers, their hope grows from their responses to practical challenges rather than from an enlightened vanguard. Carlos, a member of a recovered print shop, observed:

> Early on in the struggle to reclaim our work we started fighting for our salaries, for getting out of our severe debt loads that the boss had left us. Now, looking back on our struggle, I can see where the change in me started, because it begins during your struggles. First, you fight for not being left out on the street with nothing. And then, suddenly, you see that you've formed a co-operative and you start getting involved in the struggle of other enterprises. You don't realize it at the time but within your own self there's a change that's taking place. You realize it afterwards, when time has transpired, doing things that you would never imagine yourself doing.

About 94 per cent of ERTs self-organize under the legal framework of a worker co-operative (Ruggeri et al., 2005), but they have few close or sustained connections with Argentina's traditional co-operative sector. The main reason for this is that ERTs did not emerge from the co-operative movement but from unionized workplaces identifying with Argentina's labour movement. Indeed, most ERT members we spoke with still perceive themselves as laburantes (workers) rather than cooperativistas. As Victor, a founding member of a waste management ERT, told us:

> I feel that I am a laburante, and I will continue to be one! When we go to community meetings, we go with our overalls. And wearing our overalls all the time while at work is important to remind us of where we came from. This is one of the things we keep on reminding our younger members of the co-op, to always have their overalls on when they are at work and in the community during working hours.

Although most workers who started ERTs had no experience with any form of co-operativism (Martí et al., 2004), they were inspired by non-hierarchical social justice movements that emerged around the same time as responses to the neoliberal model. ERT workers turned to the legal and organizational framework of worker co-operatives because of the public debates that took place in the early years of the phenomenon, when a key issue on the table was what legal and administrative frameworks ERTs were to take: nationalization under workers' control or worker co-operativism. While nationalization under workers' control (modelling the Yugoslavian or current Venezuelan models of nationalization and co-management) was theoretically and historically plausible, early ERT adopters scrapped the option when it became clear that the state refused to go along with it (Ruggeri et al., 2005). The only practical and legal alternative was the already viable and long-established co-operative model.

Today, it is widely accepted in Argentina that ERTs not only save jobs and maintain a community's productive capacity, but also bring new forms of co-operative businesses into the economy that, via their social missions and the solidarity economies they forge, contribute to community economic development. Indeed, during the last decade, ERTs were able to respond to economic, political, and legal challenges, and simultaneously establish themselves as viable social economy businesses. As worker-driven and community-based organizations, ERTs' social innovations attest to their efficacy for grassroots economic and social development.

Relation to the State and the Market

Restarting production as self-managed firms in depleted or bankrupted workplaces with little or no inventory and capital, depreciated machinery, and lost market share often means that ERT workers find themselves attempting to co-operatively steer a precarious business from an unusually disadvantaged position within a competitive market. More often than not, their competitors are private firms that have not gone through the challenges that ERTs have had to, such as reviving production from within a failed firm while, at the same time, learning new skills and strategies for co-operativism and self-management. These challenges are most acute in the first year or two of an ERT as its workers face steep learning curves, the democratic restructuring of their production processes, and making do with their depleted means of production.

The challenges of restarting the firm are further compounded by the scarcity of meaningful state assistance or coherent national policies supporting ERTs. Argentina's national and regional governments tend to treat each ERT on a case-by-case basis, seeming to arbitrarily assist some while overlooking others. This is in contrast to Venezuela's state-sponsored SPUs, or the experience of worker-recuperated or self-managed firms in Brazil, which enjoy more support from the Partido dos Trabalhadores (PT) government and Brazil's main union central (Vieta & Ruggeri, 2009). The Argentine state could go a long way in helping ERT workers restart production and stabilize by, for example, setting up a national fund for the startup capital needs of ERTs, automatically expropriating failing firms on behalf of their workers when a certain percentage of the workforce desires to self-manage it, amending the country's labour laws in order to allow self-managed workers to continue to receive the same social security benefits afforded to them when working as employees, or having the state engage in purchasing policies privileging ERTs and other self-managed firms' goods and services over those of the private sector.[7]

Argentina's reluctance to implement such nation-wide policies for ERTs can be attributed to the fact that the national government still remains heavily beholden to the capitalist-entrepreneurial class (Vieta & Ruggeri, 2009). Although the governments of Néstor Kirchner (2003 to 2007) and Cristina Fernández de Kirchner (2007 to present) have left stronger social democratic imprints on Argentina in contrast with other recent national governments, the state is still caught in a conundrum: actively support these workers by setting up official policies and programs to help convert any troubled firm in Argentina into worker co-ops or continue to officially uphold, first and foremost, private property rights and treat ERTs on a case-by-case basis. To date, the Argentine state has, in actions if not in words, clearly chosen the latter.

Elena, a founding member of her ERT, underscores ERTs' myriad challenges:

> Our challenges? They are very big. Anxieties accompany us along the path [to self-management and] toward lifting ourselves out of the difficulties we faced [ever since things took a turn for the worse with our previous boss . . .] Lifting yourself out of the void is hard, and you already know that in this country there are, or I should say, *there aren't* regulatory frameworks in place that permit you – for various political reasons – to have access to the means of slowly emerging out of your difficulties, to walk along the path of production, grow, build more jobs . . . So then, you fall out of the system, you aren't a subject of credit, you don't have access to working capital (no one gives it to you), you can't access credits or funds allocated to small and medium sized businesses because we are a formerly bankrupted enterprise, and as a bankrupted enterprise now managed by its workers we are not [completely] recognized in this system.

While non-conventional sources of funding – such as community solidarity fund drives, some assistance from foreign NGOs, and some small loans and state subsidies – have helped start or sustain some ERTs, these irregular funding sources, in addition to the lack of consistent state support, have added to their tenuous existence and to the continued instability of their workers. Fajn and Rebón (2005) point out that the financial precariousness spawned by inconsistent state policies and the difficulty in meeting production demands and reaching new markets can push ERTs to focus on generating as much revenue as possible instead of on co-operative values or their social missions. During such times, ERT workers recognize that they might not generate sufficient revenues to pay salaries or the business's accounts payable, and intensify their production practices to make up for these shortfalls. These moments illustrate an implicit tension with self-managing a firm within a system made up of highly competitive markets (Craig, 1993; McNally, 1993): when staying afloat becomes the primary focus of workers in co-operatives, they risk losing sight of the collective spirit and democratic ideals that drove them to become a co-operative in the first place. Arguably the biggest challenge faced by each ERT is the risk of falling into situations of 'self-exploitation' in order to stay afloat, such as working overtime without adequate compensation, reducing salaries, not taking lunch and coffee breaks, mistreating associates, or the emergence of cadres of co-op members that behave like de facto bosses (Vieta & Ruggeri, 2009).

In light of these additional challenges, workers' autonomy to make decisions has allowed them to develop creative responses. Indeed, ERTs depend on the ingenuity and determination of their workers to ensure the ongoing operation and sustainability of the enterprise. ERT workers have 'recuperated' a variety of business practices for co-operative ends,[8] for two reasons: first, out of necessity, because low inventory and just-in-time production is a more affordable way to initially operate a depleted firm; and second, because these modes of production are, in certain sectors, efficient ways to self-manage a worker co-op, especially one that has gone through financial challenges.

Marketing and administrative needs are usually complemented by workers developing new skills and capacities through job rotation strategies, university extension programs, and sharing knowledge from workers in sympathetic social movements. The ways ERTs respond to challenges suggest that workers possess the motivation, skills, and self-actualizing capacity to contest the logic of coercion, compulsion, and forced specialization found in dominant corporate production models.

Other innovative initiatives that respond to unmet revenue goals due to underproduction, depleted machinery, lack of coherent state support, and capitalization issues, and that also differ from how most capitalist firms tend to operate, include:

- recycling left-over materials from production processes for economic and ecological purposes;
- approaching lenders as 'less risky' collective coalitions of ERTs that, in effect, creatively addresses the banking system's risk-assessment strategies;
- accessing government funding and business development programs in partnership with university research teams, local or foreign NGOs, or research initiatives working in conjunction with other recuperated enterprises;
- organizing neighbourhood solidarity fund drives;
- establishing networks of experts, facilitated by supportive university programs and technical institutes, for aid in administrative tasks and technological repair and upgrading;
- working with supportive customers and social movements to re-establish and expand market share via, for example, word of mouth; and
- developing 'economies of solidarity' among ERTs where, in the spirit of the sixth co-op principle (i.e., co-ops co-operating), production inputs, machinery, administrative needs, technological expertise and repair, and even orders are shared among ERTs in related sectors.

Internal Democracy

Most ERT workers are accustomed to hierarchical positions in capitalist enterprises. With the creation of their ERTs, workers become members of a new co-operative, even if they continue to work in the same physical space performing similar tasks. The main difference is that the previous authoritarian order has become a more democratic structure, with no direction from typical capitalist management models. Zanón, a ceramics manufacturer in the province of Neuquén and one of the most emblematic ERTs, was renamed FaSinPat, or Fábrica Sin Patrón (Factory Without Bosses) to highlight its new structure. Some of our interviewees reported that a worker co-op structure facilitates addressing the communal needs and desires that resulted from self-managing a business. Pablo, president of a print shop ERT, recalls that:

> Before, under owner-management, there was always someone marking out the rhythm of your work. Now, things are different. We have other obligations based on our own responsibility to one another and our jobs. Before we were 'workmates' but today we are like socios [associates], where the

problem of one socio affects us all. Before we were just mere acquaintances, we didn't have direct contact with all of our workmates, but now we're a much tighter unit, and what binds us together is the fact that we're all responsible for this co-operative.

These communal desires manifest in the democratic form of 'one worker, one vote' and the equitable redistribution of revenues most ERTs adopt. Although Argentine co-operative law only requires one annual workers' assembly, ERT workers often hold more frequent assemblies monthly, and, during particularly challenging periods, weekly. This practice alone generates far more administrative and managerial transparency than when these firms operated under owner-management (Fajn, 2003; Ruggeri et al., 2005). Other non-hierarchical work processes include flexible ad hoc work committees and labour processes that change with the needs of a particular order or production run and that are integrated into day-to-day decision-making processes. Looser and direct communication structures on shop floors foster flexible and open dialogue between workers.

Once the co-operative model takes hold in an ERT's workforce, most members also become committed to the equitable distribution of surpluses. Interestingly, there is a preponderance of egalitarian pay equity schemes, no matter how senior or skillful a worker is (Fajn, 2005; Palomino, 2003; Ruggeri et al., 2005).[9] This is another promising innovation that reconceptualizes work within a productive entity as it transforms organizational hierarchies while recognizing the contributions of all workers to its production processes. This is a noticeable innovation because the practice of equitable pay is not necessarily common in traditional co-operatives or even in workers co-ops (Oakeshott, 1990; Smith, Chivers, & Goodfellow, 1988).

Unlike the previous model, in recuperated enterprises revenues are distributed between workers' salaries, the material needs of workers that periodically arise (such as a worker's or family members' health costs), and pension top-ups for retired members, *before* allocating remaining revenues to the production needs of the firm. Thus, in ERTs, as in other worker co-ops, it is the workers' assembly that decides how revenues are distributed rather than management or profit logic. As such, the tendency with most ERTs in our study is to attempt to engage in forms of surplus allocation rooted in the notions of solidarity and the well-being of co-op members, their families, and surrounding communities. In short, ERTs are rooted in collective behaviours that aspire to minimize surplus value and wealth accumulation for individuals, and maximize socialized wealth and social production for all members.

Social Mission

Like all social economy businesses, ERTs have social missions and objectives. ERTs' new forms of social production and the sharing of social wealth often include the surrounding communities. Many ERTs open their workspaces to uses besides production or service delivery, including on evenings and weekends. Some of them are always open to the neighbourhood, and double as cultural and community centres, free community health clinics, education programs for marginalized children and adults, alternative media spaces, and community dining rooms run by workers, neighbours, or volunteers.

As an example, the print shop Artes Gráficas Chilavert doubles as a high school for adults and after-school programs for children. It also houses the ERT Documentation Centre, which is run by student volunteers associated with the University of Buenos Aires, and used frequently by researchers interested in the ERT movement. A vibrant community centre called Chilavert Recupera operates on its mezzanine level, hosting plays, art classes, music concerts, and community events often linked to Argentina's social justice movements. Industrias Metalúrgicas y Plásticas Argentinas (IMPA), a large metallurgic ERT, is also known as 'The Cultural Factory' because it dedicates a large portion of its space to an art school, silk-screen shop, free health clinic, community theatre, and adult education high school program. Artes Gráficas Patricios houses a primary school, a community radio station, and a dental and medical clinic, all run by neighbours, social movement groups, and health practitioners volunteering their time. Hosting such cultural and community spaces and involvment with the needs of local communities is not just a way of giving back to the neighbourhood out of self-interest or corporate goodwill. Instead, ERT members tend to see their workspaces as continuations of the neighbourhood.

While some ERTs open up their doors to the community, others (like FaSinPat and UST[10] in the greater Buenos Aires city of Avellaneda) integrate revenue sharing with the community into their social missions and their business practices, which extends their productive efforts out into the surrounding neighbourhoods. These two ERTs are renowned for dividing revenues between the needs of the firm, workers' salaries, and community service. FaSinPat frequently donates tiles to community centres and hospitals, and organizes cultural activities for the community on its premises. It built a community health clinic in three months in an impoverished neighbourhood that had been demanding such a clinic from the provincial government for two decades without success. Similarly, UST consistently redirects a significant portion of its revenues to community development projects, such as an affordable housing project for its workers and the surrounding community. This initiative has already built one hundred attractive townhomes to replace inadequate housing for its own members and other neighbours. UST's president told us that providing for the life needs of workers and the surrounding neighbourhood in areas such as decent housing, reskilling, education, and literacy are key motivators for the co-op. Indeed, he added, the co-op is in business in order to help provision the life-needs of its workers and neighbouring communities. In addition, UST built and continues to support a youth sports complex in the neighbourhood and an alternative media workshop and radio program, while also heading a unique plastics recycling initiative for the large low-income housing project located near its plant.

In conclusion, ERTs emerged during a deep economic and political crisis and, throughout their short history, have managed to survive in a hostile environment, pay back the limited loans that they have access to, generate democratic governance processes, establish a more egalitarian wage distribution system, create and preserve jobs when many other firms were firing workers, extend their work out into the community, and facilitate much needed community economic development projects. Indeed, because ERTs put people before profits, when confronted with a drop in demand, instead of downsizing (as for-profit companies typically do), they sometimes decide to absorb the drop in income evenly by, for instance, reducing working hours. Finally, the transition to self-management generated a new work ethos based on the primacy of shared responsibility, collective problem-solving, and horizontal communication (Coraggio & Arroyo, 2009).

SPUs as Social Economy Businesses

Historical Background and Current Situation

In the first decade of the twenty-first century, Venezuela witnessed an explosion of co-operatives. Harnecker (2008) reports a growth from 877 co-operatives in 1998 to 158,917 in 2006. Another study (ICA, 2010) indicates even higher growth, from 1,045 in 2001 to 286,485 in 2009. Contrasted with the ERT experience, this impressive expansion was less the result of spontaneous organizing than of public policy, including the 2001 Special Law of Co-operative Associations and the Vuelvan Caras co-operative development program (Harnecker, 2008). The proactive role of the government in relation to co-operatives was also evident in its economic support for the sector, which included granting preferential aid (Llerena, 2006) and access to government contracts (Díaz, 2006). Indeed, the main factor behind the expansion of the co-operative sector in Venezuela was strong government support, which can be traced back to president Hugo Chávez's electoral promise of breaking from the neoliberal model applied in the country in the 1980s and 1990s.

The rapid and substantial growth of the co-operative sector, however, proved unsustainable. Indeed, after a few years it was found that most of these co-operatives were inactive either because they lacked technical capacity or because they were simply fronts created to access government funds. The low percentage of functioning co-operatives (23 per cent) may justify the label 'cemetery of co-operatives' (ICA, 2010) in reference to the Venezuelan co-operative reality, but the absolute number (50,000 to 60,000) is nevertheless higher than any other Latin American country, and is also higher than all active co-operatives in Argentina, Brazil, and Colombia combined (Harnecker, 2008; ICA, 2010). Over 80 per cent of them are very small (five to ten members), and about 15 per cent of them employ between eleven and fifty people (Díaz, 2006). The majority of these co-operatives operate in the services and productive sectors, with those in transportation coming at a distant third.[11]

The rapid expansion of the co-operative sector has created several problems. In the last few years there has been a shift in government policy from supporting the traditional co-operative model to the creation of approximately 3,000 Unidades de Producción Socialistas, or socialist production units (SPUs). These were designed by the Ministry of Popular Power for the Communal Economy and are being posited as central to the country's transition to 'twenty-first century socialism' (Albert, 2008). In this transition, the Venezuelan development model for the social economy is conceptualized as a triangle that includes social ownership of the means of production, social production organized by workers, and production for social needs and purposes (Lebowitz, 2010). Social ownership of the means of production ensures that communal, social productivity is directed to the free development of all rather than to satisfy the private goals of capitalists, groups of producers, or state bureaucrats.

Social production organized by workers allows them to develop their capacities by combining thought and action in the workplace. In addition to producing products, they can recreate themselves as self-conscious collective producers. The satisfaction of social needs and purposes is the necessary goal of productive activity in the new society because it shifts the focus from self-interest and selfishness towards the needs of others and relations of solidarity. The extent to which SPUs are moving towards this ideal type of social economy is still an open question, as they operate within the orbit of the state but with relative high levels of control by workers and community representatives.

Venezuela's SPUs produce or distribute a variety of goods and services, from agricultural production to equipment rental. Most of them are relatively small, employing twenty to one hundred people. Institutionally, SPUs are nonprofit organizations owned by the state and managed democratically by a combination of three actors: the workers, local communal councils (neighbourhood associations found throughout the country), and state representatives. These characteristics distinguish SPUs from capitalist firms and from Venezuelan worker co-operatives. At the production stage, SPUs work closely with small and medium local private producers. The goods they produce are then distributed through government- and community-run discount stores known as Mercal.

Relation to the State and the Market

SPUs can be thought of as the individual parts that comprise the larger body known as social property enterprises (SPEs). In other words, each SPE is constituted by several SPUs.[12] SPUs are linked to the state through their umbrella SPEs, and SPEs, in turn, are linked to the state in several ways. First, SPEs are administered by the Registry of Social Production Enterprises (REPS in Spanish), which was created by the government in 2005 as part of the program of social production enterprises (Arenas, 2008). The Registry is, in turn, linked to the state-owned oil company, PDVSA, whose role as part of the program is to help SPEs through, among other things, preferential contracts and financing (PDVSA, 2006). Second, each SPE belongs to one of the many state corporations created by the government to promote economic and development policies that include fostering the 'popular economy,' the preferred name for the social and solidarity economy in Venezuela. For example, the three SPUs that we studied belong to three different SPEs, which, in turn, belong to one single state corporation, the Venezuelan Agrarian Corporation

(CVA in Spanish). Third, SPEs (as well as the state corporations they belong to) receive direct political guidance from the government ministry responsible for the sector of the economy they operate in. In the case of the three SPUs we looked at, the three corresponding SPEs were under the guidance of the ministry of popular power for agriculture and land.

As economic entities, SPUs, like other businesses, produce and sell commodities. These are produced through the labour of SPU workers who are hired by the SPU's administration in the context of a labour market. In other words, SPU workers sell their labour to an employer (in this case the Venezuelan state) in return for a wage. However, according to workers interviewed, wages at SPUs are considerably above the minimum, which reflects the government's commitment to provide fair and decent salaries. In order to meet its mission and support consumers and communities most in need, the commodities SPU workers produce are then sold in government and community-run 'popular markets' (Mercal) at below-market prices.[13] As a result, millions of Venezuelans have access to a variety of goods that they would not be able to afford otherwise.

The government's commitment to selling the goods produced by SPUs at below market price and to paying workers a fair salary means that SPUs do not generate enough revenue to cover their costs and therefore depend on state funds. Indeed, as noted by a state administrator, most SPUs do not generate a profit. This does not mean that there is not a conscious attempt by both the SPU's administration and their workers to produce more efficiently. Indeed, several interviewees in the SPU workforces and in the state administration argued that eventually SPUs could become self-sufficient. If SPUs were to operate without the financial help of the state and were able to generate a surplus, both the government and workers would expect that such a surplus would be managed through the SPUs' democratic structures, similarly to ERTs.

Agricultural SPUs have a particular relationship with local producers from whom they purchase raw materials. In accordance with their mission of developing the country's agricultural sector and supporting small and medium producers, SPUs purchase raw materials from local producers at a higher than average price, paralleling fair trade practices. In many cases, this price remains fixed throughout the year in an attempt to combat market-driven price fluctuations that can be devastating for farming families. Moreover, to fulfill their goals of fostering social consciousness and moving beyond market relations, SPUs engage the producers in a variety of ways. For instance, they organize educational activities on topics ranging from technical education on farming practices to political education; co-ordinate local artistic fairs; and, as will be discussed later, incorporate local producers in the SPUs' democratic structure. In some cases, SPU workers actively engage in the production process. For example, they sometimes help producers till their land and pick their crop when producers lack the means to do so or when they feel it is not worth investing time and effort into such activities because the final product would not bring enough revenue.

SPU hiring practices are also unique. Although SPU workers are hired in the context of an open labour market, in contrast to traditional businesses, all hiring is subject to a democratic process in which communal councils, SPU workers, and state management are involved. However, state managers have the final word on hiring. Although this may lead to tokenistic consultations, our interviewees suggested that the needs of communities and individuals are seriously considered in the decisions. The result is that the market logic, which dictates that only those individuals that are most capable of generating profit are hired, incorporates the logic of participatory democracy and community needs.

Internal Democracy

A distinctive feature of SPUs, similar to Argentina's ERTs, is their highly democratic character, which includes an emphasis on active participation and co-operation with local communities and producers. Democratic practices within SPUs include both formal and informal dynamics. Formally, all SPU participants, as with most worker co-operatives, have the right to vote: one person, one vote. The right to vote is exercised most prominently through the Workers' Council, a political body composed of all SPU participants and their state representative. The Workers' Council meets at general assemblies, which all SPU participants, regardless of job description, are allowed to attend. Issues that might be discussed include: production targets; the internal organization of the workplace; the election of individuals to working groups or committees that deal with specific issues at each SPU, such as housing, sports, and health; and the election of a spokesperson committee. Of all committees, this is the most important, as it represents the Workers' Council as a whole and is responsible for making smaller day-to-day decisions. The decisions at the assembly are made through a simple majority. The frequency with which assemblies are held is determined by the workers at each SPU.

Although the general assembly is the main forum where voting takes place, decisions at the committee level are also made through voting. In addition, each committee can elect a spokesperson. Spokespeople are not quite representatives, as their job is not to represent the larger political body but to simply voice its will (the word 'spokesperson' in Spanish is 'vocero' meaning the one who voices). Although spokespeople have some political representation, there is a conscious attempt on the part of SPU members to minimize it. Therefore, spokespeople can make decisions, but only after the whole committee has met and discussed the issue at hand. This is different from typical representative models where, once elected, representatives are often free to make decisions independent of those who voted for them.

In addition to the general assembly and working committees, SPU participants practice democracy within the Socialist Council of Participation. This democratic and non-hierarchical space is comprised of spokespeople from three different political bodies: local communal councils, local producers, and the SPU. The spokespeople meet regularly to discuss their activities and general concerns. The Council also participates in the hiring process at each SPU by nominating potential job candidates. The hiring process requires four spokespeople, including representatives from the local producers, the local communal councils, and the SPU Workers' Council, along with the SPU co-ordinator, who represents the state. Through a process of democratic consensus, the council nominates a small number of job candidates, and the co-ordinator then makes the final decision. This innovative hiring process sets SPU apart from other social economy enterprises in Venezuela.

In addition to the formal democratic channels of the general assembly, elected committees, and participation councils, SPU members practice democracy regularly in the workplace. Indeed, when asked about democratic practices, SPU participants referred to daily interactions just as much as to the formal processes. Paralleling ERTs' job-sharing strategies, two members of a coffee processing SPU pointed to the spontaneous and horizontal nature of these informal interactions:

If a person is needed somewhere else, we set up a meeting: 'look, who can go over there, who is available, who is ready to go over there, who can and who cannot?' It's done in a democratic manner.

My job is purchasing, but if the coffee processing assembly line is going to stop because there is a need for a set of hands, I'll go over there. If help is needed to unload [the coffee], then let's go there. If somebody needs help at Mercal [the subsidized popular shop adjacent to the SPU], they'll say, 'look, hold my post because I'm going out.' I'll say, 'yes, no problem.'

Rodrigo, the administrative assistant at another SPU, recalled an episode that also highlights spontaneity and horizontality as part of informal daily interaction. He pointed to several field operators who were moving the enterprise's fifty-six tractors from one place in the parking lot to another, and explained that this was done every day to keep the engines healthy. The idea, he recalled, came from a casual conversation with a security guard who, in this case, was part of an independent cooperative hired by the SPU, and was not technically part of the SPU itself. Rodrigo's story illustrates that part of what makes the SPU democratic is how people share information and ideas openly, regardless of their actual job description or formal rank. Rodrigo saw the security guard not as an employee that he, as administrative assistant, could boss around, but rather as 'a human being, the same as myself.'

Ana, a worker at a tomato processing SPU, noted that the ethos of participation motivated her and many others who were previously passive to become more active in democratic processes of deliberation and decision-making. As she observed, 'Now everyone participates, everyone. Here we have protagonistic participation. We all talk. In some cases, there have been people, including myself, that did not want to participate in something. But here I am participating because in the end I was convinced.' It should be noted that Ana was not upset at having been 'convinced' she should actively participate. In fact, as she went on to explain, the act of participation became a source of personal growth. This is consistent with the statements of many other SPU members, who expressed enthusiasm for being part of a collective enterprise, for having a say in decisions that affect their organizations, and for being protagonists of a new historical construction aimed at democratizing both the economy and social relations.

Social Mission

One of the defining characteristics of social economy enterprises is that they possess a social mission that goes beyond simply generating a profit. The SPU social mission is complex and emanates from various government levels and from workers themselves. The government's executive level provides the long-term vision, which has an internal and an external dimension. The internal dimension relates to key goals and principles of SPUs: non-alienated labour, no discrimination, no hierarchies, gender equity, adherence to labour rights (including a fair salary, the elimination of exploitation and access to social security), fiscal responsibility, and equality based on participation. The external dimension relates to the contribution of SPUs to Venezuelan society as a whole, and attempts to move beyond market relations while promoting local development and community participation. SPUs in the agricultural sector are also expected to contribute to the mission of the Venezuelan Agrarian Corporation (CVA in Spanish) to achieve food sovereignty and avoid dependence on food imports.

The CVA supports farmers, agricultural producers, and consumers, but is less concerned with the internal development of the corporation. This is not surprising, since the CVA is a bureaucratic organ responsible for administering the policies generated at the executive level. At the SPE level, the social mission aims at placing the means of production at the service of small and medium producers with the support of the Socialist Councils of Participation. For the government officials, the goal of these activities is to achieve integration in farming and agricultural activities so as to bring dignity to the rural producer and the surrounding communities, a process that is expected to occur with a high degree of solidarity and communal duty.

Our discussions with SPU workers about the goals of their organizations reveal both similarities to and departures from the CVA's mandate. On the one hand, workers noted that their organizations followed the food sovereignty and national agricultural development mandate articulated by the CVA. Most of the workers' comments reveal that their organization's objectives and mission revolved around four themes that directly address the food sovereignty and agricultural development mandate: (a) to increase and maximize the quantity of production, (b) to establish a close relationship with local producers, (c) to produce high quality and low cost products, and (d) to achieve agricultural self-sustainability in the country. On the other hand, many workers made references to a mission that somewhat departed from the CVA's mandate. Their extensive comments about the purpose of their organizations revolved around three themes that are closely connected with co-operative principles: (a) to feed those who need it most, (b) to foster a social consciousness among producers, communities and workers, and (c) to move from co-management to self-management.

Discussion: Commonalities and Differences

After enduring three decades of neoliberalism, in the first decade of the twenty-first century Latin America has witnessed a surge of democratically elected progressive governments, a strengthening of social movements and indigenous groups, and an expansion of social economy organizations. Some of these organizations, like the ones discussed in this chapter, are attempting to combine their economic and social mandates in novel ways, nurturing new relations (more democratic, participatory, and solidarity-oriented) internally and with the outside world.

In examining the worker-recuperated enterprises in Argentina and the socialist production units in Venezuela, it is possible to observe at least four differences. The first has to do with origin. ERTs consist of former workers of capitalist firms with an intense desire to hold on to their jobs. They turned to co-operativism and began the process of converting their firms to worker co-ops as a defensive strategy only when they realized that it was the most practical and legally recognized organizational structure in Argentina for self-managing a bankrupted firm. Eventually, however, over the course of reopening a firm as a worker co-operative, these defensive maneuvers became long-term visions, desires, and innovations that, in practice, see these workers take on the principles of co-operativism. SPUs, in contrast, were the result of a proactive design by the Venezuelan state, which provided not only much of the vision and mission, but also the technical and financial support to make them viable, as part of an overall strategy of national development that privileges the social economy and processes of local democracy. In short, ERTs are offspring of capitalist bankruptcies, whereas SPUs are creatures of an emerging socialist state.

The distinct origins connect with a second difference, which is the relationship with the state. ERTs emerged from the ashes of failing capitalist firms that workers rescued and transformed into viable co-operatives with little or no state support. In some cases, the state may help ERTs by providing modest subsidies or public sector contracts for products or services, but in other cases the state (particularly the judicial system) could put ERTs into legal limbo indefinitely. SPUs, in contrast, are created and supported by the Venezuelan state, which guarantees a market through the existence of discount stores (communal markets), and links SPUs among themselves to promote endogenous development.

The third difference is the relationship with the market. While ERTs provision some products or services to the state, they mostly sell commodities in the private market. This is primarily due to their origins as capitalist firms, but is also because there is no nationwide regulation in place facilitating or encouraging the public sector to purchase from ERTs. In many cases, ERTs have maintained relations with the same providers and clients or purchasers that they had before becoming co-operatives, or have found new providers and clients in the private market. In a nutshell, ERTs must compete in a capitalist market in disadvantageous conditions (limited access to credit, uncertain legal situations, and commitment to assist local communities), their salaries are directly derived from their revenues, and their members' wages are often below those at private firms in the same sector. SPUs, in contrast, seldom compete with capitalist firms, operate in the context of a protected market and subsidized wages, and, for the most part, provide products and services to the social economy and state-controlled markets. Their organizational logic combines elements of state companies, nonprofit organizations, and co-operatives.

A fourth difference has to do with self-management. In ERTs, workers who were used to hierarchical managerial structures suddenly experience a workplace 'without a boss' and must make decisions by themselves through participatory democracy mechanisms. They must learn self-governance and co-operative principles quickly and effectively in order to survive as organizations. In SPUs, however, a state representative is constantly present and sometimes acts in a managerial role, thereby limiting the possibility for self-management. When this happens, SPU workers may have a longer route towards self-governance than ERT workers.

In addition to these differences, both cases share four basic features. First, they emerged as direct responses by workers, other grassroots groups, and, in the case of SPUs, by a supportive state, to the crisis of the neoliberal model of the 1980s and 1990s. Second, they have weak links with the older co-operative movement. Third, they are characterized by horizontalized labour processes, democratic decision-making structures, and egalitarian pay schemes. Fourth, they have strong connections with surrounding communities and contribute to local community economic development initiatives. In some cases, particularly with some of Argentina's ERTs, they also combine productive activities with cultural, educational, and social services activities. In other cases, particularly SPUs, they incorporate multiple stakeholders in the governance and management of the organization.

Conclusion

When we look at these four features together, our two case studies suggest that the social economy businesses emerging in Latin America are somewhat different from the traditional co-operatives and the state-run enterprises of the twentieth century. At this moment, it is too early to ascertain the future contributions of these new organizations to the democratization, vibrancy, and societal relevance of the social business sector on the one hand, and to endogenous development on the other. However, although still in its germinal phase, relatively modest in size, and far from perfect in implementation, the emerging social economy business phenomenon provides examples of 'real utopias,' or prefigurative arrangements of another mode of economic and social life (Wright, 2010). They may prefigure, for example, the development of multi-stakeholder, democratic workplaces that include workers, community organizations, government agencies, consumers, credit unions, unions, technological institutes, and other co-operatives, in different aspects of the management and governance of the organization.

In any case, regardless of the particular direction that social economy businesses take in the future, the social business experiments that are taking place throughout Latin America, despite their problems and limitations, can help to counter the impact of neoliberalism while creating new possibilities for productive and economic life. Moreover, by nurturing a workplace ethos based on horizontality, caring, responsibility, and solidarity, they provide much needed inspiration for social economy organizations interested in contributing to social change and social justice.

NOTES

1 While these governments were only present in approximately half of the
   countries in the region, they managed to galvanize a rejection of the Free
   Trade Area of the Americas, advanced by the Bush administration), and
   create instead an alternative trade system known as ALBA (Alternativa
   Bolivariana para las Américas). ALBA in Spanish also means dawn, a
   metaphor suggesting a new era in Latin American history characterized by
   horizontal solidarity among member states.
2 For example, Brazil's landless movement; Bolivia's cocaleros; Peru's coffee
   co-operativess; Cuba's urban organoponicos, rural agricultural co-ops, and
   new initiatitives for other co-operative businesses; and Mexico's Zapatistas, to
   name a few.

3 The words 'recuperated' and 'recovered' appear to be used interchange-
ably when referring to these firms. We tend to use recuperated for its
etymological and political proximities to the original term in Spanish.

4 We decided to use the English acronym SPU rather than the Spanish
acronym UPS to avoid confusion with the delivery company.

5 Currently, 67.4 per cent of Argentina's co-operatives are worker co-ops
(INAES, 2008a). Considering that there were 11,371 worker co-ops as of
early 2008, ERTs represent only 1.8 per cent of all worker co-operatives. This
implies that 98.2 per cent of Argentina's worker co-ops did not originate
from workers taking over failed capitalist firms which they then had to
run themselves without any previous co-operative experience. The larger
percentage of worker co-ops in Argentina are either older co-ops not
recuperated from failed private firms or part of the wave of small worker co-
ops formed by government work-for-welfare programs since 2004 (INAES,
2008b).

6 Workers in 'second generation' ERTs learned about the processes of
workplace recuperations and conversions from the pioneering struggles
of 'first generation' ERTs. Besides receiving much sympathetic media
coverage, first generation ERTs and their strategies of recuperations and
self-management have since been discussed widely amongst political parties
of the left, social justice groups, co-operative associations and federations,
organized labour, and academic research, and these discussions have
pollinated into workplaces (especially those in trouble) in Argentina and
abroad.

7 These are the main demands that are currently being struggled over by the
various ERT umbrella organizations. For more details on these struggles and
ERT protagonists' proposals for labour and business law reform, see Ruggeri
2009 and Ruggeri et al. 2010.

8 Some examples of how ERTs mediate structural barriers to production and
lack of state assistance include the purposeful horizontalization of labour
processes and practices, such as just-in-time or day-to-day production with
minimal inventories, getting customers to pay for raw materials when
placing orders, and providing outsourced products or services for other
firms.

9 Around 71 per cent of ERTs practice complete or near-complete pay equity
(Fajn, 2003). The rest tend to practice slightly more hierarchical pay
schemes, which can be based on whether members are 'founders' or not,
with founding members getting more pay than newer members based on
the logic that they were present during the ERT's most harrowing days of
occupation and first production runs. Even in these ERTs, however, the
goal tends to be to eventually put in place a system of equal pay amongst
members, or for newer members to eventually be able to attain the same
pay as founding members. Sixteen per cent of ERTs, usually the ones that
retained their old administrative staff (such as with our newspaper ERT

case study), maintain similar salary differentials to the old capitalist firm (save for the previous owner's portion of surpluses). Other types of pay schemes are related to hours worked (7.6 per cent of ERTs) or the amount of responsibility a member has in their job tasks. In total, around 23 per cent of ERTs can be said to fall into these more hierarchical types of pay models, while the other roughly 6 per cent of ERTs practice variations on the previously mentioned schemes (Fajn, 2003). It is important to note, however, that ERTs using more hierarchical kinds of pay models also tend to cap the pay differential between highest and lowest paid members, similar to the pay practices taken up by Mondragon in Spain.

10 Union Solidaria de Trabajadores, a waste recycling and parks maintenance ERT in the city of Avellaneda.

11 Like Argentina, Venezuela has also seen the appearance of ERTs, albeit in a much smaller scale. ERTs emerged in Venezuela in 2002, and by 2006 it was estimated that there were somewhere between twenty and thirty. Most of them are small or medium in size, employing a total of a few thousand workers. In 2005, Venezuela hosted the first Latin American Encounter of Worker-Recuperated Enterprises, attended by 400 workers, unionists, and government representatives from across the region. Since then, however, the ERT movement seems to have fizzled away, having witnessed ongoing conflicts between workers and the government bureaucracy (Lucena & Carmona, 2006; El Militante, 2008; Vieta & Ruggeri, 2009).

12 For example, one of the SPEs that were included in our study has its central office in the city of Barquisimeto, with several SPUs located in nearby communities.

13 This price is 'fixed' in the sense that at any given time there is only one price for a given product, but the state does change the price periodically (usually by raising it, but never to above market value). We suggest that any analysis of the efficiency of SPUs must consider the positive impact of externalities, including the purchase of inputs at above market prices and the sale of products at below market prices.

REFERENCES

Albert, M. (2008). *Which way Venezuela?* Retrieved from http://www.zcommuni cations.org/

Amin, A. (Ed.). (2009). *The social economy: International perspectives on economic solidarity*. London: Zed Books.

Arenas, B. (2008). Capacidades societales de innovación: Su desarrollo en empresas de producción social en el contexto del socialismo del siglo XXI en Venezuela. *CIREC-España: Revista de Economía Pública, Social y Cooperativa, 60,* 121–53.

Coraggio, J.L., & Arroyo, M.S. (2009). A path to the social economy in Argentina: Worker takeovers of bankrupt companies. In A. Amin (Ed.), *The social economy: International perspectives on economic solidarity* (pp. 139–55). London: Zed Books.

Craig, J.G. (1993). *The nature of co-operation*. Montreal: Black Rose Books.

De la Barra., X., & Dello Buono, R. (2009). *Latin America after the neoliberal debacle: Another region is possible*. Lanham: Rowman and Littlefield.

Díaz, B. (2006). Políticas públicas para la promoción de cooperativas en Venezuela (1999–2006). *Revista Venezolana de Economía Social, 6*(1), 149–83.

Elgue, M. (2007). *La economía social: Por un empresariado nacional y democratico*. Buenos Aires: Capital Intelectual.

El Militante. (2008). *Venezuela's Inveval workers protest against bureaucratic sabotage*. Retrieved from http://venezuelanalysis.com/analysis/4026

Fajn, G. (2003). *Fábricas y empresas recuperadas: Protesta social, autogestión, y rupturas en la subjectividad*. Buenos Aires: Centro Cultural de la Cooperación, Instituto Movilizador de Fondos Cooperativos.

Fajn, G., & Rebón, J. (2005). El taller ¿sin cronometro? Apuntes acerca de las empresas recuperadas. *Herramienta, 28*(May). Retrieved from http://www.herramienta.com.ar/print.php?sid=300

Fontan, J.M., & Shragge, E. (2000). Tendencies, tensions and visions in the social economy. In J.M. Fontan & E. Shragge (Eds.), *Social economy: International debates and perspectives* (pp. 1–15). Montreal: Black Rose Books.

George, S. (2008). *Another world is possible if*. . . London: Verso/Transnational Institute.

Harnecker, C. (2007). Workplace democracy and collective consciousness. *Monthly Review, 59*(6), 27–40.

Harnecker, C. (2008). Principales sesafíos de las cooperativas en Venezuela. Retrieved from http://www.rebelion.org/docs/83458.pdf

Harris, R. (2000). The effects of globalization and neoliberalism in Latin America at the beginning of the millennium. In R. Harris & M. Seid (Eds.), *Critical perspectives on globalization and neoliberalism in the developing countries* (pp. 139–62). Amsterdam: Brill.

ICA. (2010). *Diagnóstico del sector de la economía social y solidaria en Venezuela*. International Co-operative Alliance-Americas and Cooperativa Gestión Participativa. Retrieved from http:// gestionparticipativavenezuela.files.wordpress.com/2010/01/resumen-diagnostico-2008-gp-para-aci.pdf

INAES. (2008a). *Cantidad de cooperativas por actividad*. Buenos Aires: Instituto Nacional de Asociativismo y Economía Social. Retrieved from http://www.inaes.gov.ar/es/Enlaces/estadisticas_c2.asp

INAES. (2008b). *Las cooperativas y las mutuales en la República Argentina.* Buenos Aires: Instituto Nacional de Asociativismo y Economía Social.

Lavaca. (2004). *Sin patrón: Fábricas y empresas recuperadas por sus trabajadores: Una historia, una guía.* Buenos Aires: Cooperativa de Trabajo Lavaca Ltd.

Lebowitz, M. (18 February 2010). Socialism: the goal, the paths and the compass. Presentation of 'El socialismo no cae del cielo: Un nuevo comienzo' at the 2010 Havana Book Fair. 'The Bullet,' *Socialist Project* e-bulletin 315. Retrieved from http://www.socialistproject.ca/bullet/315.php

Llerena, M. (2006). Empresas sociales política de competencia. *Red Venezolana de Conocimiento Economómico,* Working paper. Retrieved from http://www.redeconomia.org.ve/documentos/mllerena/resuecosocial.pdf

Lucena, H., & Carmona, H. (2006). *Empresas recuperadas: Posibilidades y limitaciones a partir de da experiencia con INVEPAL.* Retrieved from http://svs.osu.edu/documents/Hector_Lucena_y_HermesCarmona-EMPRESASRECUPERADASCASOINVEPAL.pdf

Martí, J.P., Bertullo, J., Soria, C., Barrios, D., Silveira, M., Camilletti, A., et al. (2004). Empresas recuperadas mediante cooperativas de trabajo: Viabilidad de una alternativa. *UniRcoop, 2,* 80–105. Retrieved from http://www.unircoop.org/unircoop/?q=node/35

McMurtry, J.J. (Ed.). (2010). *Living economics: Canadian perspectives on the social economy, co-operatives, and community economic development.* Toronto: Edmond Montgomery Publications.

McNally, D. (1993). *Against the market: Political economy, market socialism and the Marxist critique.* London: Verso.

Ministerio de Trabajo. (2009). *Índice boletin I de empleo y empresas (BADE).* Ministerio de Trabajo, Empleo, y Seguridad Social. Buenos Aires: Government of the Republic of Argentina.

Oakeshott, R. (1990). *The case for workers' co-op.* Basingstoke, UK: Macmillan.

Palomino, H. (2003). The workers' movement in occupied enterprises: A survey. *Canadian Journal of Latin American and Caribbean Studies, 28*(55), 71–96.

Palomino, H., Bleynat, I., Garro, S., & Giacomuzzi, C. (2010). The universe of worker-recuperated companies in Argentina (2002–2008): Continuity and changes inside the movement. *Affinities: A Journal of Radical Theory, Culture, and Action 4*(1), 252–87.

PDVSA. (2006). Guía general corporativa para la implantación Programa EPS en PDVSA. *Gerencia Corporativa de Empresas de Producción Social.*

Pearce, J. (2009). Social economy: Engaging as a third system? In A. Amin (Ed.), *The social economy: International perspectives on economic solidarity* (pp. 22–33). London: Zed Books.

Portes, A., & Hoffman, K. (2003). Latin American class structures: Their composition and change during the neoliberal era. *Latin American Research Review, 38*(1), 41–82.

Quarter, J., Mook, L., & Armstrong, A. (2009). *Understanding the social economy: A Canadian perspective.* Toronto: University of Toronto Press.

Rebón, J. (2007). *La empresa de la autonomía: Trabajadores recuperando la producción.* Buenos Aires: Colectivo Ediciones Picaso.

Reed, D., & McMurtry, J.J. (Eds.). (2009). *Co-operatives in a global economy: The challenges of co-operation across borders.* Newcastle, UK: Cambridge Scholars Publishing.

Ruggeri, A. (Ed.). (2009). *Las empresas recuperadas: Autogestión obrera en Argentina y América Latina.* Buenos Aires: Editorial Facultad de Filosofía y Letras, Universidad de Buenos Aires.

Ruggeri, A., Martinez, C., & Trinchero, H. (2005). *Las empresas recuperadas en la Argentina: Informe segundo relevamiento del programa.* Buenos Aires: Facultad Abierta, Facultad de Filosofía y Letras, Universidad de Buenos Aires, Programa de Transferencia Científico-Técnica con Empresas Recuperadas por sus Trabajadores (UBACyT de Urgencia Social F-701).

Ruggeri, A., Polti, N., Antiveros, J., Clark, G., Méndez Marichal, A., Elena, P., et al. (2010). *Informe del tercer relevamiento de empresas recuperadas por sus trabajadores: Las empresas recuperadas en la Argentina, 2010.* Buenos Aires: Editorial Cooperativa Chilavert.

Smith, P., Chivers, D., & Goodfellow, G. (1988). *Co-operatives that work: New constitutions, conversions, and tax.* Nottingham, UK: Spokesman.

Vaillancourt, Y. (2010). The social economy in Quebec and Canada: Configurations past and present. In J.J. McMurtry (Ed.), *Living economics: Canadian perspectives on the social economy, co-operatives, and community economic development* (pp. 57–104). Toronto: Edmond Montgomery Publications.

Vieta, M. (2010). The social innovations of *autogestión* in Argentina's worker-recuperated enterprises: Cooperatively organizing productive life in hard times. *Labor Studies Journal, 35*(3), 295–321.

Vieta, M., & Ruggeri, A. (2009). The worker-recuperated enterprises as workers' cooperatives: The conjunctures, challenges, and innovations of self-management in Argentina and Latinamerica. In J.J. McMurtry & D. Reed (Eds.), *Co-operatives in a global economy: The challenges of co-operation across borders,* (pp. 178–225). Newcastle, UK: Cambridge Scholars Publishing.

Wright, E.O. (2010). *Envisioning real utopias.* London: Verso.

7 Challenges for Engaging Social Economy Businesses in Rural and Small Town Renewal

LAURA RYSER AND GREG HALSETH

Northern British Columbia is an expansive rural landscape where small town communities are struggling to cope with economic, social, demographic, and political change. Many service providers and nonprofit agencies have had to address community needs in a context driven by economic restructuring and the neoliberal withdrawal of senior government supports. Drawing on examples from the communities of McBride and Smithers, this chapter explores how social economy businesses are assisting with the stabilization and renewal of rural and small town places. Despite the success of these two groups, research indicates more work is needed to improve the top-down policy and program supports to sustain institutional capacities and ensure that communities have a solid foundation for the ongoing partnerships that can broaden community and economic development.

This chapter starts with a description of Northern BC's rural and small town landscape. Rural and small town places that have been economically dependent on resource industries are struggling. To understand the roles that social economy businesses are playing in McBride and Smithers, the second section of the chapter outlines some key elements that define the social economy and the context of neoliberal policy supports for rural and small town renewal (Graefe, 2006, 2002). The third section describes the two cases we examine. In McBride this includes the McBride Community Forest, and in Smithers this includes Innovation Foods. The chapter closes with a discussion of key lessons with respect to the need for senior government policies and programs to better support local social economy initiatives.

Background

Northern BC comprises about 70 per cent of the provincial land mass and contains approximately 10 per cent of the provincial population. Its economy is similar to other northern economies, and is heavily dependent on forestry, mining, energy production, and tourism. For the purposes of this chapter, Northern BC includes everything from 100 Mile House north to the Yukon border and from the Alberta border west to the Pacific Ocean (figure 7.1). In a Canadian context, this

Figure 7.1. Map of Northern British Columbia

is a classic rural and small town region. The small towns range from 5,000 to 20,000 people, while the rural areas often have populations of less than 1,000. Prince George (population 75,000), which bills itself as 'BC's Northern Capital,' is by far the largest urban place in the region. Northern BC's most significant economic asset is its extremely rich natural resource base. It is this resource wealth (particularly forests) that facilitated the region's economic development. In part because of this comparative advantage in natural resources, and the narrow economic dependence it fosters, BC has been described as a resource periphery (Bradbury, 1987; Hayter, 2000). For more than 200 years, the region's economic dependence on resource industries has followed a long-established Canadian pattern of staples development (Barnes & Hayter, 1994; see also Marchak, 1983; Marchak, Aycock, & Herbert, 1999). Staples theory highlights the implications of transporting raw materials over long distances (causing weaknesses in other lines of development); dependency on external industrialized areas for value-added processing, markets, and supplies of manufactured goods; and dependency on external sources of capital to cover the high costs of resource development (Hayter & Barnes, 1990). The result is an increasing vulnerability over time to dramatic economic change and crisis.

The roots of the present economic and settlement landscape in Northern BC are found in two eras of development. First, through the 1950s and 1960s, BC's provincial government followed a co-ordinated public policy approach based on a model of industrial resource development (Williston & Keller, 1997). This led to a twenty-five- to thirty-year period of rapid economic and community growth across the region (Halseth, Straussfogel, Parsons, & Wishart, 2004). New communities and high-quality local infrastructure were the backbone of industrial centres mobilizing the province's rich resource base through a classic staples approach to rural development (Davis & Hutton, 1989; Horne & Penner, 1992).

The second development period, beginning around 1980, has seen considerable economic restructuring (Barnes & Hayter, 1997; Barnes, Hayter, & Hay, 2001; Halseth & Sullivan, 2002). A recession in the early 1980s marked a fundamental shift in the Fordist compromise that linked industry and government with labour and, indirectly, with rural and northern communities. Industry consolidation and centralization led to layoffs and closures. These actions soon meant that the region's population began to decline for the first time since the Second World War (Hanlon & Halseth, 2005; Hutton, 2002).

Today, Northern BC's landscape is a constellation of small, resource-dependent towns with little economic diversification. In concert with staples theory expectations, both public policy and industrial interests have kept the development focus on the extraction and export of large volumes of minimally processed raw resources (Gunton, 2003, 1997; Hutton, 1997; Munro, 2003). The result is an isolated set of small settlements that are dependent on external management for both policy and corporate decision-making. Restructuring both resource production and public service provision has meant that the past twenty years have been marked by accelerating instability, change, and job loss (Halseth, 2005; Markey, Pierce, Vodden, & Roseland, 2005). This reflects a common circumstance for staples dependent regions in developed economies (Mackenzie & Norcliffe, 1997; Marsden, Lowe, & Whatmore, 1990; Neil, Tykkläinen, & Bradbury, 1992). As a result, Northern BC is struggling with economic and public policy transitions. The two towns selected as case studies reflect the impacts of new economic and political demands that require much more of communities and local capacities.

McBride

McBride is located in the Robson Valley, between the Cariboo Mountains and the Rocky Mountains, and 200 kilometres south-east of Prince George on Highway 16. The town occupies an area within the Lheidli T'enneh First Nation traditional territory and the Simpcw First Nation traditional territory. Incorporated in 1932 (Graine, 2010), McBride was originally established as a key maintenance depot for the Grand Trunk Pacific Railway (later CN) in 1912 to 1914. Today, McBride is the economic centre of the Robson Valley, which also includes a number of smaller farming and forestry communities. The local economy includes a mix of forestry, agriculture, tourism, and small businesses.

In recent years, forest manufacturing in McBride has declined. The largest forest products mill closed in 2006, and more recently a smaller cedar mill has experienced temporary closures and reductions in the number of shifts. In addition to job losses at these manufacturing facilities, there have been spin-off job losses in the local forest harvesting and transportation sectors. However, McBride has successfully grown its tourism industry. Located less than one hour's drive from Mt Robson Provincial Park, and under two hours' drive from Jasper National Park, the town receives significant summer tourism traffic. In addition, McBride has a well-developed and expanding winter tourism industry associated with backcountry recreation and snowmobiling.

In 2006, the population of McBride was 660 within the municipal boundaries, with about the same number living outside municipal boundaries but adjacent to the town. As a result of economic crises in the local forest product manufacturing industries, the local population declined by 7 per cent between 2001 and 2006. The age structure of the population includes about 65 per cent in the working age groups between twenty and sixty-four years, and about 25 per cent under nineteen years of age. While McBride has a younger population profile than for the province as a whole, it is also aging at a faster rate, largely through the out-migration of working age households searching for employment.

Smithers

The town of Smithers is located in the Bulkley Valley against the eastern ranges of BC's Coast Mountains. Located 370 km from Prince George and 350 km from Prince Rupert, Smithers occupies a key location along Highway 16 just south of traditional Gitxsan First Nation territory and within traditional Wet'suwet'en First Nation territory.

Non-Aboriginal population growth in the area began after the arrival of the Grand Trunk Pacific Railroad in 1914. In 2006, Smithers had a population of 10,512 with a service area population of more than twice that size. One result of job losses in the forestry sector has been a small decline (about 3.6 per cent between 2001 and 2006) in the local population.

As a service centre for the Bulkley Valley, Smithers is home to numerous government agencies and community services, including the Bulkley Valley District Hospital. As a result, most local employment is found within the public sector, with healthcare alone employing about 400 people. While there have been forest products processing mill closures, the remaining mills, West Fraser Mills and New Pro, employ nearly 250 people. As in McBride, Smithers has a young population profile relative to the rest of BC. The median population age is less than thirty-eight, and more than 27 per cent of the local population is under eighteen.

Literature Review

Although the definition of rural is widely contested, in Canada, rural and small town places are generally defined as those with a population of less than 10,000 that are also located outside the commuting zone of census metropolitan areas and census agglomeration areas (du Plessis, Beshiri, & Bollman, 2004). In rural and small town places, the 'social' and the 'economic' have always been intertwined. Historically, many businesses functioned within a social economy context – that is, they needed to follow good business fundamentals in order to be profitable and survive while at the same time being good 'community citizens' and acting with civic responsibility. Since the 1980s, rural and small town places have faced dual pressures for change: economic restructuring in resource sectors (resulting in job losses and economic decline) (Hayter, 2003; Ryser & Halseth, 2010) and public policy change driven by neoliberalism resulting in the redistribution of local services and supports (Halseth & Ryser, 2006). As a result, social economy businesses have resumed their historically significant local roles. This section reviews key issues associated with the social economy and neoliberalism to set a context for our two case examples.

Neoliberalism and Rural and Small Town Restructuring

Since the 1980s, rural and small town places have been coping with neoliberal policy approaches linked with the restructuring of industries and services. Neoliberalism is defined as a 'process that aims to establish new means of accumulation and social regulation through the partial transfer of authority and/or responsibility from the public sphere to private domains' (Young & Matthews, 2007, p. 177). As part of this neoliberal agenda, governments began to regionalize, offload, or contract out services to non-governmental for-profit and nonprofit groups in order to reduce government expenditures (Halseth & Ryser, 2006). At the same time, however, social development organizations had to cope with a retrenchment of government sources of support (Meinhard & Foster, 2003). Changes in funding policies resulted in the closure of many services, which had a significant impact on vulnerable residents who were then required to commute for those services. While Klein, Fontan, and Tremblay (2009) describe how the role of the state transformed from being an initiator or provider to being a facilitator of groups addressing social needs, they also demonstrate how such changes prompted the growth of social enterprises:

> State intervention did not disappear entirely, but the State began assuming more the role of facilitator, or guide than that of initiator. The State then

became a partner. Since then, the government has been implementing new development management and financing modalities inspired by the experiments which the social movement had made in the 1980s. The place of the social organizations susceptible of participating in the development of collectivities was thus strengthened by the importance which the notion of the social economy gained and by the strength of its promoters. (p. 29)

The retrenchment of government support provided an impetus for many organizations to engage in the development of social enterprises in order to sustain their organization's services and activities. In this context, social economy enterprises can emerge to help residents cope with change, address service gaps, strengthen community resiliency, and facilitate community renewal.

The Social Economy

Rural economic change, coupled with a neoliberal policy transition, has resulted in an increasing demand for social enterprises to provide a range of services in smaller places (Kay, 2005). A wide range of authors have discussed the concept of a social economy (see chapter 1 by Mook, Quarter, & Ryan; Quarter, Mook, & Armstrong, 2009; Southcott, 2009; Teitelbaum & Reimer, 2002). While the range of definitions is quite broad, we wish to highlight the elements that we will illustrate through case examples. At the simplest level, social economy businesses fit between models of private enterprises and public services (Abele, 2009). They combine the imperative to satisfy market-driven demands for business sustainability with incorporating sets of social and community development goals (Zografos, 2007). Specific to our case examples, social economy businesses:

- seek to attain a broader distribution of collective benefits and develop collective competencies;
- distribute benefits that can target those who are unemployed, underemployed, or underprivileged;
- seek to use revenue to address social goals rather than profit-oriented goals;
- seek to address social exclusion and increase participation in democratic decision-making; and
- are often initiated by local civil society with an interest in local community and economic development.

Several researchers have outlined a suite of conditions that influence the success of social economy enterprises (Evans & Syrett, 2007; Klein et al., 2009; Quarter et al., 2009). These include the ability of leadership to adapt to change, to transform a crisis into a common cause that triggers mobilization, and to mobilize networks; mutual trust and commitment amongst all partners and participants; a diverse board membership; the innovative mobilization of resources; access to financing; entrepreneurship; the mobilization of research and training resources; the transformation of behaviours; community learning by sharing knowledge; co-ordinated citizen involvement; and synergy between actions.

Successful factors that are linked to the generation of trust and mobilization of resources and networks demonstrate the importance of social capital in community development (Kay, 2005). Social capital is generally understood as the social assets derived from norms of trust, co-operation, and networks (Reimer, 2002). Assets or relationships that have a good foundation of trust can then address the needs of individuals or groups, such as through the provision of services or social enterprises (Halseth & Ryser, 2007). During the early stages of a social enterprise, groups draw on bonding forms of social capital (the intensification of local relationships and networks), though they eventually shift towards bridging forms of social capital (linking local groups with a wider non-local network of support) during the later phases of development (Evans & Syrett, 2007). In fact, the long-term stability or success of social enterprises may be linked to the ability of leadership to 'mobilize diversified exogenous resources and to combine them with local resources' (Klein et al., 2009, p. 39).

However, to build a resilient social economy, social capital must be deployed in conjunction with other forms of capital, such as human, financial, environmental, and cultural (Kay, 2005). The mutual importance and recursive supporting relationship between these diverse sets of capital has long been recognized within community development literatures (Pierce, 1999). While neoliberal policies have provided an impetus for social enterprises to evolve, service restructuring trends have not been accompanied with an adequate institutional framework to support the success of social enterprises. The social economy must also be supported by appropriate institutional policies and program supports that has not yet been sufficiently pursued by government policy-makers (Graefe, 2002). The remaining portion of this chapter will explore the experiences of two social enterprises and gather insights that can inform future policy and program directions to support the social economy in rural and small town places.

Case Studies

McBride: McBride Community Forest

In recent years, pressures associated with job losses in the forest sector and calls for more local control over resources have resulted in the creation of many small 'community forests'[1] across the province (www.bccfa.ca). Nearly all of the community forests in BC are established as enterprises to address social goals as they employ and involve a wide group of residents, build institutional and leadership capacity, and expand access to financial and technical resources (Christoffersen, Harker, Lyman, & Wyckoff, 2008). The McBride Community Forest Corporation (MCFC) was established in August 2002 with a five-year probationary forest agreement between the community and the provincial government. That agreement ended in 2007, and the MCFC has since signed a twenty-five year agreement. Consisting of 60,000 hectares of Crown land, the MCFC is owned by the Village of McBride.[2] The goal of the MCFC is to 'provide the village and the surrounding community with a greater socioeconomic diversity within the scope of a healthy environment' (personal communication, 2010).

McBride provides direction to the MCFC through a board of directors, in which it holds four out of seven seats. The remaining three seats are 'directors-at-large' who come from the community or surrounding area. Direction is provided to MCFC staff through job descriptions, annual goal setting, and motions or policies passed in monthly board meetings. McBride hired a community forest manager and an operations supervisor to oversee day-to-day operations; however, forest management and harvesting activities are contracted out. The board of directors approves an annual budget and sales plan developed by the general manager. Revenue is generated through log sales. The operations supervisor awards contracts to loggers and truckers, monitors the operations of contracted logging crews (building logging roads and harvesting trees), and is responsible for sales (calling mills to arrange purchasing contracts). MCFC also contracts part-time help from the village to conduct day-to-day operational duties such as financial accounting, payroll, invoicing, and filing. In addition to working with landowners and the Ministry of Forests,

Lands, and Natural Resource Operations, the MCFC also works with the area's cross-country ski club, snowmobile club, heli-ski tour operators, and the provincial government's Ministry of Jobs, Tourism, and Innovation.

During the developmental stages of the MCFC, McBride contributed $50,000 and leveraged an additional $50,000 in federal funding. The MCFC also benefited from a long-term pricing arrangement for community forests which provides them with a lower stumpage rate (the resource royalties charged to forest companies for harvesting timber on Crown land) than that paid by industry. The community forest acts as a supplier for other local wood-based manufacturers. Field operations, such as road construction and maintenance, harvesting, hauling, tree planting, block layout (a harvesting plan that accounts for environmental or geographical sensitivities), timber cruising (a forest inventory conducted to determine the quality and potential value of forest resources in a given area), and mapping are contracted out with a preference to local businesses (Athey & Levin, 2001; Başkent, Kose, & Keleş, 2005; Nieuwenhuis & Gallagher, 2001).

The net income generated by the MCFC is paid to McBride as a dividend. The village then uses the money for community projects as well as for leverage to obtain other financial support. For example, the MCFC contributed $1.7 million towards the construction of a new community hall. On two separate occasions, it donated $25,000 towards the development of a community foundation. For the past four years, McBride has also used funds from the MCFC to employ an economic development officer.

The MCFC also benefits community groups. It has a fund of $10,000 per year to distribute to local service groups, clubs, and activities. In the past, such funds have been allocated to renovations for the buildings used by the Elks, Royal Purple, and the Royal Canadian Legion. Other service clubs benefit from the MCFC buying ice time for figure skating and donating funds to acquire prizes for logger sports. This money is allocated by the board of directors and its staff.

Aside from providing financial benefits, the MCFC has been able to offer in-kind support to community initiatives through staff expertise. For example, MCFC staff have been involved in the development of a tourism strategy for McBride by providing expertise, through their familiarity with government processes, and continuity of staff who work in conjunction with community volunteers. MCFC staff have also helped prepare grant applications through the Community Adjustment

Program for tourism projects such as developing recreation sites and public walking trails.

The MCFC has experienced a number of challenges since it was first established. As one of eleven pilot community forests in BC, it did not have a sufficient support network from the provincial government to draw on in its formative years. Instead, the MCFC learned through networking with other community forests and through its involvement with the BC Community Forest Association.

The MCFC also had difficulty securing financing during its start-up phase. The MCFC benefited from hiring a former district manager from the Ministry of Forests, and from acquiring small forest blocks through a small business program. These lots were already laid out, cruised, and had harvesting plans. The work that had already been done to these blocks had an estimated value of $350,000. However, banks told MCFC staff that, as a new company with no history, they would be unable to secure a loan. Furthermore, in order to secure a loan, the banks demanded a five-year projected cash flow with stumpage and log price estimates. Unfortunately, community forests cannot predict stumpage rates, which are set by the provincial government on a quarterly basis. Bank lending policies do not recognize the operational constraints of working with small scale social enterprise operations within a restructured forest industry.

Without bank financing, the MCFC relied on $50,000 obtained from the Rural Development Initiative and $50,000 obtained from McBride. During this early phase, the MCFC also relied on local contracting to finance its operations, and sold most of its log supply to McBride Forest Industries and a nearby sawmill in Valemount. While both manufacturing facilities are closed, today the MCFC sells commodity grade logs to larger companies. It also supplements its income by selling a portion of its log supply through a small market logger program in which smaller licenses are sold to people for specialty forest products. As a result, wood from the MCFC goes to fifty-three users around the province. This client base keeps the MCFC resilient during economic fluctuations in the industry, as the small market logger program is well connected and able to find niche markets emerging in a variety of places.

The expansion to more than fifty clients is a result of addressing a key economic development issue that focused on the need for transition from commodity to value-added markets in forestry. More niche products, such as the use of hemlock and fir for molding or birch for flooring, needed to be developed and supported. For example, one local company uses cedar to create landscaping materials such as mulch as well as post and rail fencing (www.cedar3products.com). Another local entrepreneur produces tonewood from Western Red Cedar and Englemann Spruce to create musical instruments such as guitars, violins, and mandolins (www.larrystamm.com).

A last critical challenge for MCFC staff is managing expectations. For example, some members of the community feel that since MCFC is a community forest, it should subsidize local businesses by supplying below-cost raw materials. Such desires need to be balanced against the reality that the community forest must be operated as a business. Due to the MCFC's involvement in community initiatives such as tourism planning and development, some members of the community expect that the MCFC can also pursue a number of tourism projects from developing mountain biking trails to acquiring a T-bar lift for a local ski hill. Financial and human capital constraints mean that staff must carefully consider all decisions with respect to local needs.

The MCFC made three key recommendations in support of the development and sustainability of community forests and social enterprises. First, administrative processes linked to the Ministry of Forests need to be streamlined. For example, regulations, monitoring, and administrative practices currently ensure community forests are practising proper silviculture.[3] However, there is a sense that such administrative practices are unnecessary, as silviculture is in the best interests of community forests and those who benefit from them. Second, the provincial government needs to reallocate more territory to community forests in order to improve their economies of scale. This would enable them to support full-time staff, acquire sufficient volume to create a 'true log market,' and attract value-added manufacturers. It is also critical to sustain government support programs to bridge workers during career transition periods. The Community Adjustment Fund and the Job Opportunities Program are examples of effective programs that assisted local workers. For example, some tourism projects, such as the construction of outhouses and boardwalks along trails, were completed with funds from the Job Opportunities Program that were used to hire local people.

Neoliberal offloading of responsibilities and the facilitation of local responses has generated 'bottom-up' interest and action in creative local social enterprises. The experience of the MCFC, however, demonstrates that such bottom-up initiatives still need assistance from appropriate and supportive 'top-down' senior government policies and programs. In addition to common sense reporting and administrative procedures, sufficient fiscal and human resources need to be allocated to the Ministry of Forests and Range to facilitate visits to community forests, particularly during the early stages of development and operation (McCarthy, 2006).

Smithers: Innovation Foods

Innovation Foods is a nonprofit social enterprise that recycles and redistributes food that is damaged or out-of-date and provides a low-cost grocery option to residents in the Smithers region (Stevenson, 2009). It was created by the High Roads Society (HRS), a nonprofit community social services organization that provides social housing placements, life skills, housekeeping, behaviour management, employment skills training, and supported employment programs for people with developmental disabilities (www.highroadservices.org).

In January 2008, HRS held a strategic planning session to determine the needs of adult clients with developmental disabilities. It identified access to safe and affordable housing as a key need. HRS discovered that many of its clients used money they would have otherwise allocated to their food budget to pay their rents. HRS heard about Quest, an organization in Vancouver that rescues and redistributes food to low-income residents and social service agencies that would otherwise be discarded. Shortly after a visit to Quest, HRS began pursuing grants to develop Innovation Foods, a similar social enterprise to provide low-cost food for adult clients with developmental disabilities. Innovation Foods was not developed to generate revenue, but to address poverty and assist with access to safe and affordable housing through increasing local access to low-cost food.

Innovation Foods' organizational structure consists of a five-member board of directors that administers the store's manager and two full-time employees, who are hired from the general public. The organization recieves advice from granting agencies as well as HRS and the Smithers and Area Recycling. HRS also provides staff support to Innovation Foods for bookkeeping, grant writing, and other operational needs. There are approximately twenty-five to thirty volunteers active with Innovation Foods, many of whom have developmental disabilities and are clients of HRS. Volunteers who are on social assistance can earn up to an additional $100 to their monthly cheque or receive food vouchers to be used at the store. In addition to memberships with churches and school programs, Innovation Foods has over 500 individual members, who receive their free and confidential memberships through the store or by referral from social service agencies. One estimate suggests that roughly 1,200 residents use the program (Stevenson, 2009).

Benefits are distributed through the provision of low-cost groceries. Any revenue surpluses are directed back to the organization as the goal of Innovation Foods is to become self-sufficient. To accomplish this, they are trying to secure a new building where multiple services from both HRS and Innovation Foods can be delivered with a lower lease cost for both enterprises.

Since its inception, Innovation Foods has benefited from the support of a diverse range of local and non-local organizations. Quest continues to provide advice about the process of building this particular type of social enterprise. HRS also received a grant from 'Community Living,' BC's Innovations Grant Program.

Local groups also provided critical financial and logistical support. HRS gave a grant to Innovations Foods, as well as no interest loans. Other grants were obtained from Smithers and Area Recycling, the Bulkley Valley Foundation, and the local branch of the Royal Bank of Canada. Other sources of funding and in-kind support came from the Bulkley Valley Credit Union, the Woodmere Nursery, Hug Farms, and other service clubs, local businesses, and individuals. A retired local grocery operator provided advice about operating a food store. Innovation Foods developed a partnership with Bandstra Trucking to transport dried goods for free. Other trucking companies bring up frozen or refrigerated foods at discounted rates.

Innovation Foods encountered a number of challenges during its development and operations. Unlike Quest, which built up its operations over time, Innovation Foods chose to develop their enterprise quickly with a large storefront. Due to their inability to secure a lower lease arrangement, this may have been a mistake.

While many enterprises are supportive, some view Innovation Foods as competition and are unwilling to share unwanted items with them. Quest is still the main source of food for Innovation Foods, which receives a 10 per cent discount, though this does not always result in a broad range of goods. Ongoing efforts are trying to develop a food supply from within the Northwest region. Innovation Foods is working with local farms, the Cattlemen's Association, and the Aboriginal fisheries to get a range of fresh vegetables, meats, and smoked, vacuum-packaged salmon.

Government policies still create environments in which organizations compete rather than co-operate. Some local organizations feel that Innovation Foods competes with them. However, some of these groups could also benefit from Innovation Foods (i.e. supplies for a soup kitchen) given that there are slim profit margins and high overhead costs. A number of improvements to policies, programs, and supports can assist the development and maintenance of social enterprises. An example is the creation of incentives for landlords to allow better lease arrangements for social enterprises.

Social service agencies need more support to develop their capacity, business knowledge, and experience. Local networks have the potential to provide timely advice. However, a venue is needed to connect social service agencies with other businesses that want to get involved in the community, not just through providing money but also through offering advice, mentoring, and in-kind support. The volunteer pool that many local organizations depend on to sustain their activities has also declined as more households experience economic stress. Innovative incentives, including more volunteer recognition, are needed to encourage community members to engage in volunteer activities associated with social enterprises.

Discussion

In a rapidly changing economic and neoliberal policy landscape, social enterprises have become important community assets as they support rural and small town renewal and social development. Our two case studies have demonstrated the contributions that social enterprises can make to small places by addressing basic needs; providing employment, training, and work experiences; providing advice and expertise; developing infrastructure; and contributing to local development strategies. The social enterprises described in this chapter benefited from both local and non-local sources of social, human, and financial capital. In addition to seed funding, both enterprises drew on other social enterprises for advice and mentorship during their early stages of development. Their expansion of networks both locally and non-locally has played a critical role in their success. However, a diverse set of expectations can question that success. As managing expectations has been a significant challenge for social enterprises, decision-makers and managers must establish a more refined scope for their enterprise's activities and operations.

However, while service restructuring and reduced government support have provided the impetus for the development of the social economy, there are too many institutional policy and program deficiencies to support a resilient social economy in rural and small town places. New policy and program frameworks are needed to help social enterprises be successful and resilient in a neoliberal era. For example, more flexible and responsive funding mechanisms and processes are needed if social economy enterprises are to fulfill their potential. This should include reconstructed financial supports that reflect the operating parameters and social goals that drive social enterprises. Current evaluation criteria used by banks are geared towards for-profit schemes and do not always provide a realistic or stable financing option for local social enterprises. Local governments, service providers, or community foundations may provide an alternative source of seed support through no-interest loans, space, and professional support services. Loan options may be through the local community futures offices. Unfortunately, the Federal Business Development Bank of Canada does not provide funding to non-profit organizations for social enterprises. While some researchers have highlighted alternative financing options for social enterprises (Quarter et al., 2009), greater promotion and awareness of such options is needed. Local governments may also play a greater role in assisting social enterprises through the provision of affordable leasing options on land and buildings. Senior governments may also establish incentive programs or cost-sharing arrangements to create more affordable leases for social enterprises.

As communities respond to change, they need both bottom-up and top-down policy and program support. Entrepreneurial mentorship is critical during the design stages of a business plan to ensure that operational expectations are both realistic and manageable. Local and senior levels of government need to provide more financial and logistical support to link social enterprises with sufficient networks of support, resources, and expertise. This may entail establishing a new institutional structure to facilitate sharing success stories, strategies, mentoring, and various forms of resources. Ongoing programs are needed to provide training and education, and to facilitate the development of human capital within social enterprises. Such programs should address the unique needs and demands of developing and operating social enterprises in rural areas and small towns. Furthermore, government policies and programs must encourage more co-operation between local groups as competition is only likely to break down social capital assets. As many organizations are coping with fewer human and financial resources, accountability, reporting, and administrative procedures need to be streamlined.

Most importantly, social economy enterprises need a louder voice and greater support (Graefe, 2002). This should include a portal to information on key issues such as developing social economy business plans; accessing funding; addressing tax parameters; maintaining relationships with community and government partners; managing succession planning; and social economy specific human resource development and training. As there is no provincial or national association for social economy enterprises, such support is especially necessary for the development of this sector. As long as they have no formal place within the mandates of senior government departments, it will remain unclear who has the responsibility to develop appropriate supportive policies and programs that will strengthen the resiliency and operating environments of the social economy enterprises that work to support the renewal of rural and small town communities.

NOTES

1 Community forests have been defined as 'any forestry operation managed by a local government, community group, First Nation, or community-held corporation for the benefit of the entire community' (www.bccfa.ca).
2 In 2003, the Government of British Columbia eliminated the appurtenance clause in order to enhance the competitiveness of industries operating in the province (Prudham, 2008). The appurtenance clause was defined as agreements that tied timber harvesting rights to specific local and regional manufacturing facilities built and operated as a condition to acquire tenure (Ross & Smith, 2002). The purpose of the clause was to generate as much local benefit as possible from local resources and avoid the problem of exporting both logs and jobs that had plagued earlier forest industry periods (Nelles, 2005). To address the loss of community benefits, the provincial government re-allocated timber volumes by taking back 20 per cent of the tenure volumes, in which half was allocated to First Nations and community forests and half was allocated to BC Timber Sales (McCarthy, 2006).
3 Silviculture practices entail reforesting harvested areas in order to achieve specific objectives and values by planting selected seeds, spacing (juvenile thinning), fertilizing, and pruning (Ministry of Forests, Mines, and Lands, 2010).

REFERENCES

Abele, F. (2009). The state and the northern social economy: Research prospects. *The Northern Review, 30*(Spring), 37–56.

Athey, S., & Levin, J. (2001). Information and competition in US forest service timber auctions. *Journal of Political Economy, 109*(2), 375–417.

Barnes, T., & Hayter, R. (1994). Economic restructuring, local development and resource towns: Forest communities in coastal British Columbia. *Canadian Journal of Regional Science, 17*(3), 289–310.

Barnes, T., & Hayter, R. (1997). *Troubles in the rainforest: British Columbia's forest economy in transition* (Vol. 33). Victoria: Western Geographical Press, Department of Geography, University of Victoria, Canadian Western Geographical Series.

Barnes, T., Hayter, R., & Hay, E. (2001). Stormy weather: Cyclones, Harold Innis, and Port Alberni, BC. *Environment and Planning A, 33*(12), 2127–47.

Başkent, E., Kose, S., & Keleş, S. (2005). The forest management planning system of Turkey: Constructive criticism towards the sustainable management of forest ecosystems. *International Forestry Review, 7*(3), 208–17.

Bradbury, J. (1987). British Columbia: Metropolis and hinterland in microcosm. In L. McCann (Ed.), *Heartland and hinterland: A geography of Canada* (pp. 400–41). Scarborough: Prentice-Hall Canada.

Christoffersen, N., Harker, D., Lyman, M., & Wyckoff, B. (2008). *The status of community-based forestry in the United States.* A report to the US Endowment for Forestry and Communities. Enterprise, Oregon: Community Forest Consortium, Wallowa Resources.

Davis, H., & Hutton, T. (1989). The two economies of British Columbia. *BC Studies,* (82), 3–15.

du Plessis, V., Beshiri, R., & Bollman, R. (2004). Definitions of rural. In G. Halseth & R. Halseth (Eds.), *Building for success: Exploration of rural community and rural development* (pp. 51–79). Brandon, MB: Rural Development Institute.

Evans, M., & Syrett, S. (2007). Generating social capital? The social economy and local economic development. *European Urban and Regional Studies, 14*(1), 55–74.

Graefe, P. (2002). The social economy and the state: Linking ambitions with institutions in Quebec, Canada. *Policy and Politics, 30*(2), 247–62.

Graefe, P. (2006). The social economy and the American model: Relating new social policy directions to the old. *Global Social Policy, 6*(2), 197–219.

Graine, M. (2010). *McBride, BC: Economic development action plan.* McBride, BC: Village of McBride. Retrieved from http://www.mcbride.ca/userfiles/file/admin/Action%20Plan%202010%281%29.pdf

Gunton, T. (1997). Forestry land use and public policy in British Columbia: The dynamics of change. In T. Barnes & R. Hayter (Eds.), *Trouble in the rainforest: British Columbia's forest economy in transition* (Vol. 33) (pp. 65–74). Victoria: Western Geographical Press.

Gunton, T. (2003). Natural resources and regional development: An assessment of dependency and comparative advantage paradigms. *Economic Geography, 79*(1), 67–94.

Halseth, G. (2005). Resource town transition: Debates after closure. In S. Essex, A. Gilg, R. Yarwood, J. Smithers, & R. Wilson (Eds.), *Rural change and sustainability: Agriculture, the environment, and communities* (pp. 326–42). Oxfordshire, UK: CABI Publishing.

Halseth, G., & Ryser, L. (2006). *Service provision in rural and small town Canada: A cross-Canada summary report.* Montreal: Initiative on the New Economy, project of the Canadian Rural Revitalization Foundation, Concordia University.

Halseth, G., & Ryser, L. (2007). The deployment of partnerships by the voluntary sector to address service needs in rural and small town Canada. *Voluntas, 18*(3), 241–65.

Halseth, G., Straussfogel, D., Parsons, S., & Wishart, A. (2004). Regional economic shifts in BC: Speculation from recent demographic evidence. *Canadian Journal of Regional Science, 27*(3), 317–52.

Halseth, G., & Sullivan, L. (2002). *Building community in an instant town: A social geography of Mackenzie and Tumbler Ridge, British Columbia.* Prince George: UNBC Press.

Hanlon, N., & Halseth, G. (2005). The greying of resource communities in northern British Columbia: Implications for health care delivery in already-underserviced communities. *The Canadian Geographer, 49*(1), 1–24.

Hayter, R. (2000). *Flexible crossroads: The restructuring of British Columbia's forest economy.* Vancouver: UBC Press.

Hayter, R. (2003). The war in the woods': post-Fordist restructuring, globalization and the contested remapping of British Columbia's forest economy. *Annals of the Association of American Geographers, 93*(3), 706–29.

Hayter, R., & Barnes, T. (1990). Innis' staple theory, exports, and recession: British Columbia, 1981–1986. *Economic Geography, 66*(2), 156–73.

Horne, G., & Penner, B. (1992). *British Columbia community employment dependencies.* Victoria: Planning & Statistics Division and Ministry of Finance & Corporate Relations.

Hutton, T. (1997). Vancouver as a control centre for British Columbia's resource hinterland: Aspects of linkage and divergence in a provincial staple economy. In T. Barnes & R. Hayter (Eds.), *Trouble in the rainforest: British Columbia's forest economy in transition: Vol. 33* (pp. 233–62). Victoria: Western Geographical Press.

Hutton, T. (2002). *British Columbia at the crossroads.* Vancouver: BC Progress Board.

Kay, A. (2005). Social capital, the social economy, and community development. *Community Development Journal, 41*(2), 160–73.

Klein, J., Fontan, J., & Tremblay, D. (2009). Social entrepreneurs, local initiatives, and social economy: Foundations for a socially innovative strategy
to fight against poverty and exclusion. *Canadian Journal of Regional Science,
17*(1), 23–42.

Little, B. (2002). BC's decades of genteel decline. (2002, April 20). *Globe and
Mail,* B1, B4.

Mackenzie, S., & Norcliffe, G. (1997). Guest editors – Restructuring in the
Canadian newsprint industry. *Canadian Geographer, 31*(1), 2–6.

Marchak, P. (1983). *Green gold: The forest industry in British Columbia.* Vancouver:
UBC Press.

Marchak, P., Aycock, S., & Herbert, D. (1999). *Falldown: Forest policy in British
Columbia.* Vancouver: The David Suzuki Foundation and Ecotrust Canada.

Markey, S., Pierce, J.T., Vodden, K., & Roseland, M. (2005). *Second growth:
Community economic development in rural British Columbia.* Vancouver: UBC
Press.

Marsden, T., Lowe, P., & Whatmore, S. (Eds.) (1990). *Rural restructuring: Global
processes and their responses.* London, ON: David Fulton.

McCarthy, J. (2006). Neoliberalism and the politics of alternatives: Community
forestry in British Columbia and the United States. *Annals of the Association of
American Geographers, 96*(1), 84–104.

Meinhard, A., & Foster, M. (2003). Differences in the response of women's voluntary organizations to shifts in Canadian public policy. *Nonprofit and Voluntary Sector Quarterly, 32*(3), 366–96.

Ministry of Forestry, Mines, and Lands. (2010). *The state of British Columbia's forests* (3rd ed.). Victoria: Province of British Columbia.

Munro, J.M. (2003). *Policies to induce structural change in the British Columbia
economy.* Burnaby: Simon Fraser University. Paper presented at the Canadian
Regional Science Association Meetings in Victoria, BC.

Neil, C., Tykkläinen, M., & Bradbury, J. (1992). *Coping with closure: An international comparison of mine town experiences.* New York: Routledge.

Nelles, H. (2005). *The politics of development: Forests, mines, and hydro-electric power
in Ontario, 1949–1941* (2nd ed.). Montreal: McGill-Queen's University Press.

Nieuwenhuis, M., & Gallagher, D. (2001). The impact of landscape design planning on the timber production and financial outputs of a forest plantation in
Ireland. *Forest Policy and Economics, 2*(3–4), 267–80.

Pierce, J. (1999). Making communities the strong link in sustainable development. In J. Pierce A. Dale (Eds.), *Communities, development, and sustainability
across Canada* (pp. 3–23). Vancouver: UBC Press.

Prudham, S. (2008). Tall among the trees: Organizing against globalist forestry in rural British Columbia. *Journal of Rural Studies, 24*(2), 182–96.

Quarter, J., Mook, L., & Armstrong, A. (2009). *Understanding the social economy: A Canadian perspective.* Toronto: University of Toronto Press.

Reimer, B. (2002). A sample frame for rural Canada: Design and evaluation. *Regional Studies, 36*(8), 845–59.

Ross, M., & Smith, P. (2002). *Accommodation of Aboriginal rights: The need for an Aboriginal forest tenure.* Edmonton: Sustainable Forest Management Network, University of Alberta.

Ryser, L., & Halseth, G. (2010). Rural economic development: A review of the literature from industrialized economies. *Geography Compass, 4*(6), 510–31.

Southcott, C. (2009). Introduction: The social economy and economic development in northern Canada. *The Northern Review, 30*(Spring), 3–11.

Stevenson, J. (2009). Innovation foods to the rescue. *Northword* (December). Retrieved from http://northword.ca

Teitelbaum, S., & Reimer, B. (2002). *The social economy in rural Canada: Exploring research options.* A report to the Concordia section of CRISES. Montreal: Concordia University.

Williston, E., & Keller, B. (1997). *Forests, power, and policy: The legacy of Ray Williston.* Prince George: Caitlin Press.

Wilson, B., Wang, S., & Haley, D. (1999). British Columbia. In B. Wilson, G. Van Kooten, I. Vertinsky, & L. Arthur (Eds.), *Forest policy: International case studies* (pp. 81–108). Oxon, UK: CABI Publishing.

Young, N., & Matthews, R. (2007). Resource economies and neoliberal experimentation: the reform of industry and community in rural British Columbia. *Area, 39*(2), 176–85.

Zografos, C. (2007). Rurality discourses and the role of the social enterprise in regenerating rural Scotland. *Journal of Rural Studies, 23*(1), 38–51.

8 Land, Self-Determination, and the Social Economy in Fort Albany First Nation

JEAN-PAUL RESTOULE, SHEILA GRUNER, AND EDMUND METATAWABIN

In this chapter we look at a project called *Land, the Environment, and Self-Determination* in James Bay, Ontario, and its implications for the field of social economy research and theory. The project developed out of ongoing conversations about the importance of land to the social and economic well-being of Fort Albany First Nation, a small Mushkegowuk Cree community located on the west coast of James Bay, about 130 air kilometres northwest of Moosonee, Ontario, which itself is 850 kilometres north of Toronto. The community is situated on Sinclair and Anderson's Islands on the Albany River, and on the mainland. The reserve population is approximately 900 (with the total population approximately 1,400). These conversations formed the basis of a community-based research initiative affiliated with the Social Economy Centre at the Ontario Institute for Studies in Education of the University of Toronto (OISE/UT). The project grew to include other academic institutional partners, primarily the Northern Ontario Research, Development, Ideas, and Knowledge (NORDIK) Institute at Algoma University, and later others such as Rural Women Making Change of the University of Guelph. The following chapter is a result of ongoing dialogue and community-based research efforts, and draws on conversations, experiences, and insights deeply rooted in applied learning and shared analysis.

We begin this chapter with an exploration of some of the key considerations relating to conceptualizing the social economy in a First Nations context. We then reflect on the research project as set out through the Social Economy Centre and its development into a broad community-based research effort. Finally, we explore some of the key concepts of land and self-determination in relation to the social economy.

**Relevance of the Concept of Social Economy
for First Nations Communities**

When this project began, we wanted to explore whether the concept of social economy would be relevant or useful to First Nations communities. We were aware of the problematic history associated with carrying out research on First Nations communities in the first place, and also knew that the discourse of the social economy did not necessarily have resonance or meaning for indigenous people in northern reserve communities. A long history of marginalization in face of mainstream economic thinking and practice is one part of the story. Another part had to do with ways of conceiving social and economic life underpinning development decisions that are particular to the locality, history, and culture of a given people, and which are perhaps more pronounced in a First Nations context. Very real and persistent goals of many indigenous communities, for example, are focused on addressing unresolved questions of indigenous land rights, governance, and self-determination. We wanted to know whether the social economy could ultimately contribute to these broader underlying goals. As for engaging in a social economy research project, we decided on a community-based approach that would allow local people to define and drive the research in ways beneficial to them, aware of what Wanda Wuttunee (2010) warned: 'Researchers may label an activity as clearly an example of social economy while a community member would not recognize that term and may have a term for that activity that is more culturally relevant . . . Again what matters most for Aboriginal communities are the results of this activity, not the conceptual framework' (p. 201).

Other authors also agree that the social economy is a term with little-known implications or relevance for Aboriginal communities in Ontario. As McMurtry (2010) notes,

> Not surprisingly, the social economy, with its conceptual roots in continental Europe, has not been embraced as a concept or as a practice by First Peoples because it lacks a clear connection to these various economic traditions. This lack of affinity is further amplified by the fact that the social economy as a policy solution, when advocated or impeded by the state, is often viewed by First Peoples as a continuation of colonialism. (p. 4)

Even beyond the application of the social economy to Aboriginal communities and practices, there is an academic under-theorizing of what the social economy is or how to characterize it (McMurtry, 2010). McMurtry proposes a definition that is intended to grow from and apply to the Canadian character of social economic activity, blending its location and its normative character. In this sense, the social economy is 'economic activity neither controlled directly by the state nor by the profit logic of the market; activity that prioritizes the social well-being of communities and marginalized individuals over partisan political directives or individual gain' (McMurtry, 2010, p. 31). This definition appears to align itself with much indigenous economic activity today and historically, particularly when discussed outside of questions of land/territoriality and self-determination. In a case study of three contemporary First Nations communities, Wuttunee (2010) found that 'what they do show is how what matters for Aboriginal communities is that when development happens, it must be both economic and social and needs to occur within the control of those communities – not under the direct control of the state or under the motivation of only making profit' (p. 206). She also noted that 'Aboriginal peoples have been practising key elements of social economy (such as economic activity in the service of community, social goals rather than profit driving economic decisions, and democratic decision making) from time immemorial' (Wuttunee, 2010, p. 206).

Russell has also grappled with questions about the relevance of social economy in a First Nations context, recognizing that mixed economic practice is often overlooked in smaller remote communities and represents significant areas that are under-researched. Russell (2007) contemplates the potential benefits as well as the dangers of the discourse for localized economies, stating that,

> the 'promise' of the social economy is certainly, in part, its potential to draw attention to causes of material hardship, but it is also in acknowledging the persistent viability of highly local socio-economic traditions to address those causes and create change. It is this latter promise, to acknowledge pre-existing economic pluralism that poses the greatest challenge to social economy practitioners and theoreticians alike. (p. 2–3)

The pervasive message among practitioners as well as community members is that this pluralism itself is in peril. Recent policy discourses favour dominant extractive development, such as the mining of minerals, metals, oil, and gas, in remote First Nations communities over traditional land practice and small-scale enterprise. If social economy discourse can make visible this problem and put it into a meaningful historical context, it could improve the situation of Aboriginal peoples in Canada who struggle against extractive development practieces and pressures to engage in such practices.

The role of social economy in indigenous communities should include not only immediate social needs such as housing, education, and small-scale enterprise alone, but also broader governance issues related to territorial and political self-determination. Governance is an important area for exploration with relation to the social economy and First Nations communities. Decisions about land and what happens within traditional territories of indigenous people must not be set aside in discussions of social enterprise, social capital, and the social economy overall. The potential for emancipatory outcomes of the social economy for Aboriginal communities lies in the assumption that land rights and governance form the base upon which any local enterprise is meaningful or indeed viable in the long run. Moreover, and not insignificantly, social economy holds potential power in a deepened consciousness among social economy practitioners outside of First Nations communities about the need to settle questions of First Nations jurisdiction and governance outside of the apparatus of the market.

The Social Economy Centre takes an interactive and organizational focus in its conceptualization of the social economy (see chapter 1). A First Nations context poses complications to looking at how the organizations in the social economy interact with the other sectors of the economy and society. It is important to underscore the specificity of experience among First Nations people with regards to the questions of land and governance within social economy definitions, if the answers to those questions are to be meaningful. It is not an exaggeration to state that any economic enterprise in a remote First Nations community under treaty, existing or proposed, is undergirded by complex institutional relations that set up the social economy debate under different terms. For instance, in most of Canada, groups may establish organizations or co-operatives without local government approval. Within a First Nations community, nearly every enterprise must legally involve some level of government oversight given the fiduciary relationship between the federal government and reserve communities, and in particular the management of traditional territories by the Crown. Hence, the same activities that originate in grassroots organizing and might be termed social economic initiatives elsewhere in Canada, are in these cases initiatives of the 'public sector.' One of the consequences of this categorization is differential access to private sector development funding (Corbiere,

Johnston, & Reyes, 2007). Another challenge is tied to the relative consistency of band council governments, who mediate relations between communities, on the one hand, and the provincial and federal governments on the other. Under Canada's *Indian Act*, a band composed of an elected chief and council is the fundamental legal unit of government for members of First Nations reserve communities. Band council governments are viewed by the Canadian government as the official governing bodies, although traditional forms of governance often exist in parallel. With elections held every three years, unless the band leadership remains stable, social enterprises, which are usually formally controlled by or strongly tied to the fates of band councils, risk volatility and disruption (Corbiere et al., 2007). Perhaps this is partly why the vast majority of Aboriginal-run social economy organizations are located off reserve and in urban areas (Newhouse, 2003).

The social economy organizations in many First Nations communities are generally more integrated with each other than in some non-Aboriginal communities, in part due to smaller populations and remote location, but also because of the distinct status First Nations people maintain as treaty holders. Moreover, there appears to be a greater sense of community and mutual self-reliance that brings together diverse local organizations within a common platform for community development. In some cases the social and economic bonds are not formalized in organizational structures, but are based on historical cultural and sustenance practices rooted in relationships to land, life, family, and community. Largely subsumed under subsistence activities, this set of relationships is variously termed as 'non-observed, irregular, unofficial, hidden, shadow, non-structured or unorganized' (Natcher, 2008, p. 3). Even the most commonly used term, the informal economy, inadequately represents the depth of the relationships formed. Natcher (2008) warns, 'While important in analytic terms, the valuation of subsistence production does run the risk of misrepresenting and devaluing the cultural significance of subsistence' (p. 4).

We agree with Russell's caution that 'the promotion of social capital can celebrate and encourage specific kinds of social action to the exclusion of other more critical and progressive mobilizations' (2007, p. 4). In face of this significant concern, we turn our attention to our specific project, which sought to create spaces for dialogue and action in relation to social and economic well-being in a remote First Nations community in Northern Ontario as part of a more radical approach to building solidarity.

Setting the Stage for Research

The objectives set out in our initial research proposal centred on: a critical assessment of social economy concepts and framework; support for local Cree participants (with an emphasis on youth) to document and value local land practice and key issues related to social, economic, and environmental change; and to share and exchange research findings with other Aboriginal communities and researchers involved in related investigations. *Land, the Environment, and Self-Determination* was designed to generate space for dialogue about meaningful social and economic practice tied to questions of land and self-determination, which were considered crucial overarching themes that could not be separated from a study on the social economy.

Alongside local researchers and partners, we set out to ask how the Mushkegowuk Cree community along the James Bay coast perceives land, the environment, and traditional cultural and economic practices in relation to social and economic well-being. Throughout the research, we were primarily asking: what is the role of land/territory, and what strategies are people developing to maintain the Mushkegowuk 'way of life,' particularly in face of pressures to enter into the world of large-scale extractive capitalism?

These are large questions for a small project to grapple with. We recognized that there were aspects of the community that might be explored in relation to businesses or nonprofit organizations, such as community social organizational efforts (health, cultural and education programming, elder and youth activities, and so forth); local small-scale enterprise in the area of lumber and value-added activities; locally developed restaurants and catering services; hunting, trapping, fishing, and other culturally meaningful practices that connected people socially and represent alternative or sustainable extractive activities; artists and artisans; and various other socially engaged organizations and efforts aimed at addressing multiple community-centred priorities. However, questions of territorial, political, and economic self-determination continue to play a key role in all of these areas and could not be separated from conversations about the social economy, woven into the very fabric of Mushkegowuk life. Arguably, these questions are also relevant for other First Nations communities, including those who maintain a historically rooted special status in federal and provincial policy as Treaty holders, and other communities whose relationship within traditional territories also continues to be a priority for local educational, cultural, and health programs. Many First Nations communities continue to fight for recognition of territorial and cultural rights in the face of provincial and federal policy and industrial development obstacles, which frame a general experience of Aboriginal people as having less opportunity or support to socially and economically organize on their own terms. Historical experiences of colonialism and racism leading to displacement and dispossession continue to undermine social and economic well-being for many First Nations people, and as such need to inform any discussion of the social economy. For many First Nations communities, the idea that the economy needs to accelerate or grow has little relevance and goes against the teachings of what Elders have said: all things we do are for those that are not yet born.

Building a Frame for Research

Before developing a formal research strategy, researchers and community members discussed issues that would support the development of a framework reflective of local aspirations. We learned that a framework aimed at contemplating social and economic well-being in this First Nations community would need to include discussion of:

- language, history, and territoriality;
- deeply rooted relationships among people and between people and nature (such as the concept of paquataskamik, explained below);
- ways of seeing and being in the world (including social and economic relationality) that lay outside of a western perspective;
- efforts of local people who struggle for self-determination in a specific place (i.e., Treaty 9 area).

We then developed a set of objectives that were achievable within the project's two-year timeframe and that could respond to the different perspectives of the specific people involved in project discussions, including university researchers, community colleagues and partners including youth, adults, elders, and other local participants. Our goal was to analyze and improve the social economy research process to benefit the community and foster ongoing alliances and social networks.

The initial research phase involved local participants in defining the research direction. The Economic Development Officer from Fort Albany First Nation encouraged the lead researcher to draw on various institutional affiliations which lead to the involvement of NORDIK Institute, a community-based research centre at Algoma University that supported the development of a broader project platform, and a group called Rural Women Making Change from the University of Guelph, which became involved in supporting the efforts of local girls to creatively express their experiences through the creation of a 'zine, or informal magazine. Diverse community members helped develop collaborative proposals that could further community goals beyond the scope of the original project discussed here. Members of community organizations formed an intergenerational community advisory group, which met over the life of the project and provided oversight and direction. The group included the band office, health centre, schools, youth, elders, and other community members who were involved in developing research protocols. It was important to the researchers to build reciprocity into the research process and to privilege Mushkegowuk social relationality.

In the early design stages, one community priority was bringing together elders and youth to discuss the role and meaning of land to social well-being. Since that time, the project has been about fostering development of meaningful space for intergenerational dialogue and community research on social and economic relationships rooted in Mushkegowuk conceptions of life and traditional territory.

Paquataskamik and First Relationships to Land

We developed a process with the participating community groups to promote youth, adult, and elder involvement with an audio documentary project about the social and economic meaning and 'value' of the Kistachowan (Albany) River. The community chose the river as a theme because of its cultural, social, and economic importance, and its centrality in the lives of many people. As part of the project, youth and elders travelled together on the traditional waters and lands, exploring history, language, issues of governance, and land management. To achieve our goal of supporting local Cree youth, the advisory group organized skill-building workshops in which youth participants made their own audio documentaries based on the interviews they carried out with community members. They received training in research and communication skills, and recorded their intergenerational learning through radio documentaries and 'zines.

Youth conducted interviews with peers, adults, and elders on key issues related to the role of land, the river, and the people for community social and economic well-being. Fifteen interviews were collected and formed the basis for a short audio documentary, titled *The Kistachowan River Knows My Name*, which aired in the local community and on Wawatay radio in northern Ontario. The key objective of this process was to bring generations together to learn about relationships to land, the river, and the community. The resulting traditional knowledge and teachings, and commitments by youth to learn more, was particularly powerful because they could be shared with the community via radio. The greater goals in this process were community building and enriching the community understanding of how the river, land, and the traditional territory provide for the people's social and economic needs.

During the development of the documentary, community members made the significance of the river more visible, in its social, cultural, economic, and spiritual senses. In particular, the physical excursion into traditional territory offered a wealth of insight into the importance of land for social and economic well-being. It also brought out how important water is to Mushkegowuk culture. As one participant explained,

> The word 'Muskeg' refers to the floating mass of land upon which we make our living. The nature of our environment attracts certain species of animals and definitely a certain kind of human character. When we hear frogs singing we know the water quality is safe for our consumption. We listen to the song of the birds to know what kind of weather is approaching. The moose will know when we need food and allow themselves to be taken. Such is the contract we have with the animal world. (Elder and community member, Fort Albany)

The group documented sites of significance to the community, travelled routes that hold great historical significance, and brought people together in the sharing of knowledge. They produced audio visual (radio, photo, and film) and written materials as part of a growing body of work valuing traditional territory, including the importance of history, current usage of the territory, and possibilities for the future.

The Kistachowan River was a site for discussing how Mushkegowuk people self-organized in the territory, binding diverse communities through sites of social, cultural, and economic activity. Through the project, participants learned that prior to contact there was a community along each tributary, with a pathway connecting each community to the next. This pathway was used by runners who carried news to a neighboring community. News could travel quickly, with fresh runners carrying it further from each community. The river itself bound people and communities together. To strengthen this traditional bond, the youth, adults, and elders on the river trip engaged in Cree mapping as they travelled the river. Names for places in the Inninowuk language were marked as an effort to bring the original names and Cree concepts to more common use among the youth.

During the river excursion the Cree-language terminology was expanded for those participating. The words 'paquataskamik' (see below) and 'Kistachowan Sipi' (Albany River's original name) were written along the sides of the raft – some were fifty feet long. There were Mushkegowuk words that were accompanied by stories for many sites along the route which were documented during the trip. Many more place names existed than the English ones that appeared on printed maps. This supported the elders' suggestion that 'every curve in the river has a name.'

The ongoing drive to orient the project to Mushkegowuk ways of knowing resulted in exploring Cree words and concepts and inserting them into key project activities and documents. The main word that arose as discussions evolved about land, the river, and life in their territory was 'paquataskamik,' which is 'an Inninowuk (Cree) word that describes the 'natural environment' and draws attention to the whole of traditional territory' (Gruner & Metatawabin, 2009). As adults involved in the project described, paquataskamik is significant partly because it references a historical relationship to land which encompassed a much larger area than the reserve or family camps. This territory has been regulated, divided, and parceled by non-Inninowuk into Crown land, treaty, and reserve spaces, which has resulted in fractures and alterations to that relationship. The resulting effects of this for social networks, economic development, and survival are felt daily. When youth lose a sense of what paquataskamik is, they may begin to lose the connections that form the complex set of relations that bind them together in a historically and geographically informed identity. The focus on the word is an explicit attempt to retain a relationship to the rivers, the lands, and the communities joined together by them.

According to one Mushkegowuk interviewee, paquataskamik is the Cree word used for traditional territory, all of the environment, nature, and everything it contains. 'Noscheemik' is the word for 'camp,' the bush, or a more specific area within paquataskamik. For project participants, it was important to remember words like paquataskamik because they spoke to the broader project of territoriality and self-determination within Mushkegowuk lands, the ability of the Mushkegowuk people to define development on their own terms, and to continue to build on a histori-cal identity in a vast area that was never 'given up' to European settlers. Historically and currently, people have derived sustenance from the land, are guided by seasons and traditional hunting routes, and consider the land as crucial to healing the Mushkegowuk people from the impacts of colonialism.

The elders and other community members were concerned that the word 'paquataskamik' was falling into disuse among the younger genera-tions, who tend to use 'noscheemik' instead, which pointed to a loss of important linguistic distinctions related to concepts of territoriality. One interviewee said:

> You use paquataskamik if you are fluent (in Cree) and if you are a young kid you use noscheemik . . . they confuse, they're not saying it properly. That's too high a word for them so they just use the simple word, noscheemik. (Community member, Fort Albany First Nation)

This change in word usage is partly because of intergenerational lan-guage loss. Residential schooling and its impact on indigenous language use drastically reduced the number of fluent speakers. A distinction be-tween 'high' Cree and 'low' Cree is made among speakers with high Cree speakers being able to use and understand highly complex sen-tence forms and descriptions that a language learner or someone who did not develop their linguistic skills deeply (one who went to residential schools at the age of five, for instance) has more difficulty with. One lan-guage instructor describes high Cree as being like '"enriched English" whereas the "watered down" form of Cree is more childish. The gram-matical structure is not there' (Greg Spence, Mushkegowuk translator, cited in Porter, 1999). Some community members worry that the de-creasing use of words like 'paquataskamik' means that the ability to form a linguistic connection to traditional territory could be at risk within a short period of time. The implications for governance, land use, eco-nomic development, and social relationships are vast.

Paquataskamik speaks to a way of relating to land based on laws and governance arrangements that were in place long before European set-tlers arrived. According to Inninowuk people, the organization of travel routes, negotiation of temporary settlements and gathering places, and planning based on availability of food sources and seasonal changes were all rooted in land-based knowledge that shaped governing practices and laws. While these laws still exist, they have been made less visible since the onset of colonialism and capitalism. Large scale extractive capitalism, in particular, has presented new problems and perceived threats to the environment. In order to protect land and the relationships to land that are integral to Inninowuk identity, territorial self-governance is a necessity. If the social economy is to successfully address environmental and cultural well-being or 'sustainability,' it must support this broader project of self-determination. As the projects demonstrate, paquataskamik fosters a connection to land and community beyond the reserve boundaries, encouraging Inninowuk ways of relating to land that are put ahead of an accumulative or extractive economy.

The Kistachowan River is included in the traditional territory that paquataskamik refers to. According to one member of Fort Albany First Nation (FAFN) interviewed by a community youth, the river is particularly important in the concept of paquataskamik:

> Well, it's very important to me as well, because I use the river for fishing, hunting, camping, being raised on it from a very early age . . . it's also very beautiful, it's pristine, and of course, it being a river, it also carries water that's important for human life; it carries water, and it's clean . . . At the same time it's a very powerful river. Every spring, when you have the spring breakup, it's quite a mighty river; I have quite a lot of respect for it. Basically, I just love the river myself. I'm on it a lot, almost every day. And just to even look at it is satisfying. (Male FAFN member interviewed by a community youth)

The river has many significant uses and meanings, physically, emotionally, and spiritually. The quotation below describes how points along the river where family are buried demonstrate the profound connection of ancestors, land, river, and paquataskamik:

> And my sister's there. My young sister is there; the third born in the family. She died when she was an infant. For him (father), the memory was so fresh, that every time he goes close to the cemetery, cleaning up the grass or fixing the fence, just doing anything to improve, then he'd finish all that and then he'd say a little prayer and cry. That was just how fresh it is. And I saw him do that until way afterwards; the last time we took him out there, and it was the very same thing. So for him the river is his daughter, lying a hundred miles up; his brother who is buried twenty miles downstream from that; his mother who's buried, probably 120 further than that . . . And his grandfather is buried about 135 miles from the north side of the river . . . along

the river. So, it's family, it's a family cemetery, it's a highway . . . there are markers along the highway to indicate significant events, significant moments; people that have passed away that are close to you and they are lying along the river. So it's a river of life; it's growth. (FAFN adult, interviewed by FAFN youth)

In this case, the part of paquataskamik that relates to the river demonstrates the profound set of personal historical relationships with the river that connects the community to the land and to each other.

The river trip helped members of the community share linguistic, cultural, historical, and geographical knowledge. It re-established respect for the meaning of paquataskamik and demonstrated how irreconcilable that meaning is with western notions of boundaries as imposed by federal and provincial reserve policy and other planning models. This points to the broad political efforts for the recognition of land and water rights that are currently underway. For the people of the community, these lands are a part of the cultural inheritance of the Mushkegowuk people, one that they feel their children and grandchildren should be able to experience. The project helped to stoke dialogues and partnerships, some pre-existing, and some catalysed by the research project itself, about the place of the river, the land, the language, and self-determination in relation to both the community of Fort Albany and to the Mushkegowuk people. While many elements of this project could be examples of the social economy in action, the added dimension of First Nations cultural and historical relationships to land and each other differentiates it from mainstream social economy discourses in two ways. First, there is a political aspect in activities that assert First Nations identities and relations to traditional territories in ways that contest dominant (western) forms of governance. Second, many of these activities take place within a non-formal set of community and kin connections. These together in other words, demonstrates that the political nature of traditional activity carried out by a First Nation community, and the often informal means in which such activities are pursued, complicates trying to subsume traditional indigenous knowledge and activities under a social economy lens.

Land, Learning, and Intergenerational Relationships

Bringing generations together to talk about the issues of land and water rights provided many learning opportunities for the community. On the subject of learning and intergenerational relationships, one interviewee said:

And I like this one (audio project), because at least you get to sit for one time in your lives, and somebody's going to show an interest in their stories, in their lives. They were just waiting for you to visit. Just waiting for young people to visit, because they have stories, they will remember good times, bad times, and dangerous times. (Community member interviewed by FAFN youth)

A project that grew out of the interviews and audio documentary was developed through NORDIK Institute, which worked with the community to develop a historical timeline, an inventory of strengths, and an ethnographic snapshot of key land issues. This smaller project became part of a broader effort to engage the community in a discussion about what activities should take place on traditional territory and how decisions about those activities should be made. In such a discussion, the framing of decision-making about territory and development is at stake. Dominant western frames that centre on an accumulation-oriented model of development (including the social economy) are at odds with Aboriginal ways of existence in cultural and geographic regions where land informs social and economic practices. Universalizing discourses do not readily transfer as they do not incorporate the diverse teachings and worldviews of many First Nations people. Common business practices elsewhere have difficulty entering into relationships derived from a different way of being, the expression of which is through language, which itself is rooted in land and territoriality. Fort Albany First Nation produces social and economic relationships that are not explicable within the usual social economy discourse. The 'social' is rooted in culture and history, carried out within practices of intergenerationality, and connects to other Mushkegowuk communities. These multiple social relationships, which span geographic landscapes, age, and kinship, are a foundational difference between indigenous communities and other communities in Canada. These relationships come from a historically-rooted identity and a specific experience of territoriality. These social elements are the driving force behind local economies, both historically and currently. Historically, people organized social and economic relations around seasonal and geographical changes, which were underscored by culture and kin relationships. Currently, jobs, housing, and social services address, either explicitly or implicitly,

multiple relationships that are rooted in a sense of identity and territoriality.

Social Economy Institutions and Networks of Solidarity

The methods behind *Land, the Environment, and Self-Determination* reflect,
in many ways, the practice of social economy as discussed in chapter 1.
Co-operation among local organizations, between local·organizations
and academic institutions, nonprofits and individuals, and regional
councils and governing bodies resulted in a set of social relations that
embody what the social economy field values most: social networking
and subverting a drive for profit to social and environmental community-oriented priorities. If these priorities are to be maintained, they
need to be explored, understood, and taken up in meaningful policy
arenas. Such priorities question the dominant trend towards opening
northern economies to large-scale development, defined elsewhere. Our
community-based research project fostered the development of the intergenerational river trip, which had tangible outcomes such as short-
term jobs for local youth in raft construction, a community mapping of
key cultural and historical sites, and education credits and accreditation
for youth and adults. The conversations between youth, adults, and elders formed the basis of a radio documentary on the deep connections
to land and life in the region. More significantly, they also deepened
the relationships community members have with each other and with
the land. These activities, organized through partnerships of small enterprises, government agencies, social economic organizations, and university bodies, still relied ultimately on the activation of friendship, kinship
relations, and indigenous knowledge, originating from a connection to
land.

The project also brought a number of social organizations together as
part of the advisory group, made up of representatives from the health
centre, educational authority, local school, band office, and the community in general. These groups discussed key aspects of the project and
how their own programming could support and benefit from it. Through
the local network created by involvement in such a project, there is a
greater possibility for generating consensus around locally driven alternative forms of development. For example, the idea of using the river as
a cultural corridor is generating interest.

As this project was discussed in various realms, the NORDIK Institute
increasingly explored new elements of the research. NORDIK was hired

by the community to collaborate on community-oriented research, and led a project supported through funding from Nishnawbe Aski Nation. NORDIK later helped shape a longer-term community-based project concerning land practice and community mapping, which involved training in community research methods and support for locally defined approaches to understanding land practice and priorities.

The Meaning for Social Economy

Our research agrees with Wuttunee's finding that 'the social economy label is a term that comes from *outside* a given community – and as such may or may not fit with the terminology used by that community for naming its experience, even though many aspects of what is labelled by the concept describes centuries-old Aboriginal practice' (2010, p. 210). The assertion that land and self-determination were crucial, overarching themes that could not be separated from our study on the social economy was maintained throughout the project.

The survival and health of Aboriginal communities and their economies are underpinned by direct relationships to land, a strong sense of community, and the drive to be self-determining people in all areas of life, including governance, education, and health. The Royal Commission on Aboriginal Peoples' Report (RCAP) and a plethora of other writing led by Aboriginal people underscore the fact that the viability of First Nations communities in Canada is dependent on a continued cultural and spiritual practice linked to land rights and political autonomy (Alfred, 2005; Battiste, 2000; RCAP, 1996). As such, economic practice is necessarily subverted to broader conceptualizations of life that take place within specific Aboriginal worldviews.

For Mushkegowuk people in Fort Albany, social economic relationships are deeply rooted in land, history, identity, and a strong sense of community. While social economy concepts have some relevance to First Nations participants, they can not adequately convey the depth of these relationships historically, socially, economically, and spiritually. This research, in collaboration and dialogue with the community, is a reminder of what many First Nations people continue to state: that listening is crucial; that going beyond the apparent is necessary; and that to approach the question of social economy in the North, history, territory, and worldview must be taken into account.

For instance, when a moose is killed, the community follows long-standing – yet largely unwritten – protocols for sharing and distributing the meat. Similarly, one participant with a small sawmill operation collects lumber and will often make a shed or table for a family who is either in need or can pay a sum. This could be considered akin to western forms of social economy, since the sharing is performed as a tradition of familial and community networks developed and sustained through cultural and linguistic traditions. These activities deepen community and familial bonds and presume the ethics of reciprocity, giving, sharing, and kindness. The redistribution of food, gifts, or other wealth is not formally organized through mainstream social economic systems. There is no formal community organization overseeing these activities, and there may or may not be formal community organizations that facilitate these exchanges, which can include teaching youth how to survive on the land; offering moose or geese to a family preparing for a funeral, marriage or graduation celebration; or extended family providing childcare in the absence of parents. Examples like these are based on relationships between people and families and are less 'organized' than they might be through the social economy's registered charities, nonprofits, and nongovernmental organizations. While such organizations exist in the community and play an increasing role in the provision of services, they do not replace other informal practices. According to some interpretations, the informal economic activities mentioned above should also be considered expressions of the social economy (see chapter 4 in this collection), as networks of social and economic relationships are activated in these non-monetary practices. Indeed, they surely can be considered as such. Yet according to some interviewees, these relationships are not quantifiable, nor should they be. This may point to a qualitative difference of importance, as they act as defining aspects of Inninowuk identity, rooted in a shared experience of land, history, and identity across vast geographical areas.

The gift-giving economy and the prioritization of land and intergenerational relations over a monetary economy shifts the focus from economic profit or gain to a deepening of relationships among people within a conception of living closely with traditional territory. Disruptions to these relationships, both social and territorial, have been the result of colonialism in sites such as residential schools and of fostering dependent relationships, as through *Indian Act* governance provisions, reserve policies, and a limited reading of Treaty 9, the document that formed a covenant between Canada and the Muskegowuk, signed in Fort Albany in 1905 and meant to uphold rights of both peoples in the territory. Unresolved governance and land issues undermine social and economic well-being, which in turn underpins the obstacles encountered in life in the community. In this fact lies another crucial difference between social economic activities in First Nations communities and the rest of Canada; namely, that there is a political nature to any activity that prioritizes indigenous cultural identity and practices. Such activities challenge the main tenets of Canadian policy towards Aboriginal peoples, which historically and currently encourages assimilation. In Canadian social economy discourse there are many latitudes to the political nature of an organization's activities. Some groups have mandates outside or beyond politics, while others take overt political positions as part of their missions and activities. The intimate connection to land and historical community relationships among Aboriginal peoples make untangling the social economy from other economic sectors and influences that play a role in the lives of Aboriginal people significantly complex.

Given that colonialism continues to operate as part of these relationships, aspects of the social economy can be a form of resistance in some contexts, and a form of dominance in others. Which role is being played might ultimately be decided by the degree to which local community agency and autonomy is exercised in any such endeavour. Such an analysis would parallel attempts to understand local indigenous struggles in achieving control of local economic development (see the examples collected in Blaser, Feit, & McRae, 2004). Another point of comparison is the distinction made in development discourses between approaches based on justice versus charity. One approach challenges hegemonic structures, while the other maintains them.

By supporting and creating a space for dialogue and learning between Cree youth and elders, *Land, the Environment, and Self-Determination* fostered learning about links between social and economic well-being and land, environment, and social and family ties. It is the bond among people in the community that has made survival possible from time immemorial. Strengthening this bond will ensure the Mushkegowuk people and culture thrive for generations to come. For other Aboriginal communities and researchers involved in related investigations, it is important to note that the findings of this project are not meant as a finished or refined critique, but as insight into one experience aimed at contemplating the social economy within a First Nation context. There is immense potential for research in this area, but it should be led by Aboriginal people and alliances of Aboriginal and non-Aboriginal scholars and practitioners who can set out parameters that are, first and foremost, relevant to community priorities, needs, and realities.

REFERENCES

Alfred, T. (2005). *Wasase: Indigenous pathways of action and freedom.* Toronto: UTP Higher Education.

Battiste, M. (Ed.). (2000). *Reclaiming indigenous voice and vision.* Vancouver: University of British Columbia Press.

Blaser, M., Feit, H.A., & McRae, G. (2004). *In the way of development: Indigenous peoples, life projects and globalization.* Ottawa: Zed/IDRC.

Corbiere, A, Johnston, R., & Reyes, J. (2007). *Aboriginal perspectives on the social economy.* Panel Presentation of the Social Economy Centre Speaker Series, Ontario Institute for Studies in Education of the University of Toronto, 28 March, 2007. Retrieved from http://sec.oise.utoronto.ca/english/lecture_archive.php

Gruner, S., & Metatawabin, C. (2009). Community Research on the Albany River. In G. Broad (Ed.), *CESD News* (pp. 1, 3). Retrieved from http://www.nordikinstitute.ca/docs/newsletter.screen.pdf

McMurtry, J.J. (2010). Introducing the social economy in theory and practice. In J.J. McMurtry (Ed.), *Living economics: Canadian perspectives on the social economy, co-operatives, and community economic development* (pp. 1–34). Toronto: Emond Montgomery.

Natcher, D. (2008). *The social economy of Canada's Aboriginal North.* Retrieved from http://www.nrf.is/Open%20Meetings/Anchorage/Position%20Papers/Natcher%20NRF%20Submission.pdf

Newhouse, D. (2003). The invisible infrastructure: Urban Aboriginal institutions and organizations. In D. Newhouse & E. Peters (Eds.), *Not strangers in these parts: Urban Aboriginal Peoples* (pp. 217–42). Ottawa: Policy Research Initiative.

Porter, J. (1999). Aboriginal language month time for celebration, preservation. *Wawatay News.* Retrieved from http://www.wawataynews.ca/archive/all/1999/3/11/Aboriginal-language-month-time-for-celebration-preservation_10883

Royal Commission on Aboriginal People (RCAP). (1996). *Report of the Royal Commission on Aboriginal People.* Ottawa: Canada Communication Group.

Russell, W. (2007). *Articulations and mis-articulations: Is this an informal enterprise, a social economy enterprise, or an extralegal harvesting operation?* Unpublished manuscript.

Social Economy Centre. (2009). *Introduction: A new research alliance.* Retrieved from http://socialeconomy.utoronto.ca/english/proj_intro.php

Wuttunee, W. (2010). Aboriginal perspectives on the social economy. In J.J. McMurtry (Ed.), *Living economics: Canadian perspectives on the social economy, co-operatives, and community economic development* (pp. 179–216). Toronto: Emond Montgomery.

9 Social Entrepreneurship: A Comparative Perspective

ROGER SPEAR

Although it could be argued that social entrepreneurship has a very long history,[1] the recent wave of interest in business with a social purpose has strong roots in the United States. In the US context, the term 'social entrepreneurship' applies to a diverse range of phenomenon from nonprofit and NGO activities, social innovation, and businesses with a social purpose. This contrasts European approaches, such as that of the EMES European Research Network (www.emes.net), which see social enterprise development as a new entrepreneurial dynamic within the social economy, or 'third sector' (Borzaga & Defourny, 2001). These viewpoints are now influencing global development of social enterprise and social entrepreneurship. Canada's engagement with the social economy, both recently in most regions (www.socialeconomyhub.ca) and historically in francophone Quebec (www.ciriec.uqam.ca), and its proximity to the United States gives it an intermediate position in which it is open to both dynamics.

This chapter is organized as follows. First, I discuss the origins and subsequent global developments of social entrepreneurship. Second, I discuss some of the major themes in the literature. Third, I discuss recent empirical research and how it informs discourse and literature. Finally, I conclude by re-establishing the importance of a comparative and theoretical approach to social entrepreneurship.

Social Entrepreneurship: A Global Perspective

Social entrepreneurship has developed rapidly in many parts of the world but has origins in the United States. James Austin, a pioneer of social entrepreneurship and a Harvard professor emeritus, co-founded the Harvard Business School Social Enterprise Initiative, which supports a range of research and educational activities, in 1993. The Initiative's approach to social enterprise encompasses the contributions any individual or organization can make towards social improvement, regardless of legal form (nonprofit, private, or public sector). Its research forums and conferences have examined a wide range of topics, including nonprofit strategy, business leadership in the social sector, consumer-driven healthcare, global poverty, public education, and the future of social enterprise. However, this approach is only one of many.

Austin, Stevenson, and Wei-Skillern (2006) argue that social entrepreneurship encompasses innovative activity with a social purpose, broadly speaking, in for-profit commercial enterprise, corporate social ventures, nonprofits, and the public sector; and, narrowly speaking, in entrepreneurial activity in nonprofits. Dees (1998) notes that it can include hybrid arrangements across business forms, and can also refer to commercial enterprise developing corporate social responsibility activities. Finally, social entrepreneurship applies equally to developed and developing global contexts, and entrepreneurial activity by NGOs in developing countries is frequently cited in the literature.

Austin et al. define social entrepreneurship 'as innovative, social value creating activity that can occur within or across the nonprofit, business, or government sectors' (2006, p. 2). Dees defines the individual social entrepreneur as someone who creates change in the social sector through:

- adopting a mission to create and sustain social value (not just private value);
- recognizing and relentlessly pursuing new opportunities to serve that mission;
- engaging in a process of continuous innovation, adaptation, and learning;
- acting boldly without being limited by resources currently in hand; and
- exhibiting a heightened sense of accountability to the constituencies served and for the outcomes created. (Dees, 1998, p. 4)

Dees recognizes this is an idealized view of a social entrepreneur, and that in practice many will not meet these requirements. Nonetheless, the idealization and individualization of the actors in this field is a persistent theme which I will return to later.

The global reach of US-inspired social enterprises is, in part, due to the spread of social entrepreneurship based in business schools. That approach has spread to other parts of the world, such as the Skoll Centre for Social Entrepreneurship in Oxford University Business School, and is also evident in several other educational institutions.

Philanthropy is an important factor behind the growth of social entrepreneurship. For example, the Skoll Centre at Oxford was founded with a donation from Jeff Skoll, the founder of eBay. In the United States, philanthropic foundations and individuals wanting to create social change have been important in fostering and shaping the growth of social entrepreneurship. One approach to an entrepreneurial relationship with sponsored social enterprise is 'venture philanthropy,' modelled on venture capitalist systems. In venture philanthropy, the investing institution builds a closer partnership with their sponsored organization, and has a more strategic role in development and a clearer focus on social returns. An example of this is the Robin Hood Foundation in New York. In some ways, social entrepreneurship is a reconfiguring of philanthropic and voluntary action to include an enterprise dimension.

Academic networks also play a role in disseminating initiatives with US origins. Practitioners are strongly influenced by philanthropic initiatives, together with university-based initiatives, such as Harvard's Social Entrepreneurship Initiative, and student member organizations, such as Harvard's Social Enterprise Club, which has held more than ten annual conferences.[2] The most renowned practitioner event is the Skoll World Forum on Social Entrepreneurship, which attracts several hundred participants. The Forum held its seventh conference in 2010 and featured Jimmy Carter, Al Gore, and Nobel Prize-winner Mohammad Yunus among its keynote speakers. The World Forum indicates its ambitions in a 2010 report: 'This year's Forum engaged the world's most influential social entrepreneurs, social investors, and thought leaders from all sectors in critical discussions, debates and work-sessions designed to create partnerships, networks, knowledge and collaborative pathways between the social, policy, academic and private sectors' (Skoll World Forum, 2010). The close involvement of philanthropic individuals and organizations with strongly committed values for social change helps explain the pronounced normative dimension in the literature, which will be addressed in the next section.

The global reach of initiatives with origins in the United States can be seen through both academic networks and philanthropic institutions and initiatives. However, the field is also marked by influential development bodies such as Ashoka, Echoing Green, Avina, Schwab Foundation, which frequently adopt a common model which identifies, develops, and supports social entrepreneur fellows globally. Ashoka was founded in 1980 and was an early promoter of social entrepreneurship, and has elected and supported over 2,500 fellows with stipends and professional support in around sixty countries. Grenier (2006) argues that networking bodies such as Ashoka play a significant role in articulating the development of the field. They typically provide status and recognition for the social entrepreneur, create vertical links to corporate and governmental national elites, and employ a language and rhetoric that is readily accessible to business and policy-makers. Horizontal dimensions of mutual support also complement Ashoka's vertical dimensions of support. As Bornstein notes, 'many of the fellows I interviewed said that the credibility, confidence, contacts and ideas they gained through Ashoka were more valuable than money' (2004, in Grenier, 2006, p. 134).

Grenier (2006) also comments on the pattern of globalization that such networks embody. Their model of entrepreneurship is derived from the US emphasis on the 'relentless' and 'visionary' individual, which may imply that 'progress' requires that Western models should be promoted, rather than locally constructed and more collective approaches to development. In practice, the strongly idealized rhetoric may be moderated by the pragmatic realities of local contexts. Nonetheless, this globalizing pattern has been influential in constructing the field of social entrepreneurship.

Academic Networks

The Harvard pioneer James Austin also founded the Social Enterprise Knowledge Network (SEKN) to advance the frontiers of knowledge and practice in social enterprise in Latin America. This network of nine Latin American university business schools plus Harvard Business School consists of more than 4,500 undergraduates, 2,600 graduates, and 140 doctoral students, together with conferences and publications.

Although business schools often teach social entrepreneurship studies, in some parts of Europe, social entrepreneurship has a different academic focus. In Denmark the Roskilde University Centre for Social Entrepreneurship has pioneered Europe's first master's degree in Social Entrepreneurship, with twenty mature students from the public and third sectors. This approach is linked to the more developed field of social enterprise and the work of the EMES Network. EMES is a research network of established university research centres and individual researchers whose goal is to gradually build up a European collection of theoretical and empirical knowledge, pluralistic in disciplines and methodology, around third sector issues. It has been a major influence in Europe, and has distinctive characteristics. The EMES approach is more interdisciplinary than the US approach, and focuses on developing a broader perspective by locating the development of social enterprise within a new entrepreneurial dynamic that is transforming the third sector and is embedded in civil society dynamics. The EMES Network explicitly views social entrepreneurship as a process leading to the creation of social enterprise. It has a nine-part ideal-typical definition (Borzaga & Defourny, 2001; Nyssens, 2006) comprising economic and social dimensions of social enterprise. Four factors define the economic and entrepreneurial nature of the initiatives:

1 A continuous activity producing goods and/or selling services
2 A high degree of autonomy
3 A significant level of economic risk
4 A minimum amount of paid work

Five factors define the social dimensions of the initiatives:

1 An initiative launched by a group of citizens
2 A decision-making power not based on capital ownership
3 A participatory nature, which involves the persons affected by the activity
4 Limited profit distribution
5 An explicit aim to benefit the community

Social entrepreneurship has developed quickly and globally for a number of reasons. First, welfare regimes have undergone restructuring in many countries, and resulted in new approaches to the public sector, such as the growth of new public management (NPG) and government as contractor in a mixed economy for the provision of public services. Second, the third sector has adapted to compete in markets created by this changing context. Third, philanthropic approaches have also been changing, and now emphasize supporting self-help initiatives rather than following paternalist models that create dependence. This can also be seen in NGOs, which operate by building local capacity (as in fair trade) and developing local NGOs and civil society. Finally, there has been a growing differentiation in the market for ethical goods and services – both in terms of ethical investment and ethical consumption, and now the further development of ethical production through social entrepreneurship. The boundary with corporate social responsibility (CSR) is becoming more blurred, and as Mulgan writes:

> more investors have sought to bridge the gap between classic business in the pursuit of shareholder value and not-for-profit ventures achieving a mix of different kinds of value; more businesses have started to use richer metrics of value; and many have become attracted to a vision of capitalism that is more founded on lasting relationships than on fleeting transactions. (2006, p. 79)

The comparative advantage of social entrepreneurship may be differentiated according to social innovation in a Schumpeterian perspective. This includes new sources or configurations of inputs, new production processes, new dimensions of product or service, new markets or market relations, and new structuring of a sector or industry:

- New inputs can include the mobilization of social capital (including volunteer labour and expertise), innovations in employment (such as work-integration social enterprises which specialize in employing trainees as workers), and the potential for lower costs (of operating as a nonprofit or profit-limited enterprise).
- Innovating processes may be through proximity (linking users and producers of services), co-production of services (Pestoff, 2009), multi-stakeholder structures that are more socially integrating, and new business models (such as employment of the homeless and disadvantaged in newspaper sales and bike courier and janitor services).
- New dimensions of products and services may include addressing state and market failures (e.g., microfinance), greater flexibility, and better adaptation to user needs.
- New markets or market relations often arise from market and state failures, such as microfinance, disadvantaged producer niches, ethical markets, and the restructuring of welfare provision to mixed economies.
- Social entrepreneurship can impact the structuring of sectors through social enterprise as a new entrepreneurial dynamic from

within the third sector, and the growth of related institutions such as
for social investment, etc. (Borzaga & Defourny, 2001).

Main Themes in the Literature and Current Research

There is a strong normative orientation in the literature on social entrepreneurship, with numerous impressive case studies, many of which
draw conclusions with an eye toward developing practical know-how.
Possibly as a result of promotional bodies playing such a major role in
social entrepreneurial developments, there is also often an emphasis on
the heroic role and individual characteristics of the social entrepreneur,
which has been a theme in conventional entrepreneurship for many
years. This section attempts to leave to one side much of the normative
case study research and concentrates on scientific studies covering the
following themes:

- Conceptual clarifications
- Stage of entrepreneurship models
- Individual vs. collective vs. organized models
- Resource mobilization (legitimacy)
- Context (embeddedness, networks, social capital, and institutions)
- Typologies of social enterprise
- Support/policy/strategy (scaling)
- Reality vs. rhetoric

Each of these themes is briefly addressed, with comparisons between the
United States and Europe where appropriate.

Conceptual Clarifications

The proliferation of definitions of the social entrepreneurial field seems
an indication of its immaturity, although it 'mirrors the multi-facets of
the phenomenon' (Mair, Robinson, & Hockerts, 2006, p. 7). A number
of authors attempt to define the scope of the field in various ways. For
example, EMES has an ideal-typical definition, developed through an
international comparitive study, which consists of four factors that address the enterprise dimension and five factors that address the social
dimension of social entrepreneurship. However, there is a need for a
definition that is operational internationally in empirical survey-based
studies.

Considerable work has been undertaken to clarify the conceptual underpinnings of the field, and this is also important as the foundation for empirical work. Nicholls (2006) develops a framework for the field based on concepts of innovation, market, and the social. Markets and social dimensions are consistent themes, but there are different approaches to innovation. As Spear argues:

> The author who has been most influential in entrepreneurship studies is Schumpeter, but he clearly ties entrepreneurship to innovation – requiring the entrepreneur to innovate in a number of respects (new service, quality, process, market, source of supplies, or industry) and thereby engage in creative destruction. This excludes a large amount of entrepreneurial activity which involves the creation of new organisations but which may not be significantly innovative. Baumol (1993) recognises this in his dual categorisation of business organisation and innovation entrepreneurship; similarly, Casson (1982) differentiates between high and low entrepreneurship: high which involves a substantial degree of innovation, and low which is basically concerned with creating a new enterprise (with no significant innovation) (2000, p. 5).

The idea of low entrepreneurship also links well with the Austrian School, which emphasizes principles of human action rather than mathematical models (Kirzner, 1997). In the context of social entrepreneurship, this applies to the replication of innovative models previously established in contexts where the potential for meeting user needs is relevant.

Stage of Entrepreneurship Models

This approach (drawing on Haugh, 2007) is common in conventional entrepreneurship research, and is adapted and used in the area of social entrepreneurship. It is based on the idea that entrepreneurship takes place when an entrepreneur recognizes, or constructs, an opportunity, and then mobilizes resources to meet that opportunity. Haugh specifies a six stage approach: opportunity identification, idea articulation, idea ownership, stakeholder mobilization, opportunity exploitation, and stakeholder reflection:

- Opportunity identification – this begins with the recognition by one, or more, person(s) that a need exists within a community.

- Idea articulation – the idea is discussed within an emerging network.
- Idea ownership – ownership is taken by a group, and intentionality takes shape through a decision to act.
- Stakeholder mobilization – resources (human, physical, financial, and technological) are mobilized, and a network develops.
- Opportunity exploitation – the enterprise is created (legally) and begins trading; individual and organizational capabilities are also developed.
- Stakeholder reflection – performance is evaluated and strategy developed for the future of the enterprise.

Austin et al. (2006) develop elements of this theme through a 'people, context, deal, opportunity' (PCDO) framework. The entrepreneur has to manage and adapt these elements for the enterprise to form and develop. These elements are similar to conventional entrepreneurship, but are slightly different in social entrepreneurship; for example the 'deal' is a negotiated agreement which includes economic benefits, social recognition, autonomy and decision rights, and delivery on altruistic goals.

Individual, Collective, and Organized Models

US studies, such as Bornstein (2004), Dees (2002), and Austin et al. (2006), as well as early writers such as Leadbeater (1997) in the UK, clearly emphasize the 'heroic' individual rather than collective models of entrepreneurship. But this emphasis is changing as some authors, such as Austin et al. (2006) and Mair and Marti (2005), adopt frameworks that focus on the processes of opportunity recognition/construction and deal-making rather than focusing on the entrepreneur (Gartner, 1989). Such an approach is drawn from conventional entrepreneurship literature and is more open to recognizing collective processes of entrepreneurship. Spear (2006) provides evidence from a number of cases that social entrepreneurship is more collective and organized than individualistic (see also chapter 4 in this collection); where organizations develop social entrepreneurship, they often sponsor a group of people who take ownership of the resulting social enterprise. Finally, Spear and Hulgard (2006) argue that collective action and social movements are important paths for social entrepreneurship, and historically social movements have been a major source driving the creation of third-sector organizations. As well, religious movements and religious institutions continue to play important roles in social entrepreneurship (Spear, 2010).[3]

Resource Mobilization (Legitimacy)

A number of authors argue that resources in social entrepreneurship are distinctive. Nicholls (2006) argues that it is crucially important that legitimacy is acquired where an innovative organizational form is attempting to become established in an institutional context. In order for the social entrepreneur to establish an innovative social enterprise in a potentially isomorphic field, different forms of legitimacy (pragmatic, moral, and cognitive) have to be used (Nicholls, 2006). As noted above, Austin et al. suggest that social entrepreneurship requires different kinds of exchanges of resources than conventional entrepreneurship. EMES emphasises the Polanyian perspective where resources may be based on three types of interactions: reciprocity, market exchange, and/or state redistribution. This typology creates the basis for analyzing the resource mix in a particular context. Finally, social capital is much more important than in conventional entrepreneurship.

Context (Embeddedness, Networks, Social Capital, and Institutions)

Granovetter (1985) argues that social entrepreneurship is typically embedded in a network of relationships within the community, and local organizations help shape and support it through social capital. Proximity to the local facilitates the recognition of unmet need and its articulation into entrepreneurial action. Drawing on such support and building social capital are important themes in social entrepreneurship. In a comparative study of several cases of social entrepreneurship, Spear argues not only that social entrepreneurship can be distributed among several people creating the enterprise, but also that some of these entrepreneurs may be outside the organization playing a sponsoring role:

> The cases show quite diverse patterns of distributed entrepreneurship with external groups or organisations playing key roles in several cases. In some ways this represents *circles of entrepreneurship* around the focal organisation, with the entrepreneurs within the organisation playing central roles, but with a wider group of *supportive external stakeholders* sometimes quite closely and essentially involved. And beyond this a supportive context of players

provides resources, and expertise some of which is conventionally supplied, but some of which may be better conceptualised as social capital. (Spear, 2006, p. 406)

The EMES network has made social capital a key theme in their work and has conducted one of the few studies of rigorous international comparative case study research (see Nyssens, 2006).

The importance of context has been recognized by a small group of researchers on conventional entrepreneurship (especially Johanisson et al., 1994); and there is an emerging network paradigm in entrepreneurship research (e.g., Hoang & Antoncic, 2003) which notes not only the positive dimensions of networks using social capital for information, expertise, and building trust, but also that such networks can have negative effects such as exclusion, restraints on non-conforming activity, and internal rent-seeking.

Institutional theory is another important theme in the literature. First, it contributes to an understanding of isomorphism, where innovative organizational forms may be subject to pressures that lead them to become more like the dominant organizational form in the field – typically the private business model. This was a theme in the EMES Network's research on work integrations social enterprise (WISE) (see Nyssens, 2006). Mair and Marti (2006) explain how innovation and change can take place by noting the theoretical challenge for institutional theory; they argue that lower levels of embeddedness can facilitate entrepreneurial action at different stages in the entrepreneurial process.

Second, a focus on institutional theory facilitates an exploration of the ways in which innovative collective action to create social enterprise in civil society can, over a period of time, overcome isomorphic pressures by reshaping the institutional context, so that public policies are better shaped for social entrepreneurship, and better contextualized for the emerging social enterprise sector.

Spear and Hulgard (2006) argue that there are three main types of institutional context shaping social entrepreneurship: new legal forms and structured public policy frameworks; self-labelling forms of social enterprise and associated networks; ad hoc constructed contexts (with new types of social enterprise sometimes adapted from other institutional forms). The creation of more developed institutional structures can be seen in the way WISE have, over a period of twenty years, achieved legitimacy and support in recognition of their effectiveness in integrating difficult-to-employ people back into the labour market (Nyssens, 2006).

Typologies of Social Enterprise

Kim Alter (2006) defines three ways in which social mission and business models can be related. In her mission-centric model, mission and business are integral, such as in WISE. In her mission-related model, the mission and business are complementary, such as in an environmental organization for reforestation with a subsidiary activity on eco-tourism. Finally, in her mission-unrelated model, the business generates income in order to support the mission.

Governance, though not a central theme for social entrepreneurship, is shaped by and in turn shapes the pattern of entrepreneurship. Multi-stakeholder governance structures indicate a collective, if not multi-stakeholder, entrepreneurial process. The choice of legal form and governance structure is an integral part of the entrepreneurial process. That choice includes forms of social capital – collective self-help initiatives are more likely to have bonding social capital, and charitable sponsored initiatives are more likely to have bridging social capital, with potential implications for resource acquisition. Spear, Cornforth, and Aiken (2007) found that there are three main types of governance structures in third-sector unitary organizations (i.e. organizations without subsidiaries): the 'pure' membership association, the self-selecting board, and the mixed organization, which combines the two previous structures. While these may have single or multi-stakeholder forms, for example, 62 per cent of the WISE studied in the EMES international study were multi-stakeholders.

In addition, hybrid structures often involve a different process of entrepreneurship. Many social enterprises are not unitary structures, but are hybrids made up of trading subsidiaries and holding structures. For instance, trading charities are typically hybrids, because one of the main ways for a charity to manage the risks from trading activities is to separate trading from its other operations and manage it within a commercial subsidiary. Trading charities can thus be regarded as third sector hybrids.

While many authors have attempted to define the key characteristics of the field, relatively few have addressed the challenge of defining the 'social.' Cho (2006) argues that defining the social is problematic in a society which has increasingly heterogeneous values, interests, and culture. He notes that well-intentioned initiatives to fundraise for social purposes can have unintended consequences, such as lotteries, which in effect are a regressive tax on the poor with harmful redistributive effects. Defining the social is problematic and in many cases contested, and so achieving compromise on the common good or general interest requires engagement with an appropriate political and institutional process. Leaving social problems to social entrepreneurs results in imposing their visions, means and ends, and it risks perverse (and unintended) effects.

While Cho's critique of social entrepreneurship recognizes that markets and state may have shortcomings regarding poverty, exclusion, and environmental degradation, it also implies the need for social entrepreneurs to recognize the problematic nature of the social, the political nature of the project they are engaged with, that they may only be addressing 'symptoms of deeper institutional and political malaise' (i.e. missing the real issue), the need for partnership and dialogue with multiple stakeholders, and engagement with relevant systems of governance.

Support/Policy/Strategy

With any innovative organizational form, it is unlikely that existing institutional and support frameworks will be appropriate. Support structures, specifically development agencies and federal structures, are important in the successful development of social enterprise, such as in the bank at Mondragon and consorzi in the Italian social co-operatives. Currently there is a lot of emphasis on braided support, where state support for small and medium enterprises is combined with specific third-sector support for social enterprise.

The UK government's policy for social enterprise is one of the most developed support strategies, and has three main goals. The first is to create an emabling environment for social enterprise through government activities (including interdepartmental liaison, enabling development, and supporting the third sector); through legal and regulatory measures (Community Interest Company Law); and through creating good access to public procurement markets. The second is to make social enterprises better businesses through business support, training, and developing infrastructure for finance and funding. The third is to establish the value of social enterprise by creating a knowledge base through research; by recognizing achievements of social enterprise; and by creating trust through, for example, social accounting and quality management.

Another interesting theme in support strategies is the link between academia and social entrepreneurship. Bloom (2006) describes the Social Entrepreneurship Collaboratory at Stanford and Harvard. Many business schools include entrepreneurship projects as part of their MBA programs, and some of these become social enterprise. Perhaps the most developed of these models is the UK's School for Social Entrepreneurs, where the one-year program is oriented towards launching a new social enterprise. Ashoka has a similar approach in its work with a range of universities.

Finally, a strong theme among advocates of social entrepreneurship is the idea of scaling to achieve greater social impact. This takes different forms, including developing growth strategies, looking for high growth potential social enterprise, and replication of the social enterprise business model, including through social franchising.

Reality vs. Rhetoric

There are relatively few ethnographic and discourse studies. But Parkinson and Howorth (2007), in a study of entrepreneurship discourse of twenty social entrepreneurs in Cumbria, a sub-region of the UK, identify the following themes in current rhetoric in strategy and policy documents:

- doing lots with very little
- financial independence through sustainability
- contributing to the mainstream economy
- bringing business discipline to social ventures
- innovating for change
- helping people take charge of their lives and futures

Only the last theme appears relevant to the meaning constructions of the social entrepreneurs in their study. They find that 'the interviewees seem to draw their legitimacy as activists, guardians or indeed entrepreneurs from a sense of social morality, rather than from the entrepreneurship discourse directly' (p. 34). Echoing the argument of Cho (2006) that the social is pluralist and contested, they argue that social entrepreneurship activities are about political engagement and collective action, and are influenced by discourses of social need and moral duty.

There are similar findings from Wallace (2005), who explores the meta-narrative of social enterprise and financial sustainability in inner-city east London. She argues that there is a disjunction between this meta-narrative and the perspectives of social entrepreneurs in the inner city, where the barriers include lack of resources, corruption, violence, and a culture of dependence on benefits. This disjunction is perhaps summarized in the following quotation: 'Break-even is utopia for most community social enterprises. The goal is to be able to cover overheads' (Wallace, 2005, p. 83).

International Comparative Studies on Social Entrepreneurship

Large-scale comparative studies on social entrepreneurship are rare, and the EMES Network is exceptional in this respect (see Borzaga & Defourny, 2001; Nyssens, 2006; www.emes.net). However, there has been some interesting survey work conducted in a number of countries by the Global Entrepreneurship Monitor (GEM). While most of their studies have been on conventional entrepreneurship, they have conducted several surveys in the UK on social entrepreneurship under this programme (see www.gemconsortium.org).

The GEM international research program conducts an annual adult population survey (APS) in each participating country. Since the survey began, the number of participating countries has steadily increased, and data are now gathered in about fifty countries. Each year, the GEM survey covers conventional entrepreneurship and explores an additional theme, such as social entrepreneurship in 2009.

The GEM survey is not completely uniform, and covers countries with variations in sample size and in the questions asked. For example, in Denmark, a survey of starters (of entrepreneurial activities), managers, and workers in social enterprises was carried out through the GEM APS in 2009. Through household telephone surveys, 4,000 adults were interviewed about their involvement in social entrepreneurship. Adult starters, managers, and workers in social enterprises were identified (Schott, Spear, & Hulgard, 2009). The social entrepreneurs in Denmark were identified through a series of questions asking whether people were involved (alone or with others, independently or as part of their job) with trying to start activities, organizations, or initiatives which have particular social, environmental, or community objectives. The survey identified starters and owner-managers of businesses and whether the entrepreneurial activity was linked to their work (sponsored entrepreneurship). The GEM approach has a typology of enterprises:

- Nascent Social Enterprise – start-ups of between zero and three months old.
- Baby Social Enterprise – those active for between four and forty-two months.

- Established Social Enterprise – those active for longer than forty-two months.

The resulting database allows an analysis of demographics as well as motivations and characteristics of the social enterprise. For example, in the UK in 2005:

- Women are proportionately more likely to be social than mainstream entrepreneurs; but overall men are more likely to be social entrepreneurs than women (3.6 per cent compared to 2.8 per cent).
- Younger people (18 to 24) are more likely to be social entrepreneurs than any other age group (3.9 per cent, compared to 2.8 per cent of over 55 year olds).
- The level of education is a strong predictor of social entrepreneurial activity, as 8.3 per cent of those with Master's degrees and 4.7 per cent of those with Bachelor's degrees were active in social enterprise.
- Those in full-time education are most likely to be social entrepreneurially active (5 per cent), compared with those with full-time employment (3.5 per cent) and the retired (2 per cent, but twice the level for mainstream entrepreneurial activity).
- People living in rural areas (1.6 times more likely to be social entrepreneurs)
- Black Africans and Black Caribbeans are, respectively, three times and two times more likely than whites to be social entrepreneurs.

There also appeared to be a culture of social entrepreneurship among many socially less privileged groups:

- Long-term registered disabled people were 2.3 times more likely to engage in social rather than commercial entrepreneurship;
- Other non-white groups were 2.2 times more likely; and
- Those out-of-work and not claiming benefits were marginally (2.9 per cent) more likely to be social entrepreneurs than mainstream entrepreneurs.

Niels Bosma and Jonathan Levie (2009) executed a comparative study across all fifty countries in the 2009 survey. Most of their report is on conventional entrepreneurship, with a small section on social entrepreneurship. Globally, they found that the average social enterprise activity rate increases slightly with economic development. They argue that there are three possible explanations. The first is that the opportunity cost of social entrepreneurship may be higher in developing countries (i.e., better returns in other occupations); but on the other hand social and environmental problems are often more prevalent in developing countries. The second explanation argues that definitions of a traditional enterprise and a social enterprise may overlap in developing countries where significant numbers of entrepreneurs want to make a profit and achieve social benefits; these definitions may be more distinct in developed countries. The third explanation suggests that the level of entrepreneurship is the same across countries, but that entrepreneurship is manifested in different ways depending on the way the institutional context shapes the forms and patterns of entrepreneurship (Baumol, 1990, 1993). Bosma and Levie find partial support for Baumol's hypothesis of substitution of one form of entrepreneurship for another (social for conventional entrepreneurship). They also find that a significant minority of social entrepreneurs, particularly in developing countries, wish to have a profitable business that at the same time addresses social issues. They argue that this demonstrates that for many people, the categories of social and business entrepreneur are artificial.

These kind of comparative studies are clearly important. But this research is only at an early stage, and more work needs to be done on questions and hypotheses; for example, the main filter question asked: 'Are you, alone or with others, currently trying to start or *owning* and managing any kind of activity' (emphasis added as the word 'owning' is likely to exclude some relevant respondents).

Conclusions

This chapter has examined the emerging field of social entrepreneurship, and specifically at its diverse origins, contrasting US and European perspectives. It has identified and critically commented on major themes in the literature and current research. The field is emerging, and as such is subject to a variety of different perspectives, definitions, and approaches. Practitioners, policymakers, and development organizations play important roles in shaping the field – typically emphasizing heroic individualistic perspectives and rhetoric. However, as the evidence base develops, distinctive features of the field can be more confidently asserted. These features include an acceptance that collective, organized, and sponsored models of social entrepreneurship are frequently effective, and that legitimacy, social capital, embeddedness, networks, and institutions are particularly important for ensuring that the social innovation can become more firmly established in civil society. Linked to this is an emphasis on appropriate support structures and policy frameworks. A substantial amount of literature is concerned with clarifying concepts and definitions that relate to business model typologies, governance, hybrids, and problematizing the social. Though they are few in number, discourse and ethnographic studies are significant as they reveal a disjunction between promotional rhetoric and the meaning of social entrepreneurship constructed on the ground. Finally, the international comparative studies, however small in number, help give a global perspective on national, regional, and local experiences.

Future research could benefit from developing comparative studies and theory. Developing databases across sectors, countries, and regions would provide a basis for addressing theoretical and policy questions. This requires standardized questionnaires and sampling methodologies. It is also important to develop more rigorous case study research. This requires developing case study templates and qualitative methods for using them. Apart from developing grounded theory from field work, it is important to link with relevant existing theory, both by exploring the similarities/differences with conventional entrepreneurship theory and by extending third-sector and social enterprise research to include the range of NGO/third-sector/private enterprise created by social entrepreneurs.

NOTES

1 For example, the development of co-operatives and mutuals in the nineteenth century. This has continued to be a strategy for addressing poverty and social exclusion globally; the growing success of microcredit in countries like Bangladesh (via BRAC and Grameen Bank) has clearly facilitated such developments.
2 The Harvard Business School and Kennedy School Social Enterprise Conference 2010 had over 1,000 participants including students, alumni, and professionals, and more than one hundred panellists and speakers addressing social issues through innovative, cross-sectoral approaches.
3 For example, the 2009 papal encyclical Caritas in Veritate (Charity in Truth) with its reflections on global progress towards the common good. The agricultural producer SEKEM's founder Dr Ibrahim Abouleish states, 'All the different aspects of the company, whether the cultural ones or the economic ones, have been developed out of Islam. We believe that it is possible to

derive guiding principles for everything from pedagogics, to the arts, to economics, from Islam.'

REFERENCES

Ackerman, S.R. (1997). Altruism, ideological entrepreneurs and the nonprofit firm. *Voluntas, 8*(2), 120–34.

Alter, S.K. (2006). Social enterprise models and their mission and money relationships. In A. Nicholls (Ed.), *Social entrepreneurship: New models of sustainable social change* (pp. 205–32). London: Oxford University Press.

Alvord, S., Brown, L., & Letts, C. (2004). Social entrepreneurship and societal transformation: An exploratory study. *Journal of Applied Behavioral Science, 40*(3), 260–83.

Austin, J.E. (2000). *The collaboration challenge: How nonprofits and businesses succeed through strategic alliances.* San Francisco: Jossey-Bass.

Austin, J.E., Stevenson, H., & Wei-Skillern, J. (2006). Social and commercial entrepreneurship: Same, different, or both? *Entrepreneurship Theory and Practice, 30*(1), 1–22.

Badelt, C. (1997). Entrepreneurship theories of the nonprofit sector. *Voluntas, 8*(2), 162–78.

Baumol, W.J. (1993). Formal entrepreneurship theory in economics: Existence and bounds. *Journal of Business Venturing, 3*, 197–210.

Bornstein, D. (2004). *How to change the world: Social entrepreneurs and the power of new ideas.* Oxford: Oxford University Press.

Borzaga, C., & Defourny, J. (2001). *The emergence of social enterprise.* New York: Routledge.

Bosma, N., & Levie, J. (2009). *Global entrepreneurship monitor: Global report 2009.* Retrieved from http://www.gemconsortium.org/about.aspx?page=pub_gem_global_reports

Cho, A.H. (2006). Politics, values and social entrepreneurship: A critical appraisal. In J. Mair, J. Robinson, & K. Hockerts (Eds.), *Social entrepreneurship* (pp. 34–56). New York: Palgrave.

Cornforth, C., & Spear, R. (Forthcoming). Hybrids and governance: Social enterprise. In D. Billis, (Ed.), *Hybrid organizations in the third sector: Challenges of practice, policy and theory.* Basingstoke, Hants: Palgrave.

Dees, J.G. (1998). *The meaning of social entrepreneurship.* Retrieved from http://faculty.fuqua.duke.edu/centers/case/files/dees-SE.pdf

Dees, J.G., Emerson, J., & Economy, P. (2001). *Enterprising nonprofits: A toolkit for social entrepreneurs.* New York: Wiley Non-Profit Series.

Dees, J.G., Emerson, J., & Economy, P. (2002). *Strategic tools for social entrepreneurs: Enhancing the performance of your enterprising nonprofit*. New York: Wiley Non-Profit Series.

Gartner, W.B. (1989). 'Who is an entrepreneur?' is the wrong question. *Entrepreneurship Theory and Practice, 13*(4), 47–68.

Grenier, P. (2010). Vision and values: The relationship between the visions and actions of social entrepreneurs. In K. Hockerts (Ed.), *Values and opportunities in social entrepreneurship*. Basingstoke, Hants: Palgrave.

Granovetter, M. (1985). Economic action and social structure: The problem of embeddedness. *American Journal of Sociology, 91*, 481–93.

Haugh, H. (2005). The role of social enterprise in regional development. *International Journal of Entrepreneurship and Small Business, 2*(4), 346–57.

Haugh, H. (2007). Community-led social venture creation. *Entrepreneurship Theory and Practice, 31*(2), 161–82.

Hoang, H., & Antoncic, B. (2003). Network-based research in entrepreneurship: A critical review. *Journal of Business Venturing, 18*(2), 165–87.

Hockerts, K. (2009). *New perspectives on social entrepreneurship*. Basingstoke, Hants: Palgrave.

Johannisson, B., Alexanderson, O., Nowicki, K., & Senneseth, K. (1994). Beyond anarchy and organization: entrepreneurs in contextual networks. *Entrepreneurship and Regional Development, 6*, 329–56.

Kirzner, L. (1997). Entrepreneurial discovery and the competitive market process: An Austrian approach. *Journal of Economic Literature, 35*(1), 60–85.

Leadbeater, C. (1997). *The rise of the social entrepreneur*. London: Demos.

Mair, J., & Marti, I. (2006). Social entrepreneurship research: A source of explanation, prediction and delight. *Journal of World Business, 41*(1), 36–44.

Mair, J., Robinson, J., & Hockerts, K. (Eds.). (2006). *Social entrepreneurship*. Basingstoke, Hants: Palgrave Macmillan.

Mosher-Williams, R. (Ed.). (2006). Research on social entrepreneurship: Understanding and contributing to an emerging field. *ARNOVA Occasional Papers Series, 1*(3), 67–87.

Mulgan, G. (2006). Cultivating the other invisible hand of social entrepreneurship. In A. Nicholls (Ed.), *Social entrepreneurship: New models of sustainable social change* (pp. 74–95). Oxford: Oxford University Press.

Nicholls, A. (Ed.). (2006). *Social entrepreneurship: New models of sustainable social change*. Oxford: Oxford University Press.

Nyssens, M. (Ed). (2006). *Social enterprise*. Abingdon, Oxon: Routledge Studies in the Management of Voluntary and Non-Profit Organizations.

Parkinson, C., & Howorth, C. (2008). The language of social entrepreneurs. *Entrepreneurship and Regional Development, 20*(3), 285–309.

222   Roger Spear

Parkinson, C., & Howorth, C. (2007). The language of social entrepreneurs. *Lancaster University management school working paper, 32*, 1–45.

Perrini, F. (Ed.). (2006). *The new social entrepreneurship. What Awaits Social Entrepreneurial Ventures?* Cheltenham, UK: Edward Elgar Publishing.

Pestoff, V. (2009). Towards a paradigm of democratic participation: Citizen participation and co-production of personal social services in Sweden. *Annals of Public and Cooperative Economics, 80*(2), 197–224.

Schott, T., Spear, R., & Hulgard, L. (2009). Organizing social enterprise in Denmark. In T. Schott (Ed.), *Social and commercial entrepreneurship in Denmark* (pp. 111–24). Denmark: University of Southern Denmark.

Seelos, C., & Mair, J. (2005). Social entrepreneurship: Creating new business models to serve the poor. *Business Horizons, 48*, 241–46.

Skoll World Forum. (2010). About Skoll. Retrieved from http://www.skollworldforum.com/about

Spear, R. (2000). The nature of social entrepreneurship – some findings. *ISTR Conference Working Papers* (pp. 1–9). Dublin.

Spear, R. (2006). Social entrepreneurship: A different model? *International Journal of Social Economics, 33*(5&6), 399–410.

Spear, R. (2009). Social entrepreneurship in co-operatives. In I. McPherson & E. Mclauglin-Jenkins (Eds.), *Integrating diversity with a complex heritage.* Victoria: New Rochdale Press.

Spear, R. (2010). Religion and value-driven social entrepreneurship. In K. Hockerts, J. Mair, & J. Robinson (Eds.), *New trends in social entrepreneurship.* Basingstoke, Hants: Palgrave MacMillan.

Spear, R., Cornforth, C., & Aiken, M. (2007). *For love and money: Governance and social enterprise.* Research Report for the Governance Hub and Social Enterprise Coalition.

Spear, R., & Hulgard, L. (2006). Social entrepreneurship and the mobilisation of social capital in European social enterprises. In M. Nyssens (Ed.), *Social enterprise, public policy and civil society* (pp. 85–108). Abingdon, Oxon: Routledge.

Sullivan, M.G., Weerawardena J., & Carnegie K. (2003). Social entrepreneurship: Towards conceptualisation. *International Journal of Nonprofit and Voluntary Sector Marketing, 8*(1), 76–88.

Thompson, J. (2002). The world of the social entrepreneur. *International Journal of Public Sector Management, 15*(5), 412–31.

Wallace, B. (2005). Exploring the meaning(s) of sustainability for community-based social entrepreneurs. *Social Enterprise Journal, 1*(1), 78–89.

10 Exploring Social Transformation, Financial Self-Sufficiency, and Innovation in Canadian Social Enterprises

TESSA HEBB, JUDITH MADILL, AND FRANÇOIS BROUARD

Writings in the field of social entrepreneurship often use concepts and terms such as social enterprise and social venture (Borzaga & Defourny, 2001). However, in keeping with the nascent status of the field, a review of the literature on those topics suggests that definitions of these terms are still being developed and are by no means agreed upon (Certo & Miller, 2008). Some academics define social enterprises by their legal form (Alter, 2006; Dart, 2004; Mendell & Nogales, 2008), however, while such definitions neatly encapsulate social enterprise, they do not fully capture the hybrid nature of many such organizations. This chapter defines social enterprise as organizations created to pursue social missions or purposes that operate with a degree of income self-sufficiency, regardless of ownership or legal structure.[1]

We will explore the defining characteristics of social enterprise, drawing on our experience and knowledge of the field as three academics familiar with these topics. Our research promotes a deeper understanding of social enterprise and its contribution to communities and society broadly. Social enterprises must have an integrated enterprise approach to their mission. We acknowledge that such a definition encompasses a wide variety of organizations, ranging from traditional not-for-profits to ventures that operate as for-profit businesses, yet are social mission centric. Further, we suggest that there are three defining characteristics of social enterprise: social transformation, financial self-sufficiency, and innovation.

While social purpose businesses are growing rapidly, in most jurisdictions they operate without a separate legal structure as small and medium sized enterprises.[2] Many social enterprises are embedded within nonprofit corporations as a form of diversified revenue for the sector.

Although a number of social enterprises within this sector, such as the Salvation Army's thrift shops, have existed for many years, there has been rapid recent growth in the quantity, type, and societal impact of social enterprises throughout the world. In 2003, it was estimated that there were 161,000 Canadian nonprofit corporations and trusts responsible for approximately 7 per cent of the GDP, with total revenue of $112 billion and earned revenues of $39 billion (Hall et al., 2005; Statistics Canada 2006). In 2008 in the United States, more than 1.4 million nonprofit organizations generated $1.36 trillion in total revenue, constituting at least 5 per cent of the GDP (Rangan, Leonard, & McDonald, 2008). In 2006 in the United Kingdom, there were 870,000 civil society organizations with a total income of £116 billion, and the total turnover of social enterprises was estimated at £27 billion, with an estimated contribution to the GDP of £8.4 billion (UK Government, 2006).

Due to growing social needs and social problems in most parts of the world, accompanied by reduced government ability to provide the funding necessary to effectively combat these social problems, social enterprises will likely continue to grow both in number and importance (Christie & Honig, 2006; Dees, 1998b; Rangan et al., 2008).

In spite of current growth in new social enterprises, academic research has been undertaken only relatively recently and has largely been case-based and anecdotal. Much of the developing literature has focused on defining what exactly is meant by social entrepreneurship and social enterprise (Dees, 1998a; Douglas, 2008; Mair & Marti, 2006; Martin & Osberg, 2007; Peredo & McLean, 2006) and much of it has focused on three dimensions considered key to social enterprises – social transformation, financial self-sufficiency, and innovation (Austin, Stevenson, & Wei-Skillern, 2006; Brooks, 2009; Dees, 1998b; Mair & Marti, 2006; Massarsky & Beinhaker, 2002). It is widely recognized that social enterprises, in contrast to commercial enterprises, are established with the primary mission of positive change through helping disadvantaged people and solving social problems. Social transformation is directly linked to the mission of the social enterprise. In effect, the output, outcome, and impact of the social enterprise result in social transformation. The challenge for most social enterprises, and those who research them, is measuring these outputs and larger impacts on society.

This notion of social transformation is embedded in most definitions of social enterprise and the closely related concept of social entrepreneurship (Alter, 2006; Alvord, Brown, & Letts, 2004; Brooks, 2009). For example, Mair and Marti give one definition of social entrepreneurship illustrating the central role of social transformation as:

a wide range of activities: enterprising individuals devoted to making a difference; social purpose business ventures dedicated to adding for-profit motivations to the nonprofit sector; new types of philanthropists supporting venture capital-like 'investment' portfolios; and nonprofit organizations reinventing themselves by drawing on lessons learned from the business world. (2006, p. 1)

As the definition further suggests, social enterprises are also differentiated from traditional nonprofit enterprises in that they seek alternate forms of financing. In contrast to traditional nonprofit organizations, which rely primarily on grants and donations to achieve their social goals, social enterprises often engage in revenue earning activities in order to fund their social missions and gain a form of financial self-sufficiency (Austin et al., 2006; Boschee, 2001; Thompson & Doherty, 2006). Lastly, social ventures are frequently described as innovative, in that they represent new organizational forms and seek new ways to accomplish social change and finance their missions (Brooks, 2009; Mair & Marti, 2006).

To assist in addressing current gaps in empirical research, this chapter investigates social enterprises in Canada along the dimensions of social transformation, financial self-sufficiency, and innovation. We explore these characteristics through interviews with twenty social enterprises in Canada. This research builds on our earlier work on these dimensions (Madill, Brouard, & Hebb, 2010).

The next section of this chapter provides a brief review of existing literature concerning the three focal dimensions of social enterprises and provides a theoretical perspective for approaching the research. Following the literature review, we describe the study methodology. We then present and discuss the research findings, and conclude by drawing conclusions and implications in the context of the strengths and weaknesses of the research.

Social Enterprises: Background Literature

Even at the basic level of defining social enterprise, there is considerable variation and no commonly held, well-accepted definition used by all social enterprise and social entrepreneurship researchers and writers. However, it is widely agreed in the literature that social enterprises are innovative organizations established to address social needs and or problems; the social mission is central and explicit; and assets and wealth are used to create community benefit (Austin et al., 2006; Babos, Clarence, & Noya, 2007; Dees, 1998a, 2001; Dees & Anderson, 2003; Douglas, 2008; Haugh, 2007; OECD, n.d.; Thompson & Doherty, 2006; Shaw & Carter, 2007; Sullivan Mort, Weerawardena, & Carnegie, 2003). While considerable concurrence exists in highlighting these basic tenets of social enterprises, there are important differences among the ways that researchers conceive of social enterprises along the basic dimensions of social transformation, financial self-sufficiency, and innovation.

Social Transformation in Social Enterprises

Social transformation refers to the impact of the social change desired or achieved by a social enterprise. Much of the literature concerning social enterprises contrasts social entrepreneurs and business entrepreneurs and underscores the major difference between the two as the social change emphasis of the social entrepreneur. Sharir, Lerner, and Yitshaki summarize this common view: The main difference between entrepreneurs operating in the business sector versus those in the nonprofit sector is that social contribution, in the sense of mission and service, becomes the main goal of social entrepreneurs, and not just profitability or financial gains (2009, p. 75–6).

Martin and Osberg (2007) use the term 'transformative benefit,' while Alvord, Brown, and Letts (2004) refer to societal transformation. The impact of social transformation can involve the number of persons affected, the scope of change, the importance of the change, the strategy, and transformation leverage (cultural, political, or economic) (Alvord et al., 2004). Social enterprises are established to address social needs and alleviate social problems, and so virtually all social enterprises seek to attain social change or social transformation (Austin et al., 2006; Babos et al., 2007; Dees, 1998a, 2001; Dees & Anderson, 2003; Haugh, 2007; OECD, n.d.; Thompson & Doherty, 2006; Shaw & Carter, 2007; Sullivan Mort et al., 2003).

Social enterprises are frequently described in terms of different levels of social transformation (Alvord et al., 2004; Martin & Osberg, 2007). The pragmatic issue of balancing the double or triple bottom-line paradigm (most often financial and social returns, and sometimes environmental returns) is frequently discussed in the literature (see for example, Neck, Brush, & Allen, 2009). The assumption is that most effective social enterprises demonstrate healthy financial and social returns, rather than high returns in one area and lower returns in the other (Thompson & Doherty, 2006). For example, as discussed in Neck, Brush, and Allen (2009, p. 17), KickStart International summarizes its social transformation on its website:

> KickStart International (www.kickstart.org) is an enterprising nonprofit that sells micro irrigation pumps in Africa, which in turn has created thousands of agricultural entrepreneurs. KickStart metrics are both economic and social, with greater focus on the impact the pumps have made on lives touched. By early 2008, KickStart featured the following statistics on its website:
> - 45,000 pumps are in use by poor farmers.
> - 29,000 new jobs have been created.
> - The pumps generate $37 million per year in new profits and wages.
> - More than 50% of the pumps are managed by women entrepreneurs.
> - 4 manufacturers produce the pumps.
> - Over 400 retailers are selling the pumps throughout Kenya, Tanzania, and Mali.

Financial Self-Sufficiency in Social Enterprises

Financial self-sufficiency refers to the ability of a social enterprise to gain financial autonomy through generating profits from income generating activities. This is often discussed in comparison to traditional nonprofit organizations that rely primarily on grants, sponsorships, and donations in order to meet their social goals. Many writers argue that earned income or financial self-sufficiency/sustainability is an essential aspect of social enterprise (Boschee, 1995, 2001) and the key characteristics defining social enterprises. Alter (2006) identifies two forms of financial self-sufficiency: cost recovery (discrete) and earned income (ongoing). While Boschee (2001) indicates a distinction between financial sustainability and self-sufficiency, he finds that sustainability can be achieved through philanthropy, donations, grants, government subsidy, and earned income, but self-sufficiency can only be achieved through reliance on earned income.

The phenomenon of applying business expertise to earn income is extensively discussed in the social enterprise literature and is used in many definitions of social enterprise and social entrepreneurship (Austin et al., 2006; Boschee, 2001; Thompson, 2002). For some researchers, social enterprises must be engaged in the production and or selling of goods and services in a market place (Thompson & Doherty, 2006).

Innovation in Social Enterprises

In many definitions of social enterprises (and the related concept of social entrepreneurship) (Austin et al., 2006; Dees, 1998a, 2001; Dees & Anderson, 2003), social enterprises are characterized by innovation. Brooks (2009) and Mair and Marti (2006) see social enterprises as using innovative behaviour to achieve social objectives. Weerawardena and Sullivan-Mort (2001) support this contention, and note that the nonprofit literature is dominated by discussion of non-technological innovation. Social enterprises themselves are seen as innovative structures to solve social problems (Fowler, 2000). Mair and Marti view social enterprise as the outcome of social entrepreneurship. In turn, social entrepreneurship is seen as innovative in that it is a 'process of creating value by combining resources in new ways,' and 'involves the offering of services and products but can also refer to the creation of new organizations' (Mair & Marti, 2006, p. 37). For example, Austin, Stevenson, and Wei-Skillern (2006) state:

> Common across all definitions of social entrepreneurship is the fact that the underlying drive for social entrepreneurship is to create social value, rather than personal and shareholder wealth (e.g., Zadek & Thake, 1997), and that the activity is characterized by innovation, or the creation of something new rather than simply the replication of existing enterprises or practices.

The term social entrepreneur is regularly used to describe individuals who initiate and run social enterprises and they are frequently characterized as innovative individuals:

> Ashoka, a premier organization that invests in social entrepreneurs, defines a social entrepreneur as an individual with innovative solutions to society's most pressing social problems. Similarly, The Skoll Foundation, which also invests in social entrepreneurs for systemic change, identifies social entrepreneurs as society's change agents: pioneers of innovation that benefit humanity. (Neck et al., 2009)

Associated with innovation, social enterprises are often described as exhibiting significant levels of social opportunity recognition,[3] proactiveness, and risk tolerance (Sullivan Mort et al., 2003).

Theoretical Approach: Development of Research Objectives

Theory concerning social enterprise is at an early stage. As noted above, even at the most basic level, a common definition of social enterprise has not been achieved. Robinson, Mair, and Hockerts (2009) 'do not prescribe to the notion that there is one meta-theory of social entrepreneurship but that there are many theories that explain and frame the activities of social entrepreneurs' (p. 3). Several of the theories that have been proffered to explain long-term survivability of social ventures include resource dependency, institutional and social capital and network theories, the resource-based view of the firm, and human capital (Sharir et al., 2009).

This research adopts the resource dependency view of social enterprises in guiding the formation of the research objectives. The resource dependence view suggests that organizations look to gain resources and minimize their dependence on the environment (Astley & Van de Ven, 1983). This theoretical approach recognizes that managing social ventures is more complicated than business ventures for two main reasons. First, social enterprises are exposed to higher resource dependence in their environments and frequently have depended heavily on financial resources obtained from governmental grants, donations, and volunteers. Second, the goods and services of social enterprises may not have easily definable commercial value (Roper & Cheney, 2005; Sharir et al., 2009). Using a resource dependency point of view focuses on understanding what resources are acquired in social enterprises to achieve social transformation. Understanding the extent to which Canadian social enterprises have diversified streams of revenue resulting in reduced dependency on government sources (financial self-sufficiency), yet still strive to achieve the social transformation goals of the enterprise, is essential to improving our understanding of resource dependency in Canadian social enterprises. Focusing on innovation also follows from resource dependency theory, in that it appears to be a key dimension that allows social enterprises to achieve both social transformation and financial self-sufficiency.

To summarize, the bulk of the literature on social enterprises is frequently case based or discussion based, with limited empirical data. Current literature suggests that both resource dependency theory and the extant literature highlight the importance of social transformation, financial self-sufficiency, and innovation. Given that importance, the current research is aimed at deepening our understanding of Canadian social enterprises along these dimensions.

Methods

As part of a larger project on social enterprises, the researchers developed a dataset of 742 social enterprises in Canada from which they selected a sample of sixty and conducted a web site analysis study (Madill et al., 2010). The research used qualitative methods (Denzin & Lincoln, 1994) and draws on Grounded Theory (Strauss & Corbin, 1998) in its approach to deepening understanding of social enterprises in Canada.

In this chapter, we briefly summarise our findings of earlier research drawn from an examination of the three defining characteristics of social enterprise using sixty publicly available profiles of social enterprises. We then discuss the results of our follow up methodology based on telephone interviews with twenty social enterprises drawn from the sixty profiles in the sample (one-third of the sample). The qualitative interviews were conducted to gain greater depth of understanding because websites may or may not reflect the reality of the organizations. For example, the focal social enterprises may have simply failed to list their accomplishments or update their websites. We interviewed the most senior member of the staff who was also most familiar with the development and mission of the enterprise. Telephone interviews were approximately half an hour in length, and were semi-structured with a set of open ended questions received by the interviewee in advance. Detailed notes were taken by the interviewer on each interview. The results of the telephone interviews reported here deepened our understanding of Canadian social enterprises along the three focal dimensions of social transformation, financial self-sufficiency, and innovation. For the purposes of this research, the three central dimensions are defined as follows:

- Social transformation is the extent to which the enterprise changes lives for the better
- Financial self-sufficiency is relying on some portion of earned income as opposed to only grants and contributions
- Innovation is utilizing new processes or behaviours to accomplish the enterprise mission

Findings and Discussion

In order to set the context for the telephone interviews reported on in this chapter, we will summarize briefly the results of the web site portion of the study published elsewhere (Madill et al., 2010). The results showed that almost one-third (31.7 per cent) of the sample enterprises were deemed to be high in social transformation. Fewer than half (41.7 per cent) were judged as exhibiting low social transformation. The findings also showed that about one-half (51.7 per cent) of the sample enterprises were high in financial self-sufficiency, defined as over 50 per cent revenues from income generating activities. About one-quarter exhibited low financial self-sufficiency. Lastly, less than one-fifth (18.3 per cent) were highly innovative. Almost two-thirds exhibited low innovation (65 per cent).

Expanding Understanding of Social Enterprises: Interview Results

BACKGROUND ON SOCIAL ENTERPRISES INTERVIEWED
The twenty enterprises interviewed operated primarily in the service sector, ranging from fair trade coffee houses to courier services. The one exception was in light manufacturing, using hard-to-employ populations in packaging assembly. Eight of the enterprises focus on food, and of those, seven engage hard-to-employ populations as their primary mission. One uses renewable energy, and another uses an innovative financing structure. The enterprises provide products or services that form the core of their mission (for example producing and distributing a board game designed to educate children on environmental issues). The twenty entities interviewed covered a variety of legal forms: sole proprietorships, for-profit corporations, nonprofit structures, charities, and businesses embedded within nonprofits.

Most of the interviewees described their organizations as social enterprises, though two indicated that their work supported other social enterprises, for example: 'My mission is to support social enterprise, to create an environment where social enterprises and community enterprises can flourish.' All interviewees with one exception were able to describe their mission in detail. While some felt their mission combined social and economic factors, most described their mission as social: 'The mission is entirely social. The courier business is just the way to accomplish it,' said one interviewee. 'Our entire purpose is social. Construction is just a means to an end. We could be in any industry. Our mission is to create quality jobs,' said another.

EXPANDED UNDERSTANDING OF SOCIAL TRANSFORMATION
While the interviewees were able to easily identify their mission, questions about degree of social transformation were the most difficult to

answer, particularly if the organization in question had either very broad societal impacts or facilitated other social entrepreneurs to achieve their mission. In one form or another they all hoped they were achieving social transformation; as one said, 'We hope we are making an impact.' However, many did not measure the impacts of their enterprise and could not point to specific social transformation as a result of their work. For many, social transformation was aspirational and ranged from 'peace in Palestine' to 'increased environmental awareness' to 'good healthy food for all.' For some, identifying their degree of social transformation meant restating the mission of the organization or the growth of the organization itself rather than the direct impacts on others that resulted from the social enterprise activities.

The interview results showed that enterprises that targeted hard-to-employ populations more readily identified their degree of social transformation and quantified it with the number of individuals whose lives had been directly impacted by the social enterprise. For example a British Columbia-based social enterprise that employs individuals with developmental disabilities in a packaging facility, uses a set of metrics called *Demonstrating Value: A Shared Framework for Assessing the Performance and Impact of Social Enterprise.* Conversely, those enterprises that affected large numbers of people or even society as a whole in a small way most often restated their mission as their degree of social transformation and were not able to provide concrete ways in which their impacts were measured. For example, one enterprise that focuses on environmental awareness impact indicated, 'Yes, it is difficult to measure, our impact is not huge but we still see the environment is being looked at by schools and other organizations, we'd like to think we play a part in supporting it.'

The measurement of social impacts varied across all interviewees. No one measurement or tool kit was referred to with any consistency. Most interviewees indicated the difficulty of measuring social transformation. Some used annual reports and published those reports on the Internet, writing that: 'To measure it, we have annual reports for the store, from a business perspective, business, sales, ongoing evaluation with store participants to see how it is working from a store perspective, meeting with customers, making changes as needed.' Others tracked numbers of participants:

> We have both quantitative and qualitative measures for our programs. In terms of quantitative measures, we look at targets met for number of trainees, number of employment hours, number of training workshops, type

of training workshops, number of participants who move on to other employment or training. In terms of qualitative measures we look at feedback from participants [and] observable changes in participants increased productivity at work; increased eye contact, confidence, self-esteem; increased hope about the future; increased support networks; able to demonstrate new skills in the workplace.

Another enterprise serving hard-to-employ populations also discussed social transformation in terms of numbers of individuals impacted: 'We have employed over 1,800 people (survivors) over the last twenty-one years. We look at things like decrease in number of hospital days, an increase in income, and feelings of self-esteem. If income is going up and wages [are] going up, then we're meeting our mandate.' However, they also looked at downstream transformation: 'We are one of the best examples of anti-discrimination. We put a different face on mental illness. It's not just the guy ranting on the street corner. That's a huge impact when people see our couriers on the streetcars.'

In spite of the small use of standardized quantitative measures, our interviewees suggest that standardized measurement tools for social impacts are increasingly common. Enterprises that use social return on investment (SROI) instruments were able to easily answer the questions on their degree of social transformation: 'In terms of job placements, we know how happy our employers are, we know we have the highest satisfaction and retention rate in the city, so we are measuring it, and we're getting better at doing that and being trained to do that.' But more often interviewees expressed a need for standardized tools and instruments to measure impact, even for those enterprises that publish detailed annual reports and track the number of individuals served by the enterprise: 'If they don't design a way where it's easy for someone to do impact analysis, it's going to be a problem because they don't have the time. Anyone running a social enterprise is over-the-top busy.'

EXPANDED UNDERSTANDING OF FINANCIAL SELF-SUFFICIENCY

All interviewees were able to easily answer questions on the degree of financial self-sufficiency within their organization. While all social enterprises must have some degree of earned revenue, these diversified revenue streams can range from a small percentage of the total revenue to 100 per cent. Social enterprises often are funded from a mix of grants, donations, and earned revenues. Seven enterprises in our sample were in the 35 to 65 per cent self-funded range. Four enterprises operated primarily with external grants and donations with only a small amount of earned revenue, seven were 100 per cent self-sufficient based on the earned revenue of the organization, and the remaining two were at the 85 per cent to 90 per cent range. These responses indicate that social enterprises themselves are well aware of their degree of financial self-sufficiency as part of their defining characteristics, but that the degree can vary from low to high within the range of organizations. The data also indicate that an external assessment can easily determine the degree of financial self-sufficiency within a social enterprise.

EXPANDED UNDERSTANDING OF INNOVATION

Most respondents reported that their enterprises are innovative. Of the twenty interviews, fifteen enterprises indicated that they were innovative; five enterprises did not answer the question. Not surprisingly, given the self-reporting nature of the interview, no enterprises said that they were not innovative. For some the whole sector is innovative as it constantly changes to meet social and community needs: 'Community development and social enterprise is inherently innovative, you are blending two aspects to make change. You are seeing people as assets in the community. Our programs are designed to give them access to do that, employment is an innovative approach to achieve this.' Interviewees themselves did not distinguish between types of innovation, such as whether their enterprise used a new process, developed a new product or whether such a social enterprise had been in existence somewhere else or over a long period of time. For some respondents the lack of competing businesses reflected innovation: 'There are very few businesses that are managed by and employ "psychiatric consumer survivors."[4] So, it is an empowerment model, a recovery model. I think the model remains innovative.' Others felt that if the enterprise was innovative at the beginning, it remained innovative today: 'Back in the 1980s, it was such a new concept and the building of this huge network of social entrepreneurs that stay in the network for life is quite innovative.' Several organizations indicated a degree of innovation in achieving financial self-sufficiency, while others indicated the problems for social enterprises when using traditional financial instruments to achieve scale: 'We try to stay away from loans. Because the last thing you want to do is getting everything up and running and you're starting from a negative balance. You're always trying to catch up to make the loan payments.'

Summary, Discussion, and Implications

This chapter presents data examining the three major dimensions noted as important but under-researched in the existing literature on Canadian social enterprises: social transformation, financial self-sufficiency, and innovation. This study builds on earlier research that examined these dimensions using a website analysis only. The analysis of the web based profile results (Madill et al., 2010) showed that approximately one-third (31.7 per cent) of the sample enterprises were judged as being high in social transformation; 41.7 per cent were judged as exhibiting low social transformation. The interview results confirm the website analysis results, which demonstrated that many social enterprises did not formally assess achievement of social transformation. Virtually all interviewees noted that social transformation was their enterprise mission and hoped they were achieving it, but most could not provide concrete measures or evidence in support of this achievement. The researchers recognize that this study may in fact understate the extent of social transformation, as the research reveals that many social enterprises do not attempt to assess social transformation themselves. Moreover, assessing their social impact is of importance to stakeholders (including funders and others).

The web profile results showed that approximately half of Canadian social enterprises sampled (51.7 per cent) are highly self-sufficient, and by diversifying their streams of revenue are less reliant than in the past on government grants, as well as donations and volunteers for the resources necessary to accomplish their social missions (Madill et al., 2010). The profile results showed that one quarter of the Canadian social enterprises sampled are low in financial self-sufficiency and still very dependent on such traditional funding. The interviews support the profile assessments. Most interviewees are aware of their enterprise's degree of financial self-sufficiency, and similar to the profile results, approximately half of the enterprises interviewed reported that earned income is greater than 50 per cent of their total revenue. Over half of the social enterprises sampled have found ways to attract resources in the form of earnings from the sale of various products and services, ranging from the sale of various food items, to provision of snow clearing and building services.

Future research is required to fully understand how these organizations manage and market their products and services within these social ventures. As well, future research is needed to investigate whether social enterprises that have a high degree of financial self-sufficiency might also have high degrees of innovation or social transformation. Testing such relationships would contribute to the development of resource dependency theory in that one can begin to understand interrelationships among key dimensions of social enterprises.

A major divergence between the interview results described in this chapter and profile assessment results published elsewhere (Madill et al., 2010) centred around the innovation dimension of social enterprises. The findings from the web-based profiles show that less than one-fifth of the sample social enterprises (18.3 per cent) were judged by the four researchers coding the data (the three paper authors and a research assistant) as highly innovative. Almost two-thirds exhibited low innovation (65 per cent). However, a high proportion of the interviewees viewed their social enterprises as innovative because they were part of a social enterprise and in their view social enterprises are by definition innovative. This self-assessment does not fit with the traditional definition of innovation and suggests that future research is required to examine what it means to be innovative in social enterprises. It may not be desirable to assess all social enterprises as innovative simply because they are social enterprises. Social enterprises competing both with other social enterprises and with traditional for profit enterprises in a sector such as catering, for example, may need to consider that simply being a social enterprise caterer is insufficient to be considered 'innovative.' However, it is recognized that for the social enterprises themselves, business type revenue generating activities are new and therefore seen as innovative within the organization.

Implications for Managing Social Enterprises

Given that relatively few social enterprises were able to provide evidence of their social transformation missions, it is important that Canadian social enterprises improve both their measurement of and their ability to demonstrate social transformation. Increasingly, sets of uniform metrics are being established that capture social return on investment (SROI). Such metrics need to be better understood and integrated into ongoing practice by social enterprises (Monitor Institute, 2008).

With regard to increasing financial self-sufficiency, bringing a market or marketing orientation to social enterprises may improve their ability to sell goods and services. A market orientation requires, first, a focus on understanding what consumers want, and second, communicating effectively with those consumers and bringing the appropriate product or service to the market in a form and place where it is most likely to be purchased by targeted consumers (Zeitlow, 2001). A marketing orientation also focuses on undertaking competitive analyses in order to better survive in the market. Accordingly, it is important to recognize that the literature concerning marketing in not for profit organizations may be helpful here. However, there is a lot left to learn concerning adapting marketing thinking to social enterprises. For example, future research is needed on positioning and branding in social enterprises. Do social enterprises emphasize positive social change in their branding, or downplay it? What should they be doing? How important is this to key target markets?

As discussed earlier, social enterprises frequently describe themselves as innovative, often simply because they are social enterprises. However, many compete with businesses and other organizations that operate in similar business sectors, such as landscaping, printing, or catering. Many such sectors are considered mature industries. Marketing approaches may assist social enterprises with remaining innovative by offering knowledge and guidance on both developing and introducing new products to such marketplaces. In turn, research is needed concerning how social enterprises have successfully developed new products and introduced them to the market – such research will build knowledge of marketing in various types of organizations and environments.

Strengths and Limitations of the Research

The findings from this study provide useful research on Canadian social enterprises. The authors recognize that the small sample size limits ability to generalize from the findings. The qualitative research approach utilized in this study suggests several approaches to be taken in future research to achieve more precise operational definitions. For example, the findings concerning social transformation point to three major subdimensions that should be further explored. The first is a deeper understanding of the goal of social transformation versus the evidence of achievement. This field lacks the ability to measure not just the outputs of social enterprises but the broader impacts of social enterprises that more closely align the mission of the organization with its transformative goals. Second, we need to gain a deeper understanding of social transformation that affects a few individuals in a major way versus social transformation that affects many individuals in a minor way. Several of the social enterprises in our sample study have deeply impacted the lives of a few individuals, while others in the study have made small changes across large populations. We find that organizations that provide opportunity for hard-to employ populations have a profound impact on these individuals; in contrast, providing fair trade products has a smaller effect on a larger population. When examining social enterprises and their dimensions, judging the relative values of such diverse outputs is difficult and should be further explored.

Finally, we feel a distinction should be made between social enterprises that focus on upstream (employee or supplier) transformation versus downstream (client or customer) transformation. Upstream transformations appear to be easier to quantify. Future research needs to explicitly recognize which sub dimensions of social transformation are being researched and focused on (Emerson, 2003; Haugh, 2005). As well, it is critical for future research to explicitly state whether it is seeking to assess the extent of the 'goal' of social transformation or evidence of the 'achievement' of social transformation. It will be critical to begin to look at social enterprises in a more granular fashion, sub-dividing the type of social enterprise with greater emphasis on the metrics used in evaluating their impact and the comparability of those metrics across the diverse field of social enterprises.

However, given the need for both qualitative and quantitative empirical research to contribute to theory development in the field of social enterprise, the current study was designed to take an important preliminary step in this research on the Canadian scene.

NOTES

1 The authors gratefully acknowledge the financial support of the Telfer School of Management, the Sprott Centre on Social Enterprises, and the Carleton Centre for Community Innovation. We thank Robert Mittelman for excellent research assistance.
2 The exception with regard to legal structure is the United Kingdom's Community Interest Corporation (CIC) and United States' Low-Profit Limited Liability Company (L3C).
3 Social opportunity recognition is a term used when business ideas and technological ideas come together to serve human needs. Serving these needs can be for profit or nonprofit. Such recognition of human needs is a key part of the social entrepreneur's tool kit.
4 The term 'psychiatric consumer survivors' is a term used by the organization to refer to post-psychiatric patients who are the social enterprise's employment target.

REFERENCES

Alter, K. (2006). *Social enterprise typology.* Retrieved from http://www.virtue venturescom/setypology.pdf

Alvord, S., Brown, D., & Letts, C. (2004). Social entrepreneurship and societal transformation. *Journal of Applied Behavioral Science, 40*(3), 260–82.

Andreasen, A.R. (2006). *Social marketing in the 21st century.* Thousand Oaks: Sage Publications.

Astley, W.G., & Van de Ven, A.H. (1983). Central perspectives and debates in organization theory. *Administrative Science Quarterly, 28*(1), 245–73.

Austin, J., Stevenson, H., & Wei-Skillern, J. (2006). Social and commercial entrepreneurship: Same, different, or both? *Entrepreneurship: Theory & Practice, 30*(1), 1–22.

Babos, P., Clarence E., & Noya, A. (2007). *Reviewing OECD experience in the social enterprise sector.* An OECD LEED Centre for Local Development international seminar held in conjunction with the Third DECIM Roundtable, November 15–18, Trento, Italy. Retrieved from http://www.oecd.org/dataoecd/22/58/38299281.pdf

Borzaga, C., & Defourny, J. (Ed.). (2001). *The emergence of social enterprise.* London : Routledge.

Boschee, J. (1995). Social entrepreneurship. *Across the board, 32*(3), 20–3.

Boschee, J. (2001). Eight basic principles for nonprofit entrepreneurs. *Nonprofit World, 19*(4), 15–18.

Brooks, A. (2009). *Social entrepreneurship: A modern approach to social value creation.* Upper Saddle River, NJ: Pearson-Prentice Hall.

Certo, S.T., & Miller, T. (2008). Social entrepreneurship: Key issues and concepts. *Business Horizons, 1*(4), 267–71.

Christie, M.J., & Honig, B. (2006). Social entrepreneurship: New research findings. *Journal of World Business, 41*(1), 1–5.

Cullen, E.T., Matthews, L.N.H., & Teske, T.D. (2008). Use of occupational ethnography and social marketing strategies to develop a safety awareness campaign for coal miners. *Social Marketing Quarterly, 14*(4), 2–21.

Dart, R. (2004). Being 'business-like' in a nonprofit organization: A grounded and inductive typology. *Nonprofit and Voluntary Sector Quarterly, 33*(2), 290–313.

Dees, G. (1998a). *The meaning of social entrepreneurship.* Retrieved from www.gsb.stanford.edu/services/news/DeesSocentrepPaper.html

Dees, G. (1998b). Enterprising nonprofits. *Harvard Business Review, 76*(1), 55–65.

Dees, G. (2001). *The meaning of social entrepreneurship.* Center for Advancement of Social Entrepreneurship. Retrieved from http://www.fuqua.duke.edu/centers/case/documents/dees_SE.pdf

Dees, J.G., & Anderson, B.B. (2003). For-profit social ventures. *International Journal of Entrepreneurship Education, 2*(1), 1–26.

Denzin, N., & Lincoln, Y. (Eds.) (1994). *Handbook of qualitative research.* Thousand Oaks: Sage.

Douglas, H. (2008). Creating knowledge: A review of research methods in three societal change approaches. *Journal of Nonprofit & Public Sector Marketing, 20*(2), 141–63.

Emerson, J. (2003). The blended value proposition: Integrating social and financial returns. *California Management Review, 45*(4), 35–51.

Fowler, A. (2000). NGDOs as a moment in history: Beyond aid to social entrepreneurship or civic innovation? *Third World Quarterly, 21*(4), 637–54.

Hall, M., de Wit, M.L., Lasby, D., McIver, D., Evers, T, Johnston, C., et al. (2005). *Cornerstones of community: Highlights of the national survey of nonprofit and voluntary organizations.* Ottawa: Statistics Canada.

Haugh, H. (2005). A research agenda for social entrepreneurship. *Social Entreprise Journal, 1*(1), 1–12.

Haugh, H. (2007). Community-led social venture creation. *Entrepreneurship: Theory & Practice, 31*(2), 161–82.

Jesson, J. (2009). Household waste recycling behavior: A market segmentation model. *Social Marketing Quarterly, 15*(2), 25–38.

Kotler, P., & Lee, N.R. (2008). *Social marketing influencing behaviors for good.* Los Angeles: Sage Publications.

Madill J., Brouard F., & Hebb T. (2010). Canadian social enterprises: An empirical exploration. *Journal of Nonprofit and Public Sector Marketing,* Special Issue on Social Entrepreneurship, 22.

Mair, J., & Marti, I. (2004). *Social entrepreneurship: What are we talking about? A framework for future research.* IESE Business School, University of Navarra, working paper #546.

Mair, J., & Marti, I. (2006). Social entrepreneurship research: A source of explanation, prediction, and delight. *Journal of World Business, 41*(1), 36–44.

Mair, J., Robinson, J.A., & Hockerts, K. (2006). *Social entrepreneurship.* London: Palgrave Macmillan.

Martin, R.L., & Osberg, S. (2007). Social entrepreneurship: The case for definition. *Stanford Social Innovation Review,* Spring, 29–39.

Massarsky, C.W., & Beinhecker, S.L. (2002). *Enterprising nonprofits: Revenue generation in the nonprofit sector.* New Haven, Connecticut: Yale School of Management.

Mendell, M., & Nogales, R. (2008). *Social enterprises in OECD Member Countries: What are the financial streams?* Alliance de recherche universités-communautés/Réseau Québécois de recherche partenariale (ARUC-RQRP) Working paper C-08-2008.

Monitor Institute, The. (2008). *Investing for social and environmental impact: A design for catalyzing an emerging industry,* pp. 1–84. Retrieved from http:// www.monitorinstitute.com/impactinvesting/documents/InvestingforSocial andEnvImpact_FullReport_005.pdf

Neck, H., Brush, C., & Allen, E. (2009). The landscape of social entrepre neurship. *Business Horizons, 52*(1), 13–19.

OECD. (n.d.). *The social enterprise sector: A conceptual framework.* Paris: Organisation for Economic Co-operation and Development (OECD) / Local Economic and Employment Development Programme (LEED). Retrieved from http://www.oecd.org/dataoecd/43/40/37753595.pdf

Peredo, A.M., & McLean, M. (2006). Social entrepreneurial: A critical review of the concept. *Journal of World Business, 41*(1), 56–65.

Rangan, V.K., Leonard, H.B., & McDonald, S. (2008). *The future of social enterprise.* Harvard Business School Working Paper. Retrieved from http://www.hbs.edu/research/pdf/08–103.pdf

Robinson, J.A., Mair, J., & Hockerts, K. (2009). Introduction. In Robinson, J.A., Mair, J., Hockerts, K., (Eds.), *International perspectives on social entre preneurship* (pp. 1–6). London: Palgrave Macmillan.

Roper, J., & Cheney, G. (2005). Leadership, learning and human resource management: The meanings of social entrepreneurship today. *Corporate Governance, 5*(3), 95–104.

Rogers, E. (1995). *Diffusion of innovations.* New York: Free Press.

Sharir, M., Lerner, M., & Yitshaki, R. (2009). Long-term survivability of social ventures: Qualitative analysis of external and internal explanations. In Robinson, J.A., Mair, J., Hockerts, K., (Eds.), *International perspectives on social entrepreneurship* (pp. 75–96). London: Palgrave Macmillan.

Shaw, E., & Carter, S. (2007). Social entrepreneurship: Theoretical antecedents and empirical analysis of entrepreneurial processes and outcomes. *Journal of Small Business and Enterprise Development, 14*(3), 418–34.

Stater, K.J. (2009). The impact of revenue sources on marketing behavior: Examining web-promotion and place-marketing in nonprofit organizations. *Journal of Nonprofit & Public Sector Marketing, 21*(2), 202–24.

Statistics Canada. (2006). *Canada's nonprofit sector in macro-economic terms.* Satallite account of nonprofit institutions and volunteering. 13-o15-XWE. Ottawa: Author.

Strauss, A., & Corbin, J. (1998). *Basic qualitative research: Techniques for developing grounded theory.* Thousand Oaks: Sage.

Sullivan Mort, G., Weerawardena, J., & Carnegie, K. (2003). Social entre
preneurship: Towards conceptualization. *International Journal of Nonprofit &
Voluntary Sector Marketing*, *8*(1), 76–88.
Thompson, J.L. (2002). The world of the social entrepreneur. *International
Journal of Public Sector Management*, *15*(5), 412–31.
Thompson, J., & Doherty, B. (2006). The diverse world of social entreprise – A
collection of social enterprise stories. *International Journal of Social Economics*,
33(5/6), 361–35.
UK Government. (2006). *Annual small businesses survey 2006/2007*. Department
of Business, Innovation and Skills, UK Government. Retrieved 19 October
2011 from http://www.bis.gov.uk/policies/enterprise-and-business-support/
analytical-unit/research-and-evaluation/cross-cutting-research
Weerawardena, J., & Sullivan-Mort, G. (2001). Learning, innovation and
competitive advantage in not-for-profit care marketing: A conceptual model
and research propositions. *Journal of Nonprofit & Public Sector Marketing*, *9*(3),
53–73.
Zadek, S., & Thake, S. (1997). Send in the social entrepreneurs. *New Statesman*,
126(June).
Zeitlow, J. (2001). Social entrepreneurship: Managerial, finance and marketing
aspects. *Journal of Nonprofit & Public Sector Marketing*, *9*(1), 19–43.

11 Education for the Social Economy

JOHN R. WHITMAN

This chapter focuses on education concerning the economic or business management dimensions of an organization that operates in the social economy in areas that overlap with the public and private sectors. This includes such social economy businesses as social enterprises, co-operatives, and community economic development enterprises. While the focus of this chapter is on education for those preparing to work in the social economy, it is important to note that there is also a need to educate policymakers and the public at large about the social economy and its distinct advantages for creating both social and economic value.

As the logic of the social economy gains strength and breadth worldwide, it is timely to reflect on the role of education for the social economy from several perspectives: to improve the collaborative and competitive performance and sustainability of social economy businesses in a time of globalization; to promote critical, academic examination of the various forms of enterprise that constitute the social economy; and to offer propositions for how education might more effectively advance the social economy. This chapter begins with a general scheme to categorize the main dimensions of education for the social economy as formal, nonformal, informal, incidental, and hybrid. I then briefly review a number of significant educational programs that address nonprofit organizations, social entrepreneurship, co-operatives, community economic development, and other educational programs in several venues – mostly in Canada, Germany, Spain, and the United States. Following this review, I will offer several suggestions for strengthening education in each of the main dimensions of education, and conclude with considerations for policymakers and entrepreneurial educators. The result suggests that now is an opportune time not only to introduce compelling and innovative initiatives to advance education in social economy businesses, but also to revise current educational curricula to include previously neglected consideration of the social economy.

Society often reproduces the forms of economic and social arrangements that are taught in schools. With the rise in prominence of professional schools of business management and administration, it is fair to ask whether and how well these schools are imparting the tools of effective economic competition as a means to increase 'human capital' (Becker, 1993/1964), or whether they are also introducing their students to effective social and economic cooperation as a way of building 'social capital' (Coleman, 1988). As Putnam suggests, building social capital more in line with the values of the social economy may be the key 'to making democracy work' (Putnam, 1993). Generally speaking, the role of building social capital in education for the social economy differentiates such education from the development of human capital in more conventional business education. Chaves and Sajardo-Moreno further explore this point in their examination of how the values instilled by orthodox capitalist business education versus a democratic, social economy oriented education can affect the lifecycle of an organization (Chaves & Sajardo-Moreno, 2004).

Following the logic of Douglass North's institution theory, education as an institution is defined by the social norms and laws of a country, which in turn reflect prevailing beliefs (North, 2005, 2005/1990). Embedded cultural norms place a limit on the emergence of practices that are seen as too far beyond prevailing norms (North, 2005). To the extent that 'culture consists of the intergenerational transfer of norms, values, and ideas' (p. 50), we would expect to see educational practices that reflect cultural preferences: cultures of co-operation would favor education that promotes co-operation (as, for example, in parts of Spain, Italy, and Canada); education that promotes competition would prevail in competitive cultures (as in the United States). As North further points out, in an uncertain world, 'institutional diversity that allows for a range of choices is a superior survival trait' (p. 42), and thus education should equip business students with multiple forms of economic and social organization. Such diversity may have survival value. Indeed, the fundamentalist commitment by the Soviet Union to the singular economic model of communism may have contributed to its demise, while China has been successful through diversifying its own economic models.

However, if the prevailing economic model of capitalism is seen as the 'victor' over communism, this obscures the fact that within a political economy of democratic capitalism there is room for diverse forms of economic and social organization, not all of which conform to the classical capitalist structure. As demonstrated in this book, nonprofit organizations, which disallow private ownership of assets (in the United States), contribute substantially to the economy. Likewise, co-operatives, which are owned by their members, lack a shareholder class interested only in a financial return on investment. The variation in these forms of economic and social organization is a good thing in the context of an increasingly globalized and uncertain world. The amorphous structure of the social economy itself means there is no royal road to educating for social economy businesses. The lack of a defining structure for the social economy is a function of its changing nature, which, in turn, impinges on the types and venues of education that pertain to the social economy. Education can both respond to institutional changes in society and create institutional change. In this chapter, I argue that education should promote a diversity of forms of economic and social organization.

Situating Education in the Social Economy

For purposes of understanding the variety of types and venues of education for social economy business, I draw on a general classification system offered by Foley (2004a) that categorizes the main dimensions of adult learning. In this schema, Foley outlines four distinct forms (2004b, p 4–5) applied here to education for social economy organizations:

1 **Formal** – an educational program led by professional educators using a defined curriculum in educational institutions. Formal education at the university level includes various types of degree programs that develop skills for social economy business. Typical degrees include the master of business administration (MBA), master of public administration (MPA), and master of science (MS) in a relevant field. Examples of topics for formal courses include social entrepreneurship, nonprofit management, co-operative management, and community economic development. Finally, certificate programs offered in higher education might include specific components of course topics such as strategic planning for social ventures, fundraising for nonprofits, designing an effective co-operative board, or grassroots organizing.
2 **Non-formal** – systematic instruction provided on an ad hoc basis. Non-formal education includes short training sessions that, for

example, update practitioners with changes in nonprofit or co-operative laws; online training; the introduction of a new methodology or technique in business practice, such as at an association conference or trade show; and non-formal, co-curricular educational activities, such as starting a social business enterprise as part of a program undertaken in collaboration with an educational organization such as the National Foundation for Teaching Entrepreneurship.

3 **Informal** – purposeful reflection on experiential, usually community-based or job-related learning. Informal education includes the systematic reflection on community organizing; for example, a group assembling after a protest to reconstruct and review what happened, what might have been done differently, and how best to proceed. A work-related example might be a group of employees reflecting together on their experience in applying a new promotional methodology. Informal education can also take place on social networking sites such as Facebook or LinkedIn through sharing information on social entrepreneurship or contacts in community economic development.

4 **Incidental** – tacit learning resulting from extensive practical experience in or exposure to businesses in the social economy. Incidental education refers to gradually gaining familiarity with the values, social norms, and practices accumulated by practical experience working in nonprofit organizations, co-operatives, or other examples of social economy organizations. A population that regularly patronizes co-operative businesses might therefore become more familiar with co-operatives and be more likely to join or even start one.

In addition to this classification, there is a fifth type, hybrid, in which two or more of the other types are combined within a single program; for example, a co-operative work/study program that combines formal and incidental learning through formal classroom instruction and on-the-job training. Another hybrid example is non-formal education combined with informal and incidental education to promote co-operatives organized by students within their schools, such as to operate food or supplies concessions or to provide functions such as dining, maintenance, and cleaning services. Additionally, programs in co-operative education, a form of work/study program in which students alternate periods of formal classroom learning with working in nonprofit organizations or co-operatives leading to incidental learning, is a hybrid type of education. See table 11.1 for generic examples under each of these five forms of education.

Table 11.1. Classification of Social Economy Business Education, Formal through Incidental

Form	Principal Characteristics	Examples
1 Formal	University degrees, e.g., BA, MS, MBA, MPA	Courses; certificate programs
2 Non-formal	Short, ad hoc training sessions	Online courses to upgrade skills; educational events and activities
3 Informal	Purposeful reflection on activities	Social networking to share information
4 Incidental	Familiarity gained through experience	Familiarity gained through exposure, such as at conferences
5 Hybrid	A combination of two or more of the above	School-based co-operatives; co-operative work-study programs

But, as Foley notes, 'If there is education there is also miseducation' (p. 5). This means that students can be misled by unfounded ideological criticism in the treatment of material, such as an unwarranted prejudice against co-operatives. Students may also be poorly served by the deliberate absence of material in an educational program, which, if included, would expand student knowledge and options. The relationship between a prevailing ideology and what is considered acceptable education should be a matter of ongoing, critical analysis (Bowles & Gintis, 1976; Brookfield, 2005). Moreover, there is much to be revealed and learned through comparative studies of education (Arnove & Torres, 2007; Mundy, Bickmore, Hayhoe, Madden, & Madjidi, 2008), through which we can see the relationship between educational policy and practice and the social economy that defines the character of the nation state (Esping-Andersen, 1990; Kangas & Palme, 2005), beginning even at the pre-school level (Tobin, Wu, & Davidson, 1989).

The above schema reveals the ways in which education can be experienced, from the formal to the incidental. While this general schema appears useful for classifying the range of educational forms that pertain to the social economy business, it is beyond the scope of this chapter to present a complete catalogue of programs and activities that could fully populate the typology. Instead, I will present a number of salient examples of educational programs from several countries, followed by a brief discussion of prospects for innovation to further diversify social economy business education.

Review of Educational Programs

Perhaps one measure of the growth in prominence of a new field is when an effort is made to compile evidence of practice. In 1995, the Kellogg Foundation provided support to Seton Hall University to study the effects of nonprofit management on the nonprofit community (Mirabella, 2007). This research entailed a census of nonprofit management education programs at colleges and universities in the United States. The results catalogue programs at some 292 institutions (Seton Hall University, n.d.). Mirabella used a slightly different classification from that inspired by Foley, mapping the growth of courses by type of program: graduate (including PhD), undergraduate, continuing education, and noncredit.

Similarly, Ashoka sponsored the first effort to compile educational resources for teaching social entrepreneurship in 2004, and the latest results are available in a handbook for teachers (Brock & Ashoka Global Academy for Social Entrepreneurship, 2008), as well as online at University Network (http://universitynetwork.org). This research has compiled information on over one hundred courses in thirty-five countries. Additionally, the Aspen Institute surveys and ranks exemplary MBA programs that stress social and environmental stewardship (The Aspen Institute, 2011).

The Canadian Social Economy Hub, which acts as a facilitator for the Social Economy Research Partnerships, funded by the Social Sciences and Humanities Federation of Canada (Quarter, Mook, & Armstrong, 2009), has commissioned a nationwide survey of post-secondary courses and programs that address the social economy and are based on community economic development. This effort will hopefully lead to a more systematic and complete compilation of such educational programs.

Additional courses in the relevant areas may be sought through other online resources including Canada's Higher Education and Career Guide (www.canadian-universities.net) and Peterson's Guide (www.petersons.com). A growing number of such studies on the topics covered here including nonprofit organizations, social entrepreneurship, co-operatives, and community development are emerging in the catalogues of Harvard Business Publishing (http://cb.hbsp.harvard.edu/cb/register), other university-based case catalogues, the Aspen Institute's Case Place (www.caseplace.org), and the European Case Clearing House (www.ecch.com).

Here I provide examples of only a few types of formal educational programs – principally education for nonprofit organizations, social entrepreneurship, co-operatives, and community economic development – offered principally through two venues: universities (including programs that grant degrees, offer courses, and provide certificate training) and other school- or community-based educational programs. In addition to these, many other educational programs in law, education, public health, social work, and other disciplines should properly be included, and indeed, many of the programs described below are multidisciplinary. However, this chapter includes illustrative examples rather than an exhaustive compendium, with greater attention given to the more recently emerging types of programs, those in social entrepreneurship, co-operatives, and community economic development.

Nonprofit Organizations

The types and number of nonprofit organizations have grown considerably since the Second World War, not only in the United States (Hall, 1992a) but globally as well, perhaps first noted by Salamon (1994) and currently tracked by the Comparative Nonprofit Sector Project (Salamon & Sokolowski, 2004) at the Johns Hopkins Center for Civil Society Studies. There has been a corresponding increase in management education and training for nonprofit organizations. However, innovation in nonprofit education was slow to arrive at some elite schools for reasons explored by Hall (1992b), including a scholarly ideology that resisted politically and culturally sensitive issues. While such institutions have since come around, educational programs that teach nonprofit management, especially those based at or affiliated with business schools, are still controversial. Some take issue with the stereotypically heroic male figure, usually drawn from outside the organization, to come in and 'fix' problems and then depart (Chetkovich & Kirp, 2001). Others are more generally circumspect about the efficacy of applying business models designed to maximize efficiency to organizations pursuing social justice missions (Eikenberry & Kluver, 2004).

Of particular note concerning the development of programs in nonprofit education in the United States has been the establishment of two key bodies that influence standards for such programs. The National Association of Schools of Public Affairs and Administration (NASPAA), founded in 1970, sets benchmark standards for graduate public service programs worldwide (its predecessor organization was the Council on Graduate Education for Public Administration, established in the late 1950s). The Nonprofit Academic Centers Council (NACC) was established in 1991 to promote and facilitate interaction among centres engaged in research and education in philanthropy and the nonprofit sector. As Mirabella points out, establishing standards for educational programs can influence their development and performance, as can conferences on specialized education, both of which factors have shaped nonprofit management education (Mirabella, 2007).

Educational programs in nonprofit management are among the more established and documented of the categories examined here. For examples, the Seton Hall source noted above would provide a wide choice.

Social Entrepreneurship

The teaching of social entrepreneurship has been increasing in popularity since the late 1970s, influenced in part by the work of Bill Drayton and Ashoka to seek out and highlight exemplary social entrepreneurs around the world, as well as by the educational initiatives of J. Gregory Dees at Yale, Harvard, and Duke, particularly in defining the field itself (Dees, 2001/1998). As was the case with some elite institutions initially shunning nonprofit education, Dees reports a similar reaction when he first moved to the Harvard Business School, noting that when he proposed a course on 'social entrepreneurship' in 1990 the 'idea was rejected as not appropriate for a business school' (Dees, 2008). This initially conservative stance has since changed dramatically.

Muhammad Yunus and his Grameen Bank represent the first example of social entrepreneurship to win the Nobel Prize (in 2006), adding cache to the field and likely increasing its educational standing. His conception of a 'social business,' a for-profit business that reinvests profits for social purposes rather than distribute them to shareholders (Yunus, 2007), has inspired a raft of new entries into the social economy, all of which are grist for educational materials such as case studies.

As noted above, Ashoka has compiled an extensive handbook of resources for teaching social entrepreneurship, which serves as a useful first stop on the way to new course development (Brock & Ashoka Global Academy for Social Entrepreneurship, 2008). David Bornstein's book, *How to Change the World* (Bornstein, 2004), is widely used as a text in such courses, and a growing number of conferences on social entrepreneurship are contributing to the substantive literature used in such courses (Mair, Robinson, & Hockerts, 2006; Nicholls, 2008/2006). A new, peer-reviewed journal, *Social Entrepreneurship*, promises to expand scholarly research as an educational resource beyond that currently covered by sources such as the *Nonprofit and Voluntary Sector Quarterly*; *Nonprofit Management & Leadership*; the *Canadian Journal of Nonprofit and Social Economy Research*; *Voluntas*, the international journal of voluntary and nonprofit organizations; and various journals of the Academy of Management.

Today, the Association to Advance Collegiate Schools of Business (AACSB) notes that thirty of its membership of 570 accredited schools of business in the United States offer programs in social entrepreneurship. Among these are Babson College (located in Wellesley, Massachusetts), which offers courses in social entrepreneurship at both the undergraduate and graduate MBA levels. The graduate level course in social entrepreneurship at the F.W. Olin Graduate School of Business focuses on innovative social entrepreneurship specifically designed to create social change. The Social Enterprise Initiative was founded at the Harvard Business School in 1993 with funding from the John C. Whitehead Fund for Not-for-Profit Management. The School of Management at Yale University offers a global social entrepreneurship course that links teams of Yale students with social enterprises in India. Among the groups studied include the SEWA (Self-Employed Women's Association) Managers School, which trains women entrepreneurs in rural and urban communities, and Udyogini, an organization working to train and develop poor women entrepreneurs in seven states in India.

Co-operatives

Co-operative forms of organization and their educational epiphenomena are probably as old as humanity. The modern stage of co-operatives is often traced to the Rochdale Pioneers in Rochdale, England, 1844, and the principles that they formulated. These principles were embraced by the International Co-operative Alliance (ICA) in 1937 and revised most recently in 1995 in Manchester, England. One of the Rochdale principles is education, training, and information, meaning that co-operatives are obliged to provide education for their members, elected officials, and the public (Shaffer, 1999; see also International Co-operative Alliance, 2010). The Whyte and Whyte case study *Making Mondragón* (Whyte & Whyte, 1991/1988) remains a widely-used text in general courses on co-operatives. Some case studies on co-operatives may be found in the same sources as those for social entrepreneurship; however, most educational materials appear to be developed de novo by course developers at the various sources of such education probably because they are of a general nature, making it more economical to create materials from scratch, and because they often reference laws that pertain to co-operatives that are unique to different jurisdictional regions, thus necessitating different versions of otherwise standard material.

In Canada, the Sobey School of Business at St Mary's University in Halifax offers a master's degree in management in co-operatives and credit unions (MMCCU). The Center for the Study of Co-operatives at the University of Saskatchewan was founded in 1984 as an interdisciplinary teaching and research institute on co-operatives. The University of Sherbrooke offers a master's degree in the management and governance of co-operatives and mutual organizations. York University's Schulich School of Business in Toronto offers a co-operative management certificate program. This nine-month course, combining online and classroom learning, was developed by the Ontario Co-operative Association with support of representatives from co-operatives and the university. The course objectives are to provide knowledge and information concerning governance, membership development, legislation, financing, and co-operative development.

In Germany, Philipps University in Marburg is the oldest Protestant university in the world, founded in 1527, and now includes about 20,000 students studying in a wide range of disciplines. The Institute for Co-operative Studies has been a leading source of training for co-operative management. The state government of Hessia established the Institute in 1963 under the faculty of law and economics. The Institute is an outgrowth of a conference in 1960, at which the initiators were convinced 'that co-operatives and co-operative self-help organizations of various types and structures play a special role in the economic and social development of the developing world. It was recognized that 'co-operative self-help organizations should be preferred to other forms of economic organizations because of their history of being particularly apt to achieving training and information effects desperately needed for the innovation process in developing countries' (Institute for Co-operation in Development Countries, 1998). The goal was to train individuals first from developing countries, and after 1989 from Eastern Europe, who could return to their countries and educate others. The resulting four-year degree program includes faculty from business administration, general economics, economic and development theory, law, and co-operative science. As of 1998, some 200 individuals had completed the program. While the program is currently suspended, the Center maintains a large library of over 15,000 volumes available to researchers from around the world.

In Spain, Mondragon University, a co-operative university owned by the MCC Co-operative Corporation, was established in 1997 after combining a polytechnic school (Mondragón Goi Eskila Politeknikoa 'Jose M. Arizmendiarrieta' S. Coop.), a business faculty (ETEO S. Coop.), and a faculty of humanities and education (Irakasle Eskila S. Coop.). The university, which is committed to 'social transformation,' provides practical education through its link to MCC, which includes 230 companies and institutions employing over 70,000 workers. The university enrolls some 4,000 students in twenty-two degree courses, and offers postgraduate courses including fifteen master's degree programs and eight specialized courses. Mondragon University employs an innovative approach to learning called Mendeberri, in which students learn in teams supported by a tutor and study material presented in an interdisciplinary manner. The goal is to promote the student's autonomy as a learner, ability to work in a team, and to develop skills in decision-making, negotiation, and communication. Students also become trilingual in Basque, Spanish, and English. Students have the option of working while studying, with part-time work offered at ALECOP, a co-operative firm specializing in producing teaching resources in Spanish. Mondragon University offers a master's program in co-operative business management and a master's program in socio-co-operative development.

The Faculty of Economics at the University of Bologna offers an undergraduate degree in social economy and a graduate degree in economics and management of co-operative firms and nonprofit organizations. In addition, together with AICCON, the faculty offers a European Summer School on Social Economy (ESSE) that tries 'to fill an important gap in the list of courses currently offered to European students in economics and social studies' (ESSE, 2011).

In the United Kingdom, the Co-operative College, an educational charity founded in 1919, focuses on four objectives: developing members and managers, working with co-operatives globally, learning from heritage, and working with schools and young people. The College's programs are central to co-operatives in the United Kingdom and internationally.

In the United States there are organizations specifically related to education about co-operatives: for example, the Association of Co-operative Educators (ACE) and the US Federation of Worker Co-operatives, which has a project called the Democracy at Work Network, a peer technical assistant network designed to promote the development of worker co-operatives.

Founded by John Logue, the Ohio Employee Ownership Center based at Kent State University 'supports the development of business across Ohio and around the world by its efforts that are proven to save jobs, create wealth, and grow the economy. The OEOC's work rests on a simple philosophy: broader ownership of productive assets is a good thing for employees, communities, and our country' (OEOC, 2011). The Center provides technical assistance, training, and outreach.

The University of Wisconsin Center for Co-operatives 'seeks to increase understanding and encourage critical thinking about co-operatives by fostering scholarship and mutual learning among academics, the co-operative community, policy makers, and the public' (University of Wisconsin Center for Co-operatives, 2011). Established in 1962, the Center engages in research, education, and outreach to a variety of business and social settings, and features the Co-operative Issues Forum as well as the Farmer Co-operatives Conference, which since 1998 has been keeping participants in such co-operatives up to date with different issues each year. The Lowell Center of the University of Wisconsin offers a course with Co-operation Works called 'The Art and Science of Starting a New Co-operative Business.'

The Institute for Co-operatives at the University of Puerto Rico's Rio Piedras campus may be the only institution of its kind in the Caribbean that integrates research and teaching (Pérez Riestra & Varela Mont, 2003). Its mission is to promote the formation, capacity building, and research of co-operatives as a means to develop social and economic solidarity in Puerto Rico. Co-operatives arrived in Puerto Rico in 1873 with the formation of the social co-operative, Los Amigos del Bien Publico founded by Santiago Andrade Caballero.

Community Economic Development

Community economic development (CED) programs in education typically represent a multidisciplinary approach to develop skills in social economy businesses. Education-Portal contains links to schools in the United States that provide education in various aspects of community development including CED.

The Canada's Higher Education and Career Guide's Canadian Universities Network, compiled by Hecterra Publishing, lists degrees in community economic development (Canadian-Universities.net, 2011).

The Department of Community, Economic, and Social Development of Algoma University in Sault Ste Marie, Ontario, offers a four-year, interdisciplinary degree program in Community Economic and Social Development with a focus on 'strategies for sustainable development in rural areas, municipalities and First Nations communities' (Algoma University, 2011). The department also offers a three-year interdisciplinary degree program in community development, a certificate in CESD, and five-day, intensive CESD Institutes.

The Shannon School of Business at Cape Breton University offers an MBA in community economic development (CED) designed 'to develop a new generation of leaders who have strong business management capabilities, well developed collaborative and interpersonal skills, and deep knowledge of accountability, social responsibility, and development issues and practices' (Cape Breton University, 2011).

Named for Moses Coady, the Catholic co-operative entrepreneur, the Coady International Institute, based at St Francis Xavier University in Antigonish, Nova Scotia, was founded in 1959 in order to address global poverty and injustice through education, research, and action partnerships. Over 5,000 professionals from 130 countries have participated in Coady programs. One of the central objectives of Coady is 'to develop a knowledge network through which to support and share the accumulation of new knowledge that supports successful development practice' (Coady International Institute, n.d.). Since 1970, the Coady Institute and the Department of Adult Education at St Francis Xavier University have offered a master's degree in adult education – community development stream. Now offered online, the program equips community development practitioners with understanding how to apply adult education principles and methods to empower communities and organizations.

Newer community development programs have emerged in Canada including the collaborative graduate program at the University of Toronto and the master of arts in community development at the University of Victoria.

In Spain, the ESADE business school's Institute for Social Innovation at Ramon Llull University in Barcelona, founded in 1956, is guided by the Jesuit principles established in the sixteenth century, 'to form leaders who would carry forth into their personal and professional lives a mission of service to others' (Delbecq, 1983). Consistent with this mission, ESADE's objectives are: to 'develop personal and organizational skills within the business community and not-for-profit organizations in order to strengthen their activities and enhance their contribution to a more just and sustainable world' and 'to transmit knowledge and provide training on integrating CSR in business strategy and stakeholder engagement, leadership, and management for NGOs and social entrepreneurship' (ESADE, 2011).

In the United States, the Center for Co-operatives and CED within the Community Economic Development program at Southern New Hampshire University is engaged in empowering communities throughout the world. The school offers a master's degree in community economic development as well as one in international community economic development. The school also offers an online graduate certificate in microfinance management. With the Center for Co-operatives, the CED provides three webinars, 'Co-operatives in Periods of Economic Crisis,' 'Preserving Main Streets through Co-operatives,' and 'How are Credit Unions Performing in the Current Banking Crisis.' In addition, the Community Development Credit Union Institute represents a partnership between the school, the National Federation of Community Development Credit Unions, and the Credit Union National Association. The Community Development Financial Institutions Fund, supported by the United States Treasury Department, provides online capacity building training for community development financial institutions.

The Educational Policy Institute for Community Development (IPEDCo) at Universidad del Sagrado Corazón in San Juan, Puerto Rico is a think tank focused on transforming public education in Puerto Rico to serve community needs. IPEDCo undertakes research on educational issues and policies; promotes discussion of educational laws and structures; identifies needs for change and proposes change strategies; and provides information to the community on educational topics through periodic open forums and through the media.

Other Educational Programs

The above programs are offered primarily through institutions of higher education. There are others that depart from the more formal programs described above and may be based in higher education, schools, or other venues.

Ashoka, the organization founded by Bill Drayton to search the world for exemplary social entrepreneurs, has initiated the Ashoka Changemaker Campus Program loosely charged with enlisting college campuses to engage their students in promoting the concept that anyone can be a socially entrepreneurial change maker. By its second year, the Changemaker Campus Consortium included Babson College, College of the Atlantic, Cornell, George Mason, Johns Hopkins, the New School, Tulane, the University of Colorado at Boulder, and the University of Maryland.

Launched in 1986, Equal Exchange sits at the intersection of farm marketing co-operatives and consumer food co-ops, and claims to be the 'largest and oldest for-profit Fair Trade organization in the United States' (Equal Exchange, 2007). In order to promote understanding of co-operatives among children, Equal Exchange has developed a curriculum for grades four to nine, which 'assists students in identifying critical topics so they can work both individually and together to create more viable systems of trade. It provides a link between personal actions and community efforts that create a more just and sustainable world' (Equal Exchange, 2007).

Puerto Rican Law 220 provides for the development of student-owned co-operatives within the public schools. These co-operatives, which number 130 at the time of writing, serve as the school store or undertake service-oriented activities in the school. Some are sufficiently successful to warrant hiring employees. This form of education exemplifies the incidental classification, and likely helps to build familiarity with the co-operative form of organization that may influence later work-related choices, a proposition that may well be studied further.

The Puerto Rican experience is not unique. Quebec has a network of student co-operatives with more than 500,000 members that operate in high schools and universities providing school supplies, stationery, and textbooks. Some operate cafeterias and offer driving and education courses (Co-operatives Secretariat, 2008). Moreover, the Centre for Co-operative and Community-Based Economy at the University of Victoria has published a compendium of various youth co-operatives from countries around the world that conveys the promise of engaging youth in distinctly different cultures in this form of social and economic organization (Smith, Puga, & MacPherson, 2005).

SOCODEVI (Société de Coopération pour le Développement International), based in Quebec, is a network of Canadian co-operatives and mutual enterprises that provide technical assistance and training with partners in developing countries. Since its founding in 1985, SOCODEVI has supported over 500 co-operatives and other enterprises in more than forty developing countries.

Perhaps exceeding the influence of even the Gutenberg Press, the Internet is democratizing people to people education worldwide. Muhammad Yunus is combining his recognition as winner of the Nobel Prize with a web site to disseminate his concepts and resources globally for creating social businesses, which shows how even individuals can contribute to education for the social economy (http://muhammadyunus.org).

Finally, a number of conferences offer a venue in which participants can learn about social economy business, if not formally and informally, then non-formally by attendance at demonstrations or incidentally by exposure to the people and content being shared. Such conferences are increasingly attended by people from other countries and may even be held in different countries, and so they are listed without reference to any particular country: the Association for Research on Nonprofit Organizations and Voluntary Action; the Association for Nonprofit and Social Economy Research; the International Society for Third Sector Research; and the Academy of Management.

Suggestions for Strengthening Education

The examples of education for the social economy that are mentioned above are a sample representing leading programs. Much more can and should be done. In this section we offer several ideas for consideration, presented according to the categories set forth by Foley.

Formal

The social economy should be addressed in more, if not all, existing traditional formal educational programs, and not only in business schools. While attention to nonprofit organizations and their management needs may be on the rise, there is virtually no mention of co-operatives as a form of economic organization that also creates social value except at specialized programs that specifically focus on co-operatives. Otherwise, co-operatives are hardly mentioned or completely missing in the orthodox introductory economics texts as an alternative form of economic organization (Hill, 2000).

To address the absence of attention to co-operatives in mainstream professional education, Babson College, with support from Equal Exchange – a Massachusetts-based co-operative that distributes fairly traded coffee, tea, and chocolate produced in turn by co-operatives – has developed an introductory curriculum on co-operatives that is freely available for use in professional graduate schools of any type, including business, law, architecture, medicine, public health, and education (Cooperative-Curriculum, 2011). Such schools could offer a course or program to provide students with an introduction to and basic literacy in social economy business. Such a course could convey an understanding of different types of economic organizations, including sole proprietorships, capital stock companies, nonprofit organizations, co-operatives, and social businesses especially in a global context. Students might learn the basics of financial reporting, including social and environmental accounting, the Rochdale principles of co-operatives, and the meaning of concepts such as 'due diligence,' 'intellectual property,' 'moral rights,' 'work for hire,' and 'employ stock ownership plan,' as well as the role of culture in influencing economic and social change (North, 2005; Rao & Walton, 2004). Providing all graduating professionals – in law, education, medicine, and other specialties, as well as in the arts and sciences – with a common literacy in business, particularly including social economy business in a global context, could conceivable increase overall communicative effectiveness and lower transaction costs. The goal is to acquaint all professional students with co-operatives in their many forms, and one outcome may be that graduates consider forming their own co-operatives rather than seeking traditional employment.

Schools need not create new courses to provide or enhance social economy business education. Existing curricula may be revised to include the social economy, especially in the global context, and to build general awareness. Additionally, existing courses might be revised to require community service that would engage students in nonprofit organizations and co-operatives. Students thus engaged could also be expected to write short reflection papers on their experiences, which in turn could provide a material for research on social economy enterprises. Such curricular revisions would then integrate education, service, and research in a way that anticipates other innovations described below.

Non-formal

There is a great opportunity for short, ad-hoc education in the form of tours for school groups and the public at actual social economy businesses. Such tours are, for example, conducted at Mondragon and at co-operatives in the Emilia Romagna region of Italy. Equal Exchange, in West Bridgewater, Massachusetts, conducts a two-hour tour of its co-operative facility, which includes a large coffee roaster as well as inventory warehouse space for its products. The tour is educational not only in raising awareness and understanding of the globalization of food

production and delivery, but also by viewing and talking to real cooperators working in their own milieu. The pride and contentment among
cooperators is palpable, and the efficiency and orderliness of operations
is remarkable. Ad hoc education resulting from opening the doors to existing co-operatives and other social economy businesses is an excellent
way for people to learn by example.

Informal

One way to advance informal education would be for cooperators and
workers in other social economy businesses to be more engaged in raising awareness of their work and the social benefits conveyed by such
work. This can be done through social networking sites, at job fairs, by
writing short articles for local newspapers, by talking to school groups
and presenting at conferences, or through the online media, as well as.
For example, searching for 'co-operatives' on YouTube resulted in over
1,300 videos, and 'co-operative' resulted in over 12,000, many of which
are rated five stars.

Incidental

An exciting way to increase understanding of social economy businesses
is to engage in working with one, thus being exposed to incidental learning. Rather than explore this category separately, I will address opportunities for incidental learning in the next section on hybrids.

Hybrid

Hybrid forms can combine two or more of the previous categories. The
collaborations described here take two general forms: one focused on
university-community partnerships; the other on combining work and
learning through co-operative education.

University-community partnerships refer to the relationship between
the university and its surrounding community in a way that advances
the interests of both. The relationship between universities, including
large research universities, and their surrounding communities has
been tenuous, as universities have become focused on creating and
disseminating knowledge rather than attending to the social and economic needs within their surrounding milieu, as was the case in the
early twentieth century (Harkavy & Puckett, 1994). But this alienation

need not continue. As part of his efforts to engage universities with their communities, Harkavy has been instrumental in establishing the Office of University Partnerships at the US Department of Housing and Urban Development, one objective of which is 'partnerships that enable students, faculty, and neighborhood organizations to work together to revitalize the economy, generate jobs, and rebuild healthy communities' (OUP, 2011). A particularly beneficial educational opportunity afforded by such partnerships is the concept of service learning, in which service to the community is provided by a student who, in turn, can reflect on the meaning of applying education to building stronger communities and increasing civic engagement. Such partnerships are widespread in Canada and other countries. For example, the University of Toronto and the University of Victoria have offices for facilitating such partnerships, and many universities in Canada have service learning initiatives. Such partnerships can be further encouraged through public policy; however, there is no reason why individual professors cannot themselves initiate a dialogue with potential community partners to explore ways to engage students in activities that would contribute to community well being, add incidental experiential learning to classroom learning, and provide an opportunity for community-based research.

Co-operative education is the second form of collaboration considered here. Co-operative education is 'a program in which students alternate periods in class with periods of related work experience, supervised by a faculty co-ordinator' (Barbeau, 1985, p. 1). The benefits of co-operative education programs are manifold: students are able to combine theory and practice, alternating between classroom and work environments; students are able to more than pay for their tuition through the salaries they receive from co-op employers; employing students in co-op programs has been shown to be sustainable during times of recession, and even during the Great Depression, when the loss of co-op placements was not as great as the loss of jobs in the larger economy; and, not least, students and employers alike are much better prepared to make full employment decisions following graduation, as each is much better known to the other.

The co-operative education concept, while not a co-operative in the ICA sense, is nevertheless an excellent example of how education can contribute to social economy businesses when such organizations – whether nonprofit, co-operative, or community development agencies – provide on-the-job working opportunities to students. It is through such exposure that students could best learn how social economy organizations work and perhaps be inspired and encouraged to start such enterprises.

The above suggestions for possible innovations or expansions of existing ideas are only a few such advances that could be made. In the concluding section, we discuss several policy and entrepreneurial implications resulting from these considerations.

Conclusion

Education for and about the social economy is likely to continue to evolve as the social economy itself expands in new ways and shapes locally and globally. Innovations in non-formal and informal education are likely to continue at the grassroots and community levels, and the Internet will facilitate expanded formal, non-formal, informal, incidental, and hybrid educational programs. More traditional formal education, particularly in elite professional schools, is likely to continue to lag behind the changes in the social economy, as we have already seen in nonprofit education, social entrepreneurship, and co-operative education. But elites and laggards will likely eventually become responsive to changing social needs served in the social economy.

Much more can be done to accelerate learning about the social economy, and this may be seen as an opportunity for public policy. The social benefits of social economy businesses should outweigh any possible compromise in economic performance, and so the forms of organization that promote both social and economic value should become a public policy priority. Traditional professional schools should be more accountable in their role in equipping new generations of leaders with the most socially and economically appropriate business models. Options to learn about nonprofit organizations and co-operatives at every business school are long overdue. Public policy makers should demand that schools provide students with opportunities to learn in their own communities by engaging in community enterprises purposefully established to improve community well being. Moreover, much more could be done to promote the model of co-operative education as a means by which to expose students to real working conditions, preferably to include social economy businesses.

Independent of policy mandates, entrepreneurial educators in the field can organize conferences on education for the social economy, establish benchmarks for quality education in the social economy, and centralize a repository of information on social economy programs that would help researchers and others identify what is underway and where gaps may indicate needs for social economy education. Establishing such institutions to promote social economy education could also, as Chaves and Sajardo-Moreno have argued, encourage others 'to emulate the social economy management model' (Chaves & Sajardo-Moreno, 2004, p. 157).

As the logic of the social economy grows in strength and breadth, accelerated in the wake of failures in both trust and performance of the orthodox capitalist model, it behooves even the most traditional schools of business management to educate their students in alternative and more democratic forms of co-operative economic organization. In the previous pages we explored several such opportunities – the nonprofit organization, the co-operative, the social business, co-operative educational programs, and university-community collaboration.

Going forward we expect to see even more innovations both in forms of co-operative social and economic enterprise as well as in the educational programs that rationalize the organization, management, and operations of such enterprises. In this process we hope that educational innovators, whether trained as scholars or experienced as practitioners, find welcoming institutions willing to experiment with new programs to develop human capital especially equipped to build social capital, and thus turn the key to making democracy work.

REFERENCES

Algoma University. (2011). *Community, economic and social development.* Retrieved from http://www.algomau.ca/departments/community-economic-and-social-development
Arnove, R.F., & Torres, C.A. (Eds.). (2007). *Comparative education: The dialectic of the global and the local* (3rd ed.). Lanham, MD: Rowman & Littlefield Publishers, Inc.
Aspen Institute, The. (2011). *Award programs.* Retrieved from http://www.aspencbe.org/awards/bgp.html
Barbeau, J.E. (1985). *Second to none: Seventy-five years of leadership in the co-operative education movement.* Boston: Custom Book Program of Northeastern University.
Becker, G.S. (1993/1964). *Human capital: A theoretical and empirical analysis with special reference to education* (3rd ed.). Chicago: University of Chicago Press.
Bornstein, D. (2004). *How to change the world: social entrepreneurs and the power of new ideas.* New York: Oxford University Press.
Bowles, S., & Gintis, H. (1976). *Schooling in capitalist America: Educational reform and the contradictions of economic life.* New York: Basic Books.

Brock, D.D., & Ashoka Global Academy for Social Entrepreneurship. (2008). *Social entrepreneurship: Teaching resources handbook.* Arlington, VA: Ashoka.

Brookfield, S.D. (2005). *The power of critical theory: Liberating adult learning and teaching.* San Francisco: Jossey-Bass.

Canadian-Universities.net. (2011). *Community development and planning master's and PhD programs in Canada.* Retrieved from http://www.canadian-universities. net/Universities/Programs/Graduate-Studies-Community_Development_ and_Planning.html

Cape Breton University. (2011). *Shannon School of Business degrees & programs.* Retrieved from http://www.cbu.ca/academics/business/degrees-programs

Chaves, R., & Sajardo-Moreno, A. (2004). Social economy managers: Between values and entrenchment. *Annals of Public and Cooperative Economics, 76*(1), 139–61.

Chetkovich, C., & Kirp, D.L. (2001). Cases and controversies: How novitiates are trained to be masters of the public policy universe. *Journal of Policy Analysis and Management, 20*(2), 283–314.

Co-operatives Secretariat. (2008). *Co-operatives in Canada.* Ottawa: Co-operatives Secretariat, Government of Canada.

Coady International Institute. (n.d.). *The Coady Institute.* Retrieved from http:// coady.stfx.ca/coady

Coleman, J.S. (1988). Social capital in the creation of human capital. *American Journal of Sociology, 94,* Supplement: Organizations and institutions: Sociological and economic approaches to the analysis of social structure, S95–S120.

Cooperative-Curriculum. (2011). *Welcome to the curriculum on cooperatives wiki.* Retrieved from http://cooperative-curriculum.wikispaces.com

Dees, J.G. (2001/1998). *The meaning of social entrepreneurship.* Retrieved from http://www.caseatduke.org/documents/dees_sedef.pdf

Dees, J.G. (2008). The joys and challenges of teaching social entrepreneurship. In D.D. Brock (Ed.), *Social entrepreneurship: Teaching resources handbook.* Arlington, VA: Ashoka.

Delbecq, A.L. (1983). *Business schools in Jesuit education: Four reflections.* Santa Clara: Leavy School of Business Administration, University of Santa Clara.

Eikenberry, A.M., & Kluver, J.D. (2004). The marketization of the nonprofit sector: Civil society at risk? *Public Administration Review, 64*(2), 132–40.

Equal Exchange. (2007). *Win win solutions: An introduction to fair trade and co-operative economics, grades 4–9.* West Bridgewater, MA: Equal Exchange.

ESADE. (2011). *Institute for social innovation.* Retrieved from http://www.esade. edu/research-webs/eng/socialinnovation

Esping-Andersen, G. (1990). *The three worlds of welfare capitalism.* Princeton: Princeton University Press.

ESSE. (2011). *Teaching objectives*. Retrieved from http://www.esse.unibo.it/teaching.html

Foley, G. (2004a). *Dimensions of adult learning: Adult education and training in a global era*. Maidenhead, UK: Open University Press.

Foley, G. (2004b). Introduction: The state of adult education and learning. In G. Foley (Ed.), *Dimensions of adult learning: Adult education and training in a global era* (pp. 3–18). Maidenhead, UK: Open University Press.

Hall, P.D. (1992a). *Inventing the nonprofit sector and other essays on philanthropy, voluntarism, and nonprofit organizations*. Baltimore: Johns Hopkins University Press.

Hall, P.D. (1992b). Obstacles to nonprofits teaching and research *Inventing the nonprofit sector and other essays on philanthropy, voluntarism, and nonprofit organizations* (pp. 233–42). Baltimore: Johns Hopkins University Press.

Harkavy, I., & Puckett, J.L. (1994). Lessons from Hull House for the contemporary urban university. *The Social Service Review, 68*(3), 299–321.

Hill, R. (2000). The case of the missing organizations: Co-operatives and textbooks. *Journal of Economic Education,* Summer, 281–95.

Institute for Co-operation in Development Countries. (1998). *The degree course in co-operative economics and the Institute for Co-operation in Developing Countries (ICDC)*. Marburg, Germany: Department of Economics, Philipps University.

International Co-operative Alliance. (2010). *Statement on the co-operative identity*. Retrieved from http://www.ica.coop/coop/principles.html

Kangas, O., & Palme, J. (Eds.). (2005). *Social policy and economic development in the Nordic countries*. Hampshire, UK: Palgrave Macmillan.

Mair, J., Robinson, J., & Hockerts, K. (Eds.). (2006). *Social entrepreneurship*. Hampshire: Palgrave Macmillan.

Mirabella, R.M. (2007). University-based educational programs in nonprofit management and philanthropic studies: A 10-year review and projections of future trends. *Nonprofit and Voluntary Sector Quarterly, 36*(4 Supplement), 11S–27S.

Mundy, K., Bickmore, K., Hayhoe, R., Madden, M., & Madjidi, K. (Eds.). (2008). *Comparative and international education: Issues for teachers*. Toronto: Canadian Scholars' Press, Inc.

Nicholls, A. (Ed.). (2008/2006). *Social entrepreneurship: New models of sustainable social change*. Oxford: Oxford University Press.

North, D.C. (2005). *Understanding the process of economic change*. Princeton: Princeton University Press.

North, D.C. (2005/1990). *Institutions, institutional change and economic per formance*. New York: Cambridge University Press.

OEOC. (2011). *Home page*. Retrieved from http://www.oeockent.org

OUP. (2011). *Welcome*. Retrieved from http://www.oup.org

Pérez Riestra, E.M., & Varela Mont, P.B. (2003). Estado actual del cooperativismo en Puerto Rico. *uniRcoop, 1*(2), 159–77.

Putnam, R.D. (1993). *Making democracy work: Civic traditions in modern Italy.* Princeton: Princeton University Press.

Quarter, J., Mook, L., & Armstrong, A. (2009). *Understanding the social economy: A Canadian perspective.* Toronto: University of Toronto Press.

Rao, V., & Walton, M. (Eds.). (2004). *Culture and public action.* Stanford: Stanford University Press.

Salamon, L.M. (1994). The rise of the nonprofit sector. *Foreign Affairs, 73*(4), 109–22.

Salamon, L.M., & Sokolowski, S.W. (2004). *Global civil society: Vol. 2, dimensions of the nonprofit sector.* Bloomfield, CT: Kumarian Press, Inc.

Seton Hall University. (n.d.). *Nonprofit management education.* Retrieved from http://academic.shu.edu/npo

Shaffer, J. (1999). *Historical dictionary of the co-operative movement.* Lanham, MD: The Scarecrow Press, Inc.

Smith, J., Puga, R., & MacPherson, I. (Eds.). (2005). *Youth reinventing co-operatives: Young perspectives on the international co-operative movement.* Victoria: British Columbia Institute for Co-operative Studies.

Tobin, J.J., Wu, D.Y.H., & Davidson, D.H. (1989). *Preschool in three cultures: Japan, China, and the United States.* New Haven: Yale University Press.

University of Wisconsin Center for Co-operatives. (2011). *Home.* Retrieved from http://www.uwcc.wisc.edu/

Whyte, W.F., & Whyte, K.K. (1991/1988). *Making Mondragón: The growth and dynamics of the worker co-operative complex* (2nd ed.). Ithaca: ILR Press, Cornell University Press.

Yunus, M. (2007). *Creating a world without poverty: Social business and the future of capitalism.* New York: Public Affairs.

Contributors

François Brouard is a bilingual chartered accountant with a bachelor's degree in business administration from HEC Montreal, a master's degree in accounting from Université du Québec à Montreal, and a doctorate in business administration (DBA) from Université du Québec à Trois-Rivières. He is currently an associate professor in the accounting group (taxation and financial accounting) at the Sprott School of Business, Carleton University, and founding director of the Sprott Centre for Social Enterprises. He is the co-founding editor of ANSERJ, a peer-reviewed journal on nonprofits and social economy in Canada. His research interests include social entrepreneurship, strategic intelligence, business transfer, SME, governance, professional education, tax, and financial planning.

Mikel Cid is the general manager of Ornalux Mexico SA de CV, and has a BBA and PhD in business administration from Mondragon University, Spain. He has conducted research on the social economy in Spain, Ireland, Canada, and Italy, and taught in the BBA program in Colegio de Estudios Superiores de Administracion (Columbia), and the MBA program in Cape Breton University.

Sheila Gruner is an assistant professor in community economic and social development at Algoma University in Sault Ste Marie. She has been working with social movements and organizations on community development initiatives and critical social transformation in Canada and Latin America for over twenty years, and with people in the James Bay region since 2005. She is completing her PhD at the Ontario Institute for Studies in Education of the University of Toronto in the area of land, learning, and the politics of policy processes in the Treaty 9 region in Northern Ontario.

Greg Halseth is a professor in the geography program at the University of Northern British Columbia, where he is also the Canada research chair in rural and small town studies and director of the Community Development Institute. His research examines rural and small town community development and community strategies for coping with social and economic change, all with a focus upon Northern BC's resource-based towns. His recent books include *Building Community in an Instant Town, Building for Success*, and an edited volume entitled *The Next Rural Economies*. His forthcoming book is *A Northern Place: Economic Renewal in Northern British Columbia* (UBC Press).

Jennifer Hann holds an honours BA in history from York University. She is currently an MA candidate in the adult education and community development program at the Ontario Institute for Studies in Education of the University of Toronto. Her thesis is on the impact of the urban reform movement on the Toronto Public Library system.

Tessa Hebb is the director of the Carleton Centre for Community Innovation at Carleton University. The Centre is a leading knowledge producer on responsible investing and impact investing tools and instruments. Her research focuses on responsible investment and impact investment, and is funded by the Social Sciences and Humanities Research Council, Government of Canada. She has published many articles on responsible investing and social finance policies. Her book, *No Small Change: Pension Fund Corporate Engagement*, was published by Cornell University Press in 2008. She is currently editing a volume for Springer Publishing, called *The Next Generation of Responsible Investing*.

Manuel Larrabure is a PhD student in the political science department at York University. He has written several articles on Venezuela's political economy with a focus on the country's new social economy organizations. He is particularly interested in understanding the relationship between participatory democracy and learning, and is extending his research to social movements across Latin America. He currently lives in Toronto, but will begin extensive fieldwork in Latin America in 2012.

Greg MacLeod is a professor emeritus at Cape Breton University, and is both founder and analyst of several successful community enterprises including New Dawn Enterprises and BCA Investment Cooperative. His community business research has carried him from Spain and Italy to Mexico and Japan. His book, *From Mondragon to America*, has been translated into Japanese.

Ian MacPherson is a professor emeritus of history, a former department chair, dean of humanities, and director of the British Columbia Institute for Co-operative Studies at the University of Victoria. His writings have focused primarily on the Canadian and international co-operative movements and on co-operative studies as a distinct field of enquiry. An elected co-operative official for forty years, he chaired the process and wrote the documents whereby the International Co-operative Alliance developed an Identity Statement for the Twenty-First Century at its Manchester Congress, 1995.

Judith Madill received undergraduate and master's degrees from the University of Manitoba, and her PhD from the Ivey School of Business, University of Western Ontario. She is a professor of marketing and holder of the Paul Desmarais Professorship in Marketing in the Telfer School of Management, University of Ottawa. Dr Madill has authored over sixty-five refereed research papers in her active research program. Recently, she has combined her ongoing research interests in the fields of social marketing and entrepreneurship in conducting work on social entrepreneurship. She is a recent winner of Excellence in Teaching and Best Paper Awards for her research.

Edmund Metatawabin attended the St Anne's Residential School for eight years from 1956 to 1963, and graduated from high school in 1968. He has a bachelor of arts degree from Trent University, and has worked at Trent University and the University of Alberta. In 1988 he was elected to a ten-year term as Chief of the Fort Albany First Nation. At present he owns a consulting enterprise. He has published two books (*Hanaway* and *Harvesting*), and has finalized a contract with Random House for a book about the Mushkegowuk people.

Laurie Mook is an assistant professor in the Nonprofit, Leadership, and Management Program of the School of Community Resources and

Development, and a research associate at the Lodestar Center for Non-profit Innovation and Philanthropy, both at Arizona State University. Laurie is a co-founder of the Social Economy Centre of the University of Toronto in Canada, and of the Association for Nonprofit and Social Economy Research. Her areas of interest are social accounting, social economy, and volunteerism.

Ana María Peredo is an associate professor at the Gustavson School of Business and Director of the Centre for Co-operative and Community-Based Economy at the University of Victoria. She has drawn on her experience as a journalist and anthropologist in her pioneering work on community-based enterprises. She has an impressive record of scholarly work on various aspects of poverty, publishing in such journals as the *Academy of Management Review, Journal of Management Inquiry, Entrepreneurship Theory and Practice, Journal of Applied Behavioral Science,* and the *Journal of World Business.* Her publications emphasize that culture need not be an obstacle to economic progress, and that successful communities are often those that use their own cultural and social energy as capital to create lasting change. Ana María's work has been recognized by a number of national and international awards.

Jack Quarter is a professor and co-director of the Social Economy Centre, OISE, University of Toronto. He is the principal investigator of both the SSHRC-funded CURA, Social Business for Marginalized Social Groups, and the Social Economy Research Alliance, which led to research in this volume. His recent books include *Researching the Social Economy* (University of Toronto Press, 2010, with Laurie Mook and Sherida Ryan), *Understanding the Social Economy* (University of Toronto Press, 2009, with Laurie Mook and Ann Armstrong), and *What Counts: Social Accounting for Nonprofits and Co-operatives,* 2nd Edition (Sigel Press, 2007, with Laurie Mook and B. J. Richmond).

Jean-Paul Restoule is Anishinaabe and French, and a member of the Dokis First Nation. He is an associate professor of Aboriginal education at the Ontario Institute for Studies in Education of the University of Toronto. His research has included Aboriginal identity development in urban areas, access to post-secondary education for Aboriginal people, HIV prevention strategies for Aboriginal youth, and the application of indigenous knowledge in academic and urban settings.

Sherida Ryan is a postdoctoral fellow at the Social Economy Centre at OISE, University of Toronto, where she teaches in the Faculty of Adult Education and Community Development. Her research focus is on the interface of emerging technology, community development, and social economy organizations. She co-ordinates the Community University Research Alliance on Social Business and Marginalized Social Groups and is the knowledge mobilization and social media director for the Social Economy Centre. Sherida is also an internet research analyst for Meta-views, a Toronto-based organization that provides research and consulting services on the relationship between media, technology, and society.

Laura Ryser is the research manager of the rural and small town studies program at the University of Northern British Columbia. She has worked extensively across northern BC and throughout Canada to explore rural restructuring and community transition, seniors' needs, innovative and voluntary services, and rural partnership development. Her current research interests include rural poverty, social learning mechanisms, institutional barriers to change, and how rural organizations are building capacity and resiliency to respond to restructuring pressures.

Daniel Schugurensky is a professor in the School of Public Affairs (College of Public Programs) and in the School of Social Transformation (College of Liberal Arts and Sciences) at Arizona State University. His teaching and research interests include community economic development, citizenship education, informal learning, migration dynamics, volunteer work, social businesses, and participatory democracy (with a focus on participatory budgeting). His most recent books are *Paulo Freire* (Continuum, 2011) and *Learning Citizenship by Practicing Democracy* (Cambridge Scholarly Press, 2010).

Jorge Sousa received his PhD from the Ontario Institute for Studies in Education of the University of Toronto. Jorge is an associate professor at the University of Alberta in Edmonton. He is the co-ordinator for the adult education program in the Department of Educational Policy Studies. Jorge's research is focused on understanding the impact that community-based initiatives and businesses have on strengthening Canada's social economy.

Roger Spear is a professor of social entrepreneurship and founder member and vice-president of the EMES research network on social enterprise. He teaches organizational systems and research methods at the Open University, and is a visiting professor in a master's degree program in social entrepreneurship at Roskilde University, Copenhagen. His most recent research projects are a study of governance and social enterprise; OECD projects on the social economy in Korea and in Slovenia; and 'Civil Society and the Commanding Heights,' a paper for the Carnegie Trust Commission of Inquiry into the Future of Civil Society.

Marcelo Vieta is completing his PhD in the Program in Social and Political Thought and is a research fellow with the Center for Research on Latin America and the Caribbean (CERLAC), both at York University. Vieta researches and has published on the phenomenological, historical, and political economic environments of the worker-recuperated enterprises of Argentina and the social and solidarity economies of Latin America. He is also a member of the board of the Canadian Association for Studies in Cooperation. As of January 2012, Vieta will be a visiting postdoctoral researcher at the European Institute for Research on Cooperatives and Social Enterprises, University of Trento.

John R. Whitman teaches social entrepreneurship at Georgetown University and taught related courses at Babson College and Harvard University. He has worked in international environmental management, started and sold an international software company, and conducts research in co-operatives, nonprofit organizations, and philanthropic foundations. Dr Whitman has lived in Canada, Egypt, Israel, Japan, Norway, and Pakistan. He has a PhD from the University of Toronto, an EdM from Harvard University Graduate School of Education, and an AB in philosophy from Boston University. He has published with the American Library Association, written book chapters on social entrepreneurship, and authored articles in peer-reviewed journals, including *Nonprofit Management & Leadership*.